KU-067-706

OTTO
in the Time of the Warrior

A tale of the Karmidee
Charlotte Haptie

WITHDRAWN
FROM STOCK

Hodder
Children's
Books

a division of Hachette Children's Books

Laois County Library
Leabharlann Chontae Laoise

Acc. No. 08/19777

Class No. JF

Inv. No. 10328

Text copyright © 2006 Charlotte Haptie
Map copyright © 2006 Hodder Children's Books
Map artwork by Trevor Newton

First published in Great Britain in 2006
by Hodder Children's Books

The rights of Charlotte Haptie to be identified as the Author of
the Work has been asserted by her in accordance with the
Copyright, Designs and Patents Act 1988

1

All rights reserved. Apart from any use permitted under UK copyright law,
this publication may only be reproduced, stored or transmitted, in any form,
or by any means with prior permission in writing from the publishers or in the case of
reprographic production in accordance with the terms of licences issued by the
Copyright Licensing Agency and may not be otherwise circulated in any form of
binding or cover other than that in which it is published and without a similar
condition being imposed on the subsequent purchaser.

All characters in this publication are fictitious and any resemblance to real persons,
living or dead, is purely coincidental.

A Catalogue record for this book is available from the British Library

ISBN-10: 0 340 89417 2
ISBN-13: 978 0340 89417 0

Typeset in Perpetua and Tekton by Avon DataSet Ltd,
Bidford on Avon, Warwickshire

Printed and bound in Great Britain by Clays Ltd, St Ives plc

The paper and board used in this paperback by Hodder Children's Books
are natural recyclable products made from wood grown in sustainable forests.
The manufacturing processes conform to the environmental regulations
of the country of origin.

Hodder Children's Books
a division of Hachette Children's Books
338 Euston Road
London NW1 3BH

For
Sheila
Joe
Peggy
Des
with
love

Contents

The City of Trees

CrabFace

TumbleMan

The Rainmaker

The Ice King

Key

1 SteepSide
2 HighNoon
3 WorkHouse
4 ClockTown
5 The Gardens
6 The Heights
7 The Whispering Park
8 Parry Street
9 BlueCat Wood
10 Skinker's Mint
11 Deux Visages
12 Cloudy Town
13 The Watchers
14 BirdTown

11
12
7

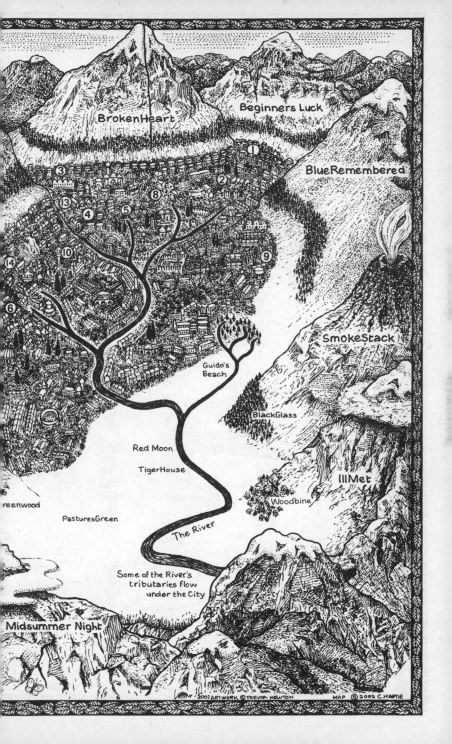

Otto Hush

Ice-makers and fire-makers. Lamp eyes, dammerung, mat flyers, artists, whisperers, counterfeiters. Multiples. These are the Karmidee. The last truly magical people, hidden and far away in their secret City of Trees, their last refuge from our world, where they would be put in laboratories, or zoos, or worse . . .

Once there were many such people and creatures living among us. They are all there in the stories. Even mermaids. Even fire-breathing dragons, dreaming on the edge of volcanoes. But those are stories for children now.

Don't be deceived. Magical people exist and they are called Karmidee. But they are not like the people in the fairy tales. They do not twinkle. They are real flesh and blood and bone.

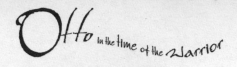

Otto in the time of the Warrior

Their City was discovered in the end, of course. Humans get everywhere. There was an earthquake, a crack opened in a mountain and explorers found their way through. They took over, as explorers often do.

However the Karmidee managed to seal the City again. And now three hundred years have passed. The outsiders, now known as Citizens, are very many and very powerful. They believe that the City has always been theirs. But they are wrong. And even though it is their home, the City of Trees is far greater and far more mysterious than they know.

The Karmidee have a King. He is a gentle, mild-mannered person who lives as a Citizen among the Citizens and comes to the aid of his people in times of trouble. He was chosen, like all Karmidee Kings and Queens, because he was born with a birthmark in the shape of a butterfly.

His name is Albert. Albert the Quiet.

His son is Otto Hush.

Strange Events ON THE Roof Garden

'. . . and one of them was carrying a bicycle in its beak,' added Otto Hush, over his shoulder.

His father, Albert, librarian and quiet King, was climbing up the creaking stairs behind him. This was the last flight, up to the roof garden on the top of Herschell Buildings. It was nearly midnight and the air hung very still. There was a mutter of thunder in the distance.

'That way,' whispered Otto, pointing.

Not that any pointing was needed. Two crate birds were making a nest in among the neglected flowerbeds and the chaotic garden furniture. Already, it loomed impressively over the smaller trees. The penny-farthing bicycle could be seen clearly, interwoven with some pieces

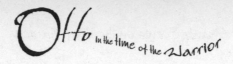

of drainpipe and a great many mattress springs.

'Isn't it great?' whispered Otto. 'We'll be able to see her eggs, and the babies, really close.'

He and Albert both suddenly ducked and tripped over things. A crate bird, really close, had come gliding in to land. He hit the ground on splayed feet, swayed slightly, shook his massive wings and nodded peaceably to Otto and his father. Crate birds look like giant storks. They are usually about three metres tall. Fortunately they are vegetarians.

'Perhaps time to go,' said Albert, softly, as the crate picked his way over to the nest on his long legs.

'What's that?' whispered Otto.

'What's what?'

'There, coming towards us . . .'

There was something coming. Very hard to see.

Many of the roof gardens in the City of Trees are joined by narrow rope bridges. There was a bridge across Parry Street leading to the much tidier gardens on the roof of Owen Mansions. Otto knew that it was possible to go from Owen Mansions to the gardens above the street behind and, by other bridges and along other rooftops, all the way to the Boulevard. It was dangerous. Some of the bridges were in poor repair.

Someone, or something, didn't seem concerned about the seven-storey drop on to Parry Street. The bridge swung from side to side. A shape came over the tops of the lime trees. It moved slowly and awkwardly. It was small.

Not a person. Otto realized. A dog?

The dog, if it was a dog, came over the parapet with a scrabble and a thud. Then it seemed to become entangled with the bushes. Finally it rolled across the stone floor and came to a stop right in front of Albert.

The bushes kept rustling as if they had come alive.

'Well, what have we here . . . ?' muttered Albert in his calm way. 'Ah, a bear cub,' he added. 'A very young one . . .'

He crouched down and the bear cub stayed still, looking up.

There was a crack of thunder. The bear cub made a small sound and the bushes shivered, although there was no wind.

'Hard to see in this light . . .' murmured Albert. 'I wonder where the parents are.'

He stood up slowly and looked back across the bridge. No longer swaying.

'It looks as if it's got a pattern on its back,' said Otto. Even in the night-time shades of black and silver and grey he could make out shapes behind the bear cub's ears. Repeated again, along the spine and flank. These shapes now began to shift and change.

'It's going stripy,' he whispered.

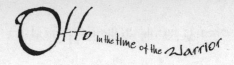

'I believe you are right,' said Albert, as if bears did this all the time.

There was a small sound, like the breaking of a small, dry twig.

'The bushes,' whispered Otto.

'That'll be them,' said Albert. 'Ssh . . .'

He picked up the bear cub and it licked his face.

'Honourable greetings,' said Albert, rather more loudly, addressing the bushes. 'I, Albert, King of the Karmidee, known as Albert the Quiet, am honoured that this bear cub has been brought to me for my protection. I undertake to shelter her in my family and care for her as I know her parents would . . .' he paused. The bushes had become completely still. 'If they could.'

Albert is known for his ability to help and care for Impossible animals. There was a moment of silence on the roof.

Then Otto heard something move and turned in time to see the rope bridge sway, very gently to and fro.

'What the skink—'

'Time for us to go home I think,' said Albert. 'Try to avoid the word skink, Otto.'

'But what the—'

Albert kept his voice to a whisper. 'You've heard stories about chameleon animals, all completely Impossible, of

6

course. Well, except for actual chameleons, which are a sort of lizard, I think—'

Otto was still gazing at the bridge. Without doubt something had just walked back across it.

'I saw a chameleon fish once,' he said, looking back at the little bear. 'At least I think I did. I saw the tank.'

'Well, this is a chameleon bear. Of a very small variety. There would no doubt have been much bigger ones too. Maybe there still are. They used to talk about them in the mud towns when I was a kid. Different chameleon animals. The bears were supposed to live in the forests above the mud towns . . .' Albert stroked the cub's nose. 'I thought they'd died out long ago, if they'd ever been there at all. No one can see them, obviously. They can change colour, blend in. Makes them invisible. Safe from hunters and so forth. When the Normals came they hunted everything.'

'Well it's not exactly hard to see this one, Dad.'

'Exactly. Something's wrong. She keeps changing, look now, hard to see in this light, anyway she's not only not invisible, she's very visible. Not safe for her. Not safe for the others with her. Not safe at all. It looks like her mother has kept her as long as she dared. Now they're asking us to look after her, which is quite an honour, when you think about it, poor little thing.'

There was another crack of thunder. The storm was

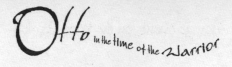

coming closer. The bear cub made a snuffling sound and Otto patted her head, feeling large and protective.

In truth, strange dangers awaited them both, as yet unknown. Otto reached down again now, and felt the anxious beat of the little bear's heart through her fur. He did not imagine that she would one day save his life.

They all stood there on the roof garden for a moment longer, under the clouds and stars, while around them the great City of Trees mirrored the sky, with lamps and lights and mysteries of its own.

'I'll stay a bit,' whispered Otto. 'Just for a minute.'

Two massive shapes loomed ponderously out of the darkness.

'Look, Dad, they've got an old sink—'

'I'll see you down there,' said Albert, pitching his voice below the noise of the mighty wing beats.

The crates were taking off again, cooing hoarsely to one another.

'They might bring something really big next, like, you know, a bath.'

The bear cub yawned. Albert carried her to the stairs, leaving the door standing open.

Almost immediately there was a crack and a jolt of lightning and thunder and, in the same moment, a gust of cooler air rushed across the roof garden, spinning and twisting, and Otto, amazed, saw a funnel of blue light spiral into existence between where he stood and the foundations of the crate nest.

He ducked down, watching through leaves, as the light spread, paler now and very clear, revealing a tall boy, almost a man, standing looking down at something in his hand. He wore dark, sparkling clothes and a billowing cape. His feet were bare. His black hat was pushed back on his head. He looked up and then, slowly, as if searching, he looked around him. Not close by. Into the distance. He turned and Otto saw him very clearly. He had a pale, freckled face.

He stayed quite still.

Otto didn't even breathe.

The boy glanced up at the storm clouds and muttered a curse. It seemed that he had no wish to be on this shabby roof garden. He was holding what looked to be a sphere of blackglass. He tossed it in the air with one hand and caught it with the other. Smiling to himself, all grace and menace, he put it back into his pocket, jumped into the air and disappeared.

Otto didn't move. He stared at the place where the boy had stood, while the light that had surrounded him faded into darkness.

Then it started to rain. Massive, splattering drops. The crate birds returned, bringing umbrellas, and began trying

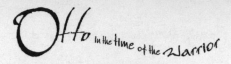

to open them and build a roof. Otto stood up slowly. He had no umbrella. He decided to go back inside. He walked backwards to the doorway.

Telephone Calls

Perhaps Otto would have mentioned what he had seen. However, things were going on in the flat.

'What's that on your head, Mum?'

'Ottie, thank goodness, could you just check on the girls? I thought I heard Zebbie, but I'm not sure, and we've got a bit of a problem in the kitchen . . .'

Dolores's hair was wound up in a scarf. Not unusual. However she also had a large golden insect sitting on her head. A bit like a grasshopper. Or was it a praying mantis?

'Giant crickets,' she hissed, finger to her lips. 'Getting in through the ventilation thingy. Your father's trying to catch them.'

The winter had been long and terrible and ever since

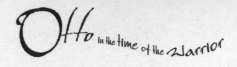

it had ended the City had been whirring and buzzing and blooming with Impossible insects and new and extraordinary plants.

There wasn't much point in trying to be quiet. Now all sorts of sounds were coming from the kitchen. A series of beautiful, creaking notes, crockery breaking, Albert swearing—

Then the telephone, a large black and brass affair, began to ring loudly right next to Otto. The twins immediately started protesting and enquiring from their bedroom.

Albert appeared at the kitchen door, followed by an emerald green cricket the size of a small cat.

'Ah, Otto,' said Albert, raising his voice in order to be heard, 'I think the little bear has woken up. Don't let the twins annoy her.' And he whispered something friendly over his shoulder to the bear cub, presumably in the kitchen, and then lifted the receiver and said, 'Old Town 4022, Mr Hush speaking,' as he always did, even though at this time of day it was almost definitely Granny Culpepper, who knew very well who he was.

'Good evening, Chief Librarian,' he added, pleasantly, a moment later.

Hepzibah and Zeborah came out of their room.

'Inspect!' yelled Zebbie, clapping her hands. 'Big inspect!'

Several crickets had assembled in the kitchen doorway

and were turning their shining heads from side to side, looking slowly up and down the corridor.

Now Dolores came out, stepping over them, and crouched down, a sieve in one hand and a casserole dish in the other. She started waving the sieve about, trying to coax the nearest cricket into the casserole dish.

'Are you going to cook them, Mum?'

'NO. And please help instead of just standing there grinning.'

'I think they're amazing.'

'Then I suggest you go into the kitchen and get really amazed. There are at least five more on the dresser . . . Hepzie! They won't like you doing that! You realize your father has brought a bear cub home, Ottie. A real bear cub . . .'

She wiped her forehead with the back of her hand.

'It's Mr Paxton,' hissed Otto.

She straightened up and looked at him sternly. 'The bear is Mr Paxton? That man has changed into a bear?'

'On the phone, Mum. It's Mr Paxton on the phone.'

Mr Paxton was the newly appointed Chief Librarian. A man much preoccupied with rules, statutes and regulations.

'Well it's very late for him to be phoning,' said Dolores, still stern. 'I can only presume he isn't having to cope with a kitchen full of crickets.'

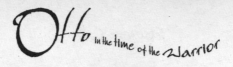

'Of course, Mr Paxton,' Albert was saying. 'A matter of grave concern. But as I am in charge of Ancient Documents I am confident that I can deal with it to your satisfaction . . . Yes, I see . . . Mmm . . . Yes, I see.'

Obviously Mr Paxton had a lot to say.

Otto peered round the kitchen door. His mother's grey cat, Wishtacka, was sitting on the fridge, cool and aloof as ever. A number of very large crickets were glittering and swaying on the table. More, as Dolores had said, were on the dresser. Some were gold, some bright green. Others were a burnished black with copper-coloured heads. As he stood there admiring them one of the black ones raised its wings slightly and began to rub them together. Then a second one did the same thing. Like musicians tuning their instruments.

The bear cub was sitting on a piece of blanket in the corner by the laundry basket. She rubbed her eyes and then, still blinking, fixed her gaze on the crickets. Her fur, Otto realized, was striped in the same colours as the scarf around Dolores's hair. Now it began to change. She became gold and green and black. She scratched under her chin with a coppery paw.

Dolores rushed back into the kitchen, slammed the empty casserole dish down next to the cooker, seized the oven mitts, put them on, and advanced slowly towards the bear.

'She's not hot, Mum,' said Otto.

'I'll leave at once,' shouted Albert into the phone. 'But I'm sure it is not a matter for concern, Mr Paxton.' The crickets had begun to sing. A mournful and beautiful sound. Loud.

'She may be carrying some disease. We must all be very careful.' Dolores picked up the bear cub, who immediately snuggled into her arms and licked her face all over.

'Got to go to the library,' said Albert, putting the phone down.

'At this time of night?'

'The dome has been struck by lightning apparently. No damage up there but one of the lightning conductors must have been incomplete, possibly borrowed by crates. Anyway some bits of masonry have fallen off above the Western Door—'

'And he wants you to go out in this weather for that? This is in his Big Book of Rules for Small-Brained Bosses, I presume?'

'No.' Albert was pulling on his raincoat and searching for his umbrella.

Dolores stared at him. The bear cub started licking her ear.

'This damage above the door has revealed some sort of space in the wall, a cavity that's been sealed off. They've found

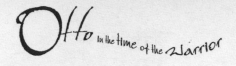

a book He thinks it may be of interest to my department.'

'Something to do with the Karmidee?'

Albert was Senior Librarian in charge of the Department of Ancient Documents. A good number of these documents are Karmidee. However, much of the history of the Karmidee has been forgotten or lost since the Outsiders came. It was told in stories and songs that were never written down or pictures that were worn away.

'Almost definitely,' said Albert. He paused, his hand on the bolt on the front door. 'Mr Paxton is rather agitated. Apparently the front and the back of this book have panels of carved blackglass.'

Dolores and Otto both gasped. Blackglass, of course, is another name for obsidian, the mysterious rock which is found in sleeping volcanoes and the only place where the Karmidee can store magical energy. It is a substance of great importance to them which is feared by the Citizens, who do not understand it.

'It sounds like one of those books of pictures. The blackglass cover was just their way of protecting the pages,' added Albert. 'He says the pictures are of very good quality, mainly birds and animals apparently, and he thinks it should probably be put straight into one of the humidity controlled cabinets. I've got the keys, I'm going to take them over there now.'

'Is he going to report the blackglass to the Normal Police?'

'I hope that I've persuaded him that it won't be necessary.'

'Oh, do be careful, Al . . .'

Hepzie came pottering out of the living room. Otto picked her up.

'Flowers,' she informed him, pointing to the daisies on her night dress. 'Heppie cuddle bear?'

'I shouldn't be too long,' said Albert, at the door.

'Heppie cuddle bear now?'

'No, NO, Bear must have a BATH now,' said Dolores.

'Why?'

'Bear may have germs.'

'Why?'

'Because we don't know where she's been.'

'Germs!' yelled Hepzie, pointing to the bear. Daisies were blossoming all over her fur, white and gold on a field of green.

'Pretty germs!'

The phone began ringing again and Dolores threw up her hands and one of the oven mitts flew off.

She picked up the receiver, gesturing to Otto. He was to put Hepzie back to bed.

'Hello,' she said fiercely, and then added in a kinder voice, 'Oh, hello, Miss Fringe.'

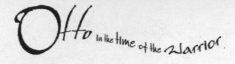

Just then the lights went out and the crickets, all of them, fell silent. Otto, still carrying Hepzie, went to get a worm torch from under the sink. It was not unusual for the electricity to fail during storms.

He went back to the corridor as the worms began to wake up and to glow softly. Dolores was rattling the telephone cradle. The call was already over, then.

'It's stopped working,' whispered Dolores, as if they might be overheard. 'That was Miss Fringe, she's at the library. She rang to warn your father. It's the obsidian covers on the book, apparently after Perfect Paxton phoned here he decided he should phone the Normal Police after all, just to be on the safe side. So he did and they're on their way to the library now. They could get there before him.'

Otto stared at her in horror. The Normies would confiscate the book, because, of course, obsidian isn't Respectable, even though most Citizens don't know its powers. But that was not the worst of it. Nor was it the reason that Dolores had whispered to her husband to be careful as he set off for the library.

Albert is the King of the Karmidee. His people call him Albert the Quiet. His task, as a matter of honour, is to advise the Karmidee in times of danger. The Normal Police would delight in an excuse to arrest him. This book and its Non-Respectable cover would be a very good excuse indeed.

'We've got to tell him, Mum.'

'There's not time.'

Hepzibah tried to grab the torch. The beam swung around the corridor, throwing shadows against the walls. It steadied on Dolores's face.

'Go and tell Mayor Crumb, Ottie,' she said in a rush. Mayor Crumb, despite being a Citizen and holding high office, had become a friend to the Karmidee.

'You mean on the mat?'

'Yes. On your carpet. There's no other way.'

'Are you sure, Mum?' Dolores usually disapproved of mat flying.

She nodded. 'Just check to see if it's stopped raining. And be very, very careful.'

Otto pushed Hepzie into her arms. Then he ran to his room, shut the door behind him, took down the screen and opened the window wider, as wide as it would go.

No one in sight. Everything wet and glistening. Streetlights flickering on and off.

He unrolled the mat, crouched down on it and sailed out over Parry Street.

Fetching Mayor Crumb

It was not long before Otto could make out the craggy bulk of the Town Hall on the Boulevard and, a little further on, the dome of the City Central Library. He flew over the Western Door and saw the Normies in their new uniforms, already clustering nastily around his father on the pavement. Then he hurtled on, too angry to be afraid.

Two minutes more and he was at Mayor Crumb's flat. Not at the door. That would have taken too much explaining to the concierge. At the window. Clocks, near and distant, began to chime midnight. The whole building was in darkness, the lights must have failed here too.

He rapped on the glass. It was dangerous hovering like this. A gust of wind could blow him against the side of the building, or someone might see him. He reached out, about to knock again, and at the same moment the window opened outwards and he was jolted back and down through the air, spinning right over and back and then over again.

'Remain calm!' called a sturdy voice, already alarmingly far above.

'I'm OK,' Otto gasped, inaccurately, dragging on the fringe of the mat as the loyal carpet fought to save them both and the side of the building lurched past at new and terrifying angles.

Suddenly he was stopped. And the right way up. Almost touching the cold wet glass of a window next to a fire escape. The lights in the building flickered on and then off again and Otto, in that moment, saw a girl staring at him. Eyes round in amazement.

'On my way,' called the Mayor from somewhere.

Otto spiralled frantically upwards.

'Someone watching,' he hissed.

A massive shape rocketed down towards him and then bounced to a halt about one storey below.

Mayor Crumb had no need of a carpet. He was wearing the flying jacket especially made for him by Roxie and Mattie Mook of the Mook Family WoolShop. The jacket, actually the size of a full-length coat, was made from a secret and magical combination of colours designed to make use of the cosmic

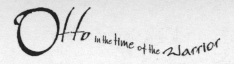

properties of the wool. The buttons down the front were the size of saucers. Doing them up caused the Mayor to ascend. Undoing them, one by one, was supposed to allow for a stately and dignified return to the ground. All this required skill and was absolutely Impossible. The Mayor, of course, would never use the jacket in daylight.

'Exact art, this button business . . . right . . . oh dear . . . too many . . .'

The Mayor shot past, going up, with impressive acceleration, fumbling with a button near the collar, and Otto shot after him, past the open window, on up past the roof gardens and into the rain-washed night.

'There we are . . .' said Mayor Crumb, beaming and bobbing.

They were horribly, unnecessarily high. Otto kept his eyes almost closed. His teeth were chattering. He is one of the few mat flyers in the City but he still doesn't like heights.

'How can I help?' enquired the Mayor.

At The Library

'. . . and a trusted member of the library staff,' boomed Mayor Crumb. He looked very large and impressive. His flying jacket, which reached his ankles, was unbuttoned for landing, revealing evening dress – a black brocade frock coat and breeches and a cherry-red embroidered waistcoat. He had landed in an alleyway behind the Town Hall. Otto knew this because he had almost landed on top of him.

Mr Paxton, a pale-faced man, nodded, swallowing vigorously. Face pinched as a clothes peg.

'We were called to the scene,' said Mr Eight, one of the Normal Police, 'because Impossible Artifacts were reported to have been discovered of a Non-Respectable Nature and Not Normal. On our arrival my colleague

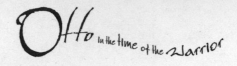

recognized this gentleman who, as you may be aware, your Mayorfulness, is not only a person of magico origin but is also their King, although you wouldn't think he was a King to look at him—'

'A RELIABLE, TRUSTED AND RESPECTABLE member of the library staff and therefore a City employee, and a man whose judgement I admire, whose intellect I admire . . .'

'Quite so, quite so,' said Mr Paxton, who was looking rather smaller than usual. 'I do not consider it a matter for the library to concern ourselves with any *hobbies* Mr Hush may have outside working hours, however, er, well, out of the *ordinary*—'

'Being the King of the Karmidee is NOT a HOBBY,' yelled Otto, unable to restrain himself. Albert frowned at him.

'SO,' continued the Mayor, staring at Mr Paxton, 'I am not at all clear why you found it necessary to disturb these gentlemen from their sleep—'

'The Normality Monitoring Department never sleeps, your Mayorfulness,' said Mr Six, all badges and buttons.

Mr Paxton spoke rapidly. 'The guidelines issued by the Town Hall on the handling of artifacts made from or including elements made from obsidian are very clear, your Mayorfulness. Such items must be reported. The assistance of the Normal Police must be sought. I summoned them in accordance with these guidelines and then they became, well, they became rather preoccupied with Mr Hush, here, and started to accuse him of hiding this book in the building in the first place with the intention of using the obsidian for some Impossible Purpose. A suggestion which, I have to say, I find most unlikely.'

Mayor Crumb snorted. He spun round, his jacket billowing, and Albert, Otto, Miss Fringe and the two Normal Police all stepped neatly backwards.

'Such items must be reported,' repeated Mr Paxton doggedly, now face to face with the top button of Mayor Crumb's elegant waistcoat, 'for inspection in case of the need for collection——'

'And detection and rejection by all right-minded people,' added Mr Six and Mr Eight in unison.

'But Mr Hush raised an objection to the inspection,' finished Mr Paxton.

'If I could make a correction, it was a question of protection——' began Miss Fringe.

'BE QUIET ALL OF YOU!' thundered Mayor Crumb.

Everyone became quiet.

'As elected Mayor of the City I request Mr Six and Mr Eight to leave at once.' He glared at the Normal Police. During the winter they had taken orders from a rival in the

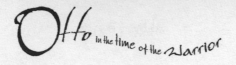

Town Hall and kept the Mayor under house arrest. He didn't like them.

They stared back at him mutinously.

'At once,' said Mayor Crumb.

They began to walk slowly along the wide pavement of the Boulevard, as if they had just had the idea of taking a stroll, swinging their torches and pretending to look in shop windows.

Albert held out the book. 'It appears that it has been concealed in this cavity in the wall above the door,' he said. 'It may well have been here since these doors were repaired following, er, problems with some buildings about three hundred years ago.'

Otto guessed that his father was referring to the time of the earthquake three hundred years before, when the Northern Mountain BrokenHeart split in two and outsiders invaded the City and made it their own. These outsiders were, of course, normal human beings, and the ancestors of those now living in and ruling the City today. The ones known as Citizens. The Citizens do not believe that the Karmidee built the City. They do not believe that there was an earthquake. They think that the City has always been theirs.

Mayor Crumb carried the book into the vestibule of the Western Door. Miss Fringe handed him a worm torch and he scanned the parchment pages, delicately turning from one to the next with his big careful fingers.

'Beautiful,' he muttered. 'Extraordinary . . .'

Everyone was gathered around him, craning to see. Otto caught glimpses of gorgeous, brightly coloured pictures crowded with animals, people, buildings and trees.

'And this sort of thing is very rare?' murmured Mayor Crumb.

'Very few books have been found from this period,' said Albert. 'As you can see, it is almost entirely made up of pictures, which was common at the time. Some pages appear to have fallen out. I suggest that we examine the cavity thoroughly in the morning.'

'My concern is with the cover,' said Mr Paxton. 'I've never seen such large pieces of obsidian. It has Impossible properties that are not understood. Who knows what might happen if we keep it here in the building. It could start to smoke and smoulder. It could change into something else. I will not be responsible—'

'But,' said Mayor Crumb, not looking up from the book, 'Mr Hush as Senior Librarian in charge of Ancient Documents *will* be responsible. I entrust this book to his care, on behalf of all the people of this City, in the certain knowledge that he will look after it in the proper manner and investigate any meaning it may have for us today.'

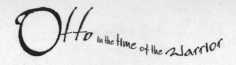

Mayor Crumb handed the book back to Albert and Mr Paxton followed it with his eyes.

'And may I add,' said the Mayor, 'may I add that the Town Hall Committee for the Propagation of Books wrote to me this week to say how delighted they are with your services since you took over as Chief Librarian last month, Mr Paxton.'

Mr Paxton squared his shoulders.

'Has the Minister for the Maintenance and Repair of Municipal Buildings been informed about the damage to the building?' asked the Mayor.

'Yes indeed, your Mayorfulness,' said Mr Paxton. 'According to Library Rule 72b.'

'Excellent. Excellent. Well, I'll be making my way home then.'

'Shall I accompany you to your steam car, your Mayorness?' Mr Paxton looked up and down the Boulevard. In vain.

'Thank you, no,' said the Mayor, gravely. 'I will enjoy the night air, I think.' And with a flicker of a wink at Otto he set off down the Boulevard, his stride becoming longer and considerably more bouncy as he went, presumably starting to do up the buttons on his remarkable jacket. The streetlights were flickering back to life.

'I think I'll go home myself now, Mr Hush,' said Mr

Paxton, as they all stared after the mysteriously buoyant Mayor, now brightly illuminated under a cluster of lamps designed to look like a giant bunch of flowers. (One of many pieces of art work celebrating the final arrival of the spring that year, after a particularly long and terrible winter.)

At that moment the Mayor suddenly shot upwards and appeared to seize a wrought iron daisy on the way past. He flailed about upside down. Presumably he had done up too many buttons. He dropped halfway to the ground and stayed like that briefly before landing again and immediately sitting down.

A thoughtful silence fell among those standing outside the Western Door of the library.

'Our Mayor is indeed a Remarkable Man,' said Mr Paxton after a moment.

Blue

The last hour of darkness was coming to an end. Already the sky was pale in the East. Soon the street traders would come down to the markets with their carts and kiosks and tents.

Soon. But not yet.

This was the quietest time of all.

Otto landed his carpet near the crate nest. The garden smelt of damp soil and flowers.

He made his way slowly to the door to the stairs. He felt very tired.

There was a sound behind him, almost like a footstep.

Then, without doubt, he heard someone breathe.

He spun round and found himself dazzled by bright blue light. He put up a hand to shield his eyes. The air felt hot.

'Honourable greetings,' said a voice. And then rushed on in a tumble of words. 'I can't believe it, Otto, I've found you! I thought I might have to try many times to find you and here you are, the first visit I make! Greetings to your family!'

Otto squinted into the turquoise light. Someone stood silhouetted in the middle of it. He backed a step towards the door behind him, still shading his eyes, and as he did so the turquoise melted and became paler and cooler and lost itself in the air.

A girl was standing, smiling, in front of him.

Otto stared at her. She seemed lightly balanced there on the stone paving, as if she could leap forward at any moment.

'Honourable greetings, Otto Hush,' she said again, with the formal grace of the Karmidee.

She was, he guessed, a year or so older than him. She wore a loose shirt, and narrow trousers that ended, tattered, well above her ankles. There were padded canvas patches over her elbows and knees. Her hair stood up in black spikes, her eyes were brown and her skin was very dark. Little fragments of something bright sparkled on her face and hands, as if she had flown down through a storm of sand and diamond dust. But she had no mat, he had not seen her coming towards the roof, he couldn't understand how she was there at all.

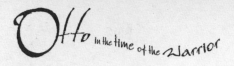

There was a pattern embroidered on the front of her shirt. It was made up of three creatures which could, perhaps, be mistaken for long-legged rabbits. They were leaping in a circle, one behind the other. Or maybe there was only one, travelling round and round, as the moon circles the earth.

Otto knew the creature by its true name. It was a hare. And this was the sign of the Blue Hare, one of the mountain spirits, an ancient and mysterious figure in the forgotten history of the Karmidee. Commonly seen as a carnival costume, especially in the spring.

'Have you given the KeepSafe to the King, Otto Hush?' she asked him. 'Did all go well?'

'Who are you?' asked Otto. 'And how do you know my name?'

Her wide excited eyes narrowed in alarm.

'Don't you remember me?' She stepped towards him and put her hand on his arm, bringing her face close to his, staring intently. 'It is you, Otto, I know it is—'

'Yes, I am me, I mean, you're right, my name is Otto—'

'And you really don't remember what happened, Otto?'

Otto, slowly, shook his head.

'You are Otto Hush, son of Albert the Quiet, Karmidee King, and you don't have something secret that I entrusted to you . . . ?' Her grip tightened on his arm, she lowered her voice, it was fierce now, '. . . something of great importance to our people?'

'Look, I'm sorry, but—'

'Perhaps you think I am talking rubbish? I am mad?'

He couldn't place her accent. Obviously she was a Karmidee and yet she seemed foreign and strange.

'Well, no, no, I'm sure you're not—'

'You have a little bear who travels with you? A little bear who changes colour?'

'How do you know about the bear—'

'She has an unusual name . . .' The girl frowned. She was still clutching his arm, standing very near him. Suddenly, he felt sure that she possessed great magical energy. He sensed it like heat from a fire.

'I can't remember it,' she bit her lip, 'if only I could remember it. I can only remember that your mother chose the name and then your sisters couldn't pronounce it and it ended up being this, this . . . word.'

Otto found his voice. 'We haven't chosen a name for her yet,' he said, hoarsely. 'She only arrived this evening.'

She let him go. Only a few moments before she had been smiling and young. A kid. Older than him, but still a kid. Now she was ageless. She could have been a statue or a painting. Her face was grave and beautiful and wise.

'Then it is not over as I hoped, Otto Hush,' she said softly.

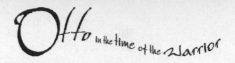

'And for you it has not yet begun. Listen to me now. There is a struggle, a battle, going on. For the future, the present and the past. Do you understand? It is going on now, here and across time.

'There are two in this struggle, Otto. I am one of them. The other is someone who has the power to sweep all this away,' she gestured across the glowing City. 'He will sweep it all away as if it had never been. Not because he hates our people. No, he wants to make it as if the Citizens never came here. As if they never found a way into the City.'

She stepped back and looked at him. As if she was measuring him in some way.

'But they did come, Otto Hush. And I believe that if they had not come through the broken mountain then they would have come some other time, some other way. That is a terrible truth. I have travelled and seen many things. And this is what I know. We must live together or die.'

There was a diamond on a strip of cloth around her neck. It was shaped like an arrow head.

'My name is Blue,' she whispered. 'I will call for help. And you will not fail me. I will call for help . . . And you will save my life. You will be a hero, Otto Hush.'

Suddenly, moving so fast he could barely see her, she crouched down and leapt towards him. In a blaze of blue light he flung himself sideways, falling into bushes, wet leaves in his face, branches snapping. He waited for the flicker of time that it would take her to crash into the frame of the door just behind him . . . He heard nothing.

He heaved himself to his feet. Turned round, dripping and scratched, ready for the next thing. Whatever on earth that was going to be.

But nothing happened. He was alone. The last of the light spread over the roof garden from where he was standing, swirled among the flowerbeds and was gone.

Back Home

Otto crept back into the flat. Through the half-open kitchen door he saw Dolores asleep at the table. Wishtacka was on her knee. One cricket, the only one left apparently, was sitting in Wishtacka's basket.

Signs of struggle and mayhem and twin activity lay here and there around the floor. Bits of banana, the unhelpful casserole dish . . .

'Ottie?' whispered Dolores. 'Are you all right?'

He nodded. 'Go to bed, Mum.'

She rubbed her beautiful, sleepy eyes. 'Your dad phoned,' she said, yawning. 'I was just waiting for you both . . . Do you want anything to eat or anything . . .'

'No thanks.' Definitely not.

'I was worried.' She smiled at him, peering as if the room were full of fog.

Otto wanted very much to speak to Mab, his loyal, proud and scornful friend. A Karmidee from TigerHouse, she always knew more about Impossible things than he did; but surely, surely nothing like this had ever happened to her.

However, Mab and her grandmother were very busy with something and she had told him almost two weeks ago that she would see him soon and please not to try and contact her until then. Whatever all that was about.

He closed his bedroom curtains against the dawn.

His neck and shoulders ached, probably after the tumbling fall on the carpet when he went to fetch Mayor Crumb. But Mayor Crumb, the strange book at the library, the crickets and the crate bird nest and even the smiling, dangerous boy had all been driven from his mind. He lay in the half-dark, exhausted, dazzled by blue light every time he closed his eyes.

Hearing the girl's voice. *I will call for help. And you will save my life . . . You will be a hero, Otto Hush.*

Fly Posting

Meanwhile, two unknown children were skidding, scurrying and gliding up the Boulevard from the distant southern end.

One, a girl, was running backwards and forwards, swinging into trees and leaping out again. She kept returning to her companion, a boy, barely visible inside a large wheeled chair.

This chair was gliding gently through the air about two metres off the ground. It had four large iron wheels and a fifth smaller one which was out on its own at the front and used, by the occupant, to steer. Apart from these wheels and the long bar for steering, it was all made out of woven wicker. The back and sides continued upwards and met in a curved roof.

Fly Posting

The boy inside had a pile of rolled posters on his knees. He kept sticking his arm out and pointing at particular trees. Now he had chosen a huge chestnut outside the House of Dancing. The girl, who seemed full of elastic energy, sprang up on to a low branch and he threw her a poster. She deftly unrolled it and pinned it on to the trunk of the tree using tacks from a bag hanging on her belt.

They progressed up the Boulevard, stopping and starting, gradually using up their pile of posters.

The cold daylight seeped between the buildings and flooded the City of Trees. They reached the corner of Whisper Street and there were no posters left.

'Let's go back, Morwenna,' said the boy in the chair. 'That's our patch done.'

'I want to look at things,' said the girl, grinning. 'See,' she pointed at a shop selling traditional striped and spotted wedding clothes. 'That wasn't there before.'

She ran over and pushed her small face up against the window. A family of unicorns came down the middle of the Boulevard, their reflections streaming black and silver across the curved glass.

'Well, at least there's a few of them around,' she said quietly.

'We need to go,' said the boy. 'We don't want to be late like we were last time—'

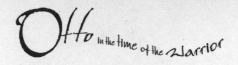

'Oh but last time we got lost, Cal,' said the girl, grinning again, 'There weren't all these lovely sign posts.' And she pointed to where *Whisper Street* had been carved in the stone wall of the wedding shop. But the letters were ancient, worn by wind and rain.

She stood on her hands and her small round hat stayed neatly on her head. She was dressed all in scarlet silk. Trousers, jacket, hat and shoes.

'Come on, you know it'll be me that gets blamed—'

'AND you lost the map, or sat on it, or something—'

'I don't remember that—'

'Well it was a long time ago,' said Morwenna, very solemn, and, for some reason, they both laughed.

Then there was a rattle of wood on wood as someone opened a window to let the morning inside. Morwenna jumped nimbly up into the wicker chair and it swung round the corner. Gathering speed, silent as an owl, the chair sped down the waking streets, turning towards the South West. On and on, and then up through the alleyways that spread across the feet of TumbleMan Mountain, which sat so gilded and golden and innocent in the early sun.

Hovering

Hepzie and Zeb were hovering just above the ground. It was a new skill. Almost twelve months before, at about the age other small children were perfecting their walking skills, they had both suddenly started to float up into the air and to fly about, causing great consternation and turmoil in the Hush household.

Then, during the winter they had stopped flying altogether because they were sad.

In the last few days they had started to rise up, only a few centimetres, and stay like that, their faces as solemn as if they were still on the floor with everybody else. The first time had been in the elegant tea rooms on the top floor of Banzee, Smith and Banzee, the famous department store on the

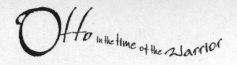

Boulevard. A certain amount of consternation and turmoil
had followed there too. After all, flying, even low level
hovering, is not Possible, Respectable or Normal.

'Down!' cried Dolores, all ready to go out. 'How can I
take them shopping if they're going to do that? They
promised not to do that. You promised, didn't you, and then
we're going for a little treat, if you *don't do that*.'

'Just a little bit,' suggested Zeborah. 'Nobody see?'

'Of course somebody see! Everybody see! Even a little,
tiny bit off the floor is not Respectable! If you do it you're
going straight in the buggy!'

'They just look taller,' said Otto.

'Until you look at their feet. Then they look Impossible.
Don't encourage them, Ottie. And don't forget to take your
dad's lunch to the library as soon as you've had
your breakfast.'

Otto had woken up late. Now he was waiting for a chance
to say something about what had happened on the roof . . .
Although it was hard to predict how his mother would react
to hearing about a boy and then a girl who came Impossibly
in and out of nowhere in blasts of blue light.

Dolores was brought up as a Citizen. The previous
summer she had found out that her quiet husband, Albert, a
librarian, was actually a Karmidee, even though he lived in
the City among the Citizens and seemed so Respectable. Not

only that, he was the King of the Karmidee. Then she had discovered that her own highly Respectable mother was secretly a Karmidee too. Life had been unpredictable ever since. So had Dolores.

'There was this amazing girl on the roof,' said Otto, putting down his toast.

Dolores was now trying to put a sun hat on Hepzie's head.

Hepzie began bouncing up and down as if she were on springs.

'Mum, listen, this girl was on the roof. She recognized me. It was incredible——'

'HEPPIE! STOP IT! GET DOWN!' cried Dolores.

Hepzie stopped in mid-air, nose to nose with her mother, and stayed absolutely still.

'Don't forget Dad's lunch,' said Dolores, still staring at Hepzie who was staring back, unblinking.

Otto left his toast.

As he went down the corridor and closed the door behind him he could hear his mother, wrestling with her voice to keep it calm, saying, '*Now*, I am going to count to *three* . . . one . . . two . . .'

'THWEE!' cried a small, cheerful voice, joining in.

THE Beatle ON THE Boulevard

The Boulevard was sparkling. It is the most magnificent of all the shopping streets in the City. Very wide, lined with cherry and chestnut trees and with ornate awnings in front of all the shops. These are elegant and, in some cases, enormous. There are also pavement cafes, squares, statues, fountains, aquariums underfoot, street conjurors and every shape of building. There are trams, of course. But Otto chose to walk.

He bought a mango sorbet from Fozzard's Ice Cream Soda Bar and ate it sitting in the shade of the elephants at the base of the Karmidee Tower. As soon as he had delivered Albert's lunch he would go and see his excellent friend Sween, Citizen, musician and also the son of a secret outlaw. Sween would have time to listen.

A white butterfly dodged parasols and floral hats and landed on his head.

'Very cunning,' he whispered. 'Now you can't be seen.' Otto's hair was completely white. Then another insect landed on him too. Not a butterfly this time. A blue and gold beetle. It thudded down on the back of his hand, closed its wings and hid them under the shimmering armour of its back. Then it walked thoughtfully down on to his finger. A jewel on his light brown skin.

This was no ordinary visit from an insect. This was the beetle which Mab the Moth, his friend in TigerHouse, sent to him when she wanted to see him. When they had first met she had given him a green beetle to summon her in the same way. It was resting in its box at home.

The second beetle, the one on his hand now, was a new event. She had only shown it to him recently, when she had appeared on her mat outside his window very early one morning.

'Not that I'll want to use it much,' she had said, with a quick smile.

'Not that I'll come if you do,' he had replied.

He put the beetle on his shoulder where it clung to his dark red shirt. That was also when she had told him, in a different voice, that there was something she had to do for her grandmother and she would be in touch soon. She was

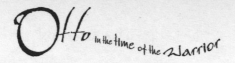

in a hurry, too much of a hurry, or maybe too worried, to explain any more.

Otto grinned with excitement.

He hurried off towards the library, so that he could go on to TigerHouse, and see Mab, as soon as possible.

As he went, despite the fact that he was walking fast, he saw that there were posters surprisingly high up the trunks of some of the trees. Had someone been all the way along here with a ladder?

People were stopping to peer up at them. The big purple lettering was bordered with stars which flashed and twinkled and, from time to time, burst into sparks and showered the pavement below with tiny boiled sweets. This attracted attention.

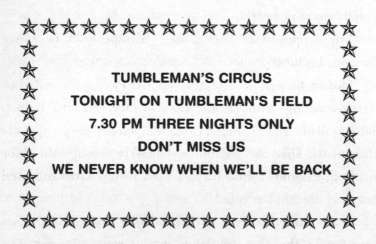

☆☆☆☆☆☆☆☆☆☆☆☆☆☆☆☆☆
TUMBLEMAN'S CIRCUS
TONIGHT ON TUMBLEMAN'S FIELD
7.30 PM THREE NIGHTS ONLY
DON'T MISS US
WE NEVER KNOW WHEN WE'LL BE BACK
☆☆☆☆☆☆☆☆☆☆☆☆☆☆☆☆☆

Message AT THE Library

Miss Fringe came and found him in the Reading Room. A massive, domed place, piled with silence, rustling and the scribbling of pencils.

'I'm supposed to meet Dad,' whispered Otto. 'I've brought his lunch.'

'I know, he sent me to fetch you. Mr Paxton has called an extra meeting with all the Senior Librarians to discuss Library Rule 221b.' Miss Fringe had spoken more quickly than usual. Then she led the way briskly through the door marked, in gold: LIBRARIANS ONLY. And Otto followed her into the familiar office.

Last summer, a year ago, his father had almost been arrested by the Normal Police in this room. Almost. The

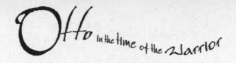

window, which had been completely shattered by a dragon, had been replaced since then. It was made up of small squares of glass.

'I don't remember that little picture in the window.'

'It wasn't there, Otto. They found some pieces of stained glass when they were renovating the cloisters at the Town Hall. All incredibly old, of course. Fragments. Mayor Crumb had it sent down here and suggested that your father might like it in his office.'

Otto peered at the jagged fragment of yellow glass, set into one pane near the side of the window. A picture had been painted on to it with thin black lines, like scratches. It showed three small figures standing beside some trees. One was holding something which might be a fishing rod. There was a faint jagged 'w' on his chest and his hand rested on the head of what looked like a dog. Another was slightly taller. His clothes were striped. The third was the tallest of all.

Miss Fringe spoke. Almost into Otto's ear. She, too, was examining the picture. Like Albert, she is a Karmidee living in the City among the Citizens. Not an easy thing to do.

Some cherry blossom was stuck to her sleeve and the hair around her face.

'It's very exciting,' she said. 'We think it represents the Warrior and the Traveller and the Giant, but of course we can't be sure. They were supposed to have met by the edge of a forest, although we don't know which one.'

Otto wondered what Mab wanted. Maybe it was to tell him about that Circus . . . Well, for once he had something to tell her. Several things. Several amazing things.

'The story is, of course, that the Warrior was saved by the Traveller . . . and the Giant.' Miss Fringe frowned and flicked at a white petal, now on the back of her hand. It floated reluctantly to the polished wood floor. 'You've heard the story?'

'Yes,' said Otto. Every Karmidee had, even him.

'Well it was after Araminta sealed the City with her Gates, you know, the Gates across the split in BrokenHeart Mountain, the Gates that stop any more Outsiders getting in, not that the Citizens realize it, of course, it's all magic—'

'I know about the Gates, Miss Fringe,' said Otto quickly. He had never seen her so nervous.

Miss Fringe blushed under her many freckles.

'Of course you do,' she said, in a lower voice. 'Anyway, Araminta disappeared, as you know, after that, and the Karmidee found someone else with the mark, you know, the birthmark that shows they must be the next King, or Queen, and he became known as the Warrior. Very fierce, presumably. The Outsiders were still taking over, we think,

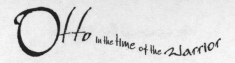

and someone called the Crow, or something, a sort of Citizen King, a terrible person, plotted to kill the Warrior. But the Traveller came out of the forest—'

Why on earth was she chattering on like this? Otto tried to cover up the fact that he was yawning. 'And he's the one with the striped clothes?'

'That's right. They're always drawn like that. I imagine stripes must have been a sort of traditional clothing in those days. Not that giants exist, of course.'

All Karmidee have magical energy, which doesn't always stay within the limits of their bodies. Miss Fringe's energy allowed her to draw objects towards her. At times of emotion, however, magical energy can show itself unbidden.

The petal of cherry blossom which Miss Fringe had flicked off her hand drifted back up from the floor and settled on the end of her nose. She brushed it off, blushing again.

Then, worryingly, a pencil rose off the nearest desk, spinning gently in the air, and landed on her shoulder.

'Miss Fringe,' began Otto, 'are you all right?'

'And then, according to the stories, of course, this Traveller summoned forest spirits of some sort and the Crow fled the spot, never to return. Terrified, presumably,' said Miss Fringe rapidly, swatting at the pencil. A number of silvery paper clips leapt up on to the front of her cardigan.

Albert came quietly into the room.

'I've got your lunch, Dad,' said Otto, getting the parcel out of his bag.

'Thank you,' said Albert. He took it and put it down on his desk without looking at it. Perhaps he wasn't hungry.

Miss Fringe was still by the window. Albert glanced at her.

'We were examining the stained glass, Mr Hush,' she said.

'I'm in a bit of a hurry,' said Otto.

Albert ignored this. 'This little fragment is very old,' he said, touching the tiny picture very lightly with his long fingers. 'They have discovered some large windows at the Town Hall in the last few days, completely intact, I believe.'

Otto was clenching his teeth.

Then Miss Fringe marched over to the wall opposite the desk and the window and opened it. The library is an ancient building containing many narrow secret passages. This one did not have pleasant memories for Otto. Puzzled and frustrated, he followed Albert and Miss Fringe inside.

'Miss Fringe was examining the cavity today, the place where the book was found last night,' said Albert. 'It is just a space over the frame of the Western Door where a stone block is missing. The damage from the lightning strike revealed it. She found some loose pages in there which seem to have fallen out of the book. The binding has become

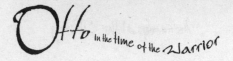

fragile with time. The pages are from the back.'

The worm lanterns along the ceiling were filling the passage with a honey-coloured haze.

'This appears to have been the very last page.' He paused. Choosing words. He was holding a page of parchment.

'There are no pictures on it. Just some very scrawled handwriting.'

'So it's really old, too,' suggested Otto helpfully.

'Yes. We think the book dates from the time of the earthquake and the arrival of the Citizens. Maybe repairs were made to the library after the earthquake. For some reason this book was hidden in the cavity above the door. In the period we call the Time of the Warrior.'

Otto had finally noticed just how tightly his father was holding the piece of parchment.

'Only Miss Fringe and myself have seen what is written here, Otto. We think you should have it.'

'Me?'

'Take a look.'

Otto took the page in his hand. His heart was beginning to thud under his ribs.

The parchment was crisp and brown. The writing looked as if it had been written in a scrawling hurry. Just a few words. Slanting and falling away off the page. Not properly finished . . .

Otto Hush, I hope you'll see this.
Come and help me to get out. I'll be in the dome

Otto stared at the words. At his own name at the beginning. He felt the sweat start to prick under his hair.

There was silence.

'Someone else called Otto Hush. I can't be the first,' he said in a rush.

'That might be the explanation,' said Albert.

'Let's hope he got the message,' said Miss Fringe heartily.

'Nevertheless, I thought you should see it,' said Albert.

'But it can't be me, Dad. That book they found in there is three hundred years old, isn't it, and . . .'

Otto, shifting about, banged his elbow on the wooden panelling of the wall. They all seemed to be standing so close together.

'We think the book is three hundred years old. The writing is harder to place. Either the message was written in the back of the book *before* it was hidden in the cavity three hundred years ago, *or* someone has been here since last night, written the message on this loose page and left it here for us to find today. The cavity was open over night,' said Albert.

'Could someone have been trapped in the Reading Room?' asked Otto, rapidly. 'That's got a dome. What

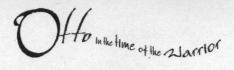

dome? Why haven't they put their name? Why haven't they finished it?'

'I think it was written in a great hurry. Perhaps in secret,' said Albert. 'It looks to me as if the person might have written a bit more and then didn't get the chance for some reason.'

There was the sound of a door opening in the office outside the passage. Footsteps.

'Mr Hush?' called a voice. Otto recognized the busy sound of Chief Librarian Paxton.

Albert and Miss Fringe at once became completely still. Then, when Mr Paxton had left and closed the door behind him, Albert led the way out of the passage and back to his desk.

'Let me know if you want to talk about this again,' he said. And his voice was quiet but very clear, as if each word were very important. He picked up his paper bag of sandwiches.

And they did talk about it again. But not until after many extraordinary and dangerous things had happened and Otto had understood the message only too well.

Norah at the Library

Otto Hush was not the only person to receive a strange and disturbing message that day. Norah Sargasso, Junior Chess Champion, was also in the library.

She had gone there with her usual intention, to examine medical books on rare diseases. She had examined them all already, but there might be a new one. She entered one of the small reference departments next to the mighty domed Reading Room at about the same time that Otto and Miss Fringe were making their way along a nearby passage inside the wall.

Norah walked on briskly. Then something caught her eye. Her mother had recently become acquainted with the handsome and famous Max Softly, Theatrical Agent. This

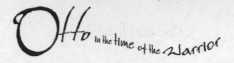

Max person lived in BlueCat Wood, an area of the City which Norah had only visited to play chess, which meant that she had not really seen it at all since she and her mother always went to and from games in a specially hired steam car with curtained windows.

Here, left out on a table with a number of other guide books and maps and things, was a very old looking pamphlet called *BlueCat Wood, Essential Information for the Inexperienced Adventurer*.

Norah strode past the table, realized what she had seen and turned back. In the few seconds it took for her to reach the scattered books they seemed to rearrange themselves. This often happened. Just as she could see all the possible sequences of moves in a chess game she now, without wanting to, saw these books and papers pile themselves according to size, then colour, then in a flurry of movement, alphabetical order . . .

Sighing, Norah sat down and picked up the small book about BlueCat Wood. It seemed to be very old, the print was hard to read. There had been far fewer buildings and streets when this was written, and many more trees. The castle where her mother's friend, Max Softly, now lived was described in detail. It was already ancient even then. There were supposed to be hidden passages. The author of the guide book had heard rumours that there was a secret cupboard in the wall of one room and that no one knew how to open it any more.

Norah was about to close the book and had absentmindedly flicked through to the last page. Then she saw something which electrified every byway, nook and cranny in the dense and intricate labyrinth of her brain.

'Ah, Miss Sargasso,' said a neat, crisp voice in her ear. 'I see you have found one of the mysteries of the Reference Section.'

Norah managed to nod politely. She was feeling very shaken.

The man who had spoken leant forward and pointed to the handwriting. He was wearing a badge which informed Norah that he was the Chief Librarian, Periculus Paxton. His eyes looked tired and red.

'Obviously we don't encourage readers to write in our books,' said Mr Paxton, smiling slightly before his face sprang like elastic back to a serious frown. 'But this piece of, ah, antique vandalism is rather fascinating and has no doubt puzzled many historians. This little book is over three hundred years old.'

Norah nodded again. Surely no one had ever been as puzzled as she was now.

'We believe that it was written when the book was almost new. It is a simple guide book. Just covering one area. And as

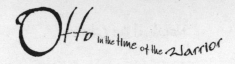

you will see inside the front cover, it was donated to the
Reference Section by someone who chose to remain
anonymous but who wrote here . . .' Norah had not noticed
this entry at the front. She blinked. Her mouth felt dry.
'. . . in a perfectly straightforward manner, that the book
should be kept for reference and not loaned out. However
then at the back, seemingly in the same, ah, hand, we have
this little message in code. To my knowledge no one has ever
deciphered it.'

Mr Paxton raised his eyebrows. 'A person with your
natural intellectual gifts, Miss Sargasso, and a logical way of
thinking, might well succeed where others have failed.'

'Are you sure it was written all that time ago?' asked
Norah suddenly, more loudly than she intended.

'As you can see, the book has been damaged recently.
All the guide books and maps here on the table were the
victims of an unfortunate leak in the spring when the
snows thawed. Some of the coded message has been, well,
washed away.'

'Are you sure it was written all that time ago?'
repeated Norah.

'Yes, indeed. There is no doubt that both the book itself
and the handwritten additions are at least three hundred
years old. The ink used has been examined at length. Miss
Fringe, our Under Junior Assistant Librarian in the

Department of Ancient Documents has a particular interest in these matters.'

'But it can't be—' began Norah, without meaning to say anything.

However Mr Paxton didn't hear her. 'Which reminds me, do excuse me, I need to see a colleague about a modification I want to make in Rule 64d . . .' And Mr Paxton marched briskly away.

Norah was left with the coded message. It disappeared in a blur towards one side of the page where, as Mr Paxton had explained, the paper had recently been wet. It began:

Three hares. Music Room. Nine of surrounding blocks carved. Nine mountains. Blue Remembered three blocks above hares and two to the right. Smoke Stack two blocks to the left. Midsummer Night three Tumble Man one block to left. Rainmaker four to left. Crab Face two down and one to right Broken Beginner's Luck, one down, one to left. Press in order of mountains as really are. starting in North, going East. Repeat

Mr Paxton had been right. Norah could read it. But not because of the superior and extraordinary nature of her deductive abilities. She could read it because it was written in her own code which she used in her own diary at home. And this message, which was three hundred years old, was in her own handwriting. And somehow, in some unimaginable way, she must have written it herself.

THE New Dress

Otto hurried out of the library by the Northern Door, on to a quiet side street. He came to a square with very tall trees where he and his mat could sneak into the sky without anyone noticing.

Soon he was high over the Boulevard. A great cloud of dragonflies shimmered in the sunshine. He hid above them and took the mat as fast as he dared over to HighNoon and up over SteepSide and then on and on to the South until he came to the last houses, and the great City lay behind him.

Then he traced the river, dirty and twinkling across the Wasteland, until at last it was crowded with barges and boats and wooden houses lay below him. Rooftops piled together, walkways and jetties and narrow streets winding inland.

These were the stilt houses of the Karmidee. The homes they had built on the mud plains by the river after the Outsiders, the ancestors of the Citizens, had invaded and taken over their City. There were two of these settlements, known as the mud towns. This was TigerHouse. Red Moon was further down the river. Places where Citizens rarely showed their faces.

Below Otto now, were people linked to him by ancient blood. His people. Three of his grandparents are Karmidee. But he has been brought up on Parry Street, living as a Citizen among Citizens and talking like one. Today he would not even have to speak, his clothes would give him away. As he circled down to land he felt the familiar lack of ease. He walked to Mab's house with his face set, fearing hostile glances, not meeting anyone's eye.

Mab's house was set on high stilts, stained by the rise and fall of the river water. The door could be reached by a ladder from the walkway below, which stood in the mud on lower stilts of its own. At night the ladder was pulled up for safety. Now it was down.

He climbed up and knocked on the carved door and Genevieve, Mab's grandmother, opened it at once. Grinning, bony, sharp elbows, pale skin long ago tanned like parchment. Blurred purple tattoos on the backs of her fingers.

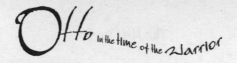

'Honourable greetings,' she said, muffled. What on earth?
Pins. She was holding pins between her teeth.

'She had her invitation two weeks ago,' said Genevieve.
'They don't give you much time. There's two days left. I'm
making her a new dress.'

Otto nodded. Not understanding.

'Honourable greetings,' he said. What invitation?

'Wait here,' said Genevieve, losing a number of pins.
'She's just trying it on.'

Otto waited.

The front door opened into the small living room. The
walls were painted with pictures of the Mountain Spirits. He
knew now that Mab had painted these herself. She had told
him only recently, although they had been friends for a year.

He continued to wait.

Voices from the next room.

Albert had seen the paintings too. Everyone who saw
them thought they were very good. Mab wasn't grown up
yet but her pictures were.

Otto waited.

There was a big pile of papers on the low table by the
stove. Otto had a look and found more pictures. Animals
and so forth.

Mab came in. Followed, triumphantly, by Genevieve.

'I've got an interview for the Guild,' said Mab immediately.

'Honourable greetings,' said Otto.

Mab generally wore the same black and green dress. Now she was wearing a dark red one, the colour of bloodberry wine.

'The Artists' Guild,' said Mab. She waved at the pile of paintings. 'You only get one chance. Gran wanted me to do a lot of extra pictures. I've been painting for days.'

Otto knew that the Karmidee Artists were members of a Guild, a sort of society or something, and he knew, because she had told him, that it was very important to be in it. However . . .

'But you're just a kid,' he said, bending down to pick up pins.

Her pale face was flushed. She was all washed and clean looking. Her long fair hair, unusually, had been brushed a lot.

'Now's the time when they join, Otto,' said Genevieve. 'Then they get help to learn. The Guild is powerful. Takes care of them.' She waved her big hands as she talked, snatching at the air.

Genevieve herself was an Artist, although of a very different kind. She had designed and built the Whispering Park. She made figures out of scrap metal, which moved and floated by themselves. However, Otto had never heard of her being a member of the Artists' Guild.

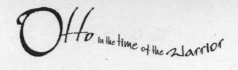

'It's her one chance,' said Genevieve now. 'I put her name down last year.'

'I have to go and be interviewed and show them my work,' added Mab. She was holding the thick folds of her new dress in one hand. Her knuckles were clenched white.

Genevieve suddenly clapped.

'I've forgotten the flowers! I'll have to go out, Otto, to get some flowers. Won't be long. Take care in that dress, Moth, don't let it get dirty.'

She snatched a bag from a hook by the door and they heard the ladder rattle as she went down.

The small room fell silent. It was very hot.

'Something incredible happened on the roof,' began Otto rapidly, whispering for some reason, picking up a moonstone from the floor. 'I met this girl. Last night. She just appeared. She knew my name. She said we'd met before. She knew my Dad's name too . . .' He glanced at Mab to make sure that she had heard him.

She was looking down at the wooden floor and her own feet in their old patched shoes, half hidden by the luxurious dress. She was on the edge of crying. Mab never cried.

'What's wrong?'

She kicked at the hem of the dress, all fringed with dark lace.

'She's set her heart on it,' she said. 'She's absolutely

desperate for me to be accepted. She's absolutely desperately set her heart on it. I've never seen her like this about anything.'

'Well your pictures are so good. You're sure to get in, aren't you?'

'I'm delighted you think so. The only problem is you don't know what you're talking about. I'm going to change out of this.'

She walked out of the room and closed the door.

He looked at the Mountain Spirits all around the walls. The Ice King, Midsummer, CrabFace. The he saw that there was a new one. The Blue Hare, the spirit of BlueRemembered Mountain. Mab had painted it in the traditional way, a hare with silver-grey fur, standing as tall as a man with a starry sky behind it and the sign, the hares running in a circle, inside the moon.

Otto had seen this sign very recently, of course.

Mab came striding back into the room wearing her familiar dark dress.

'She once told me that she did try to join when I was little but they turned her down because she makes all her things out of scrap metal and they fly about. They don't approve of it. They think it's showy. They're very, incredibly particular——'

'But her stuff is brilliant, the Whispering Park, that fountain in Red Moon——'

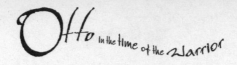

'I know.' Mab went to the window. 'They sound full of airs and graces to me, very strict, but she really wants me to be admitted. And, you know, she was so ill in the winter, she's only just got better really——'

The ladder rattled outside.

'I just can't let her down,' whispered Mab. 'It would be terrible.'

'Is this why you sent the beetle?'

'Yes.' She flushed. 'It's horrible. She keeps going on about how they look after children if they join. It's like she thinks something bad is going to happen.'

The door opened.

Genevieve stood on the threshold.

She was not holding any flowers. She wasn't holding anything. Her arms hung at her sides and her hands were empty and still.

'What's the matter?' said Mab.

'It's nothing, Moth,' said Genevieve.

She stood there a moment longer and stared at Mab.

'The Circus is here,' said Genevieve.

'Yes, I know,' said Mab. 'I've never been to one.'

'It's been at least twelve years,' said Genevieve blankly.

'I've read about them,' said Otto. 'But I didn't know there was one here. I thought they were only in stories. They travel about, don't they? From place to place? This one must travel around the City . . .'

His voice seemed big and clumsy, like something echoing in a well.

Genevieve hadn't looked at him yet. She continued to stare at Mab. And even Otto, who notices things, could see no clue to her thoughts in her face.

'Oh, it travels all right,' she said, very, very quietly.

Many more alterations had to be made to the dress. Genevieve, the flowers forgotten, began storming from one small room to another with bits of lace and jars of little jet buttons. Mab was to put the dress back on again. Otto was to go now. Honourable greetings to his family. She was sorry but Mab had to help with the dress and then finish packing her paintings and deliver them to the Guild and then they had to get her some new shoes.

Otto stood a moment at the door. He held it open and the sounds and smell of the river washed across the threshold. Mab was standing on the table while Genevieve tugged and fought with the hem of the dress. She looked over at him and rolled her eyes.

'See you tomorrow,' she mouthed.

He had agreed to go to the interview with them, friends and family were allowed.

'The library was struck by lightning,' whispered Otto in

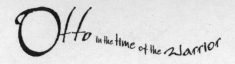

a rush. 'They found a book of pictures hidden in the wall.
Over the Western Door. It's got these obsidian covers. It's
very old. And then they found this message in the same place
the next day. And it seemed to be for me. And I met this girl
called Blue on the roof. Our roof. She knew my name. She
was incredible—'

'Incredible?' said Mab.

'Well, I mean, strange.'

'Strange *and* incredible,' said Mab with a slight smile.

'What's that?' exclaimed Genevieve, taut as a tight rope.
'There's something spilt.'

But it was only the beetle that Mab had sent to
fetch Otto, roosting on the bodice of the dress among
the moonstones.

'I think you should get on home now, Otto,' said
Genevieve. 'We've so much to do.'

Crystal Communication

Otto did not go straight home. He still had time to try and visit his friend Sween Softly, up in BlueCat Wood.

Sween was a Citizen and a child prodigy. He played the guitar and other similar stringed instruments. His father was the well-known theatrical agent and socialite Max Softly, a secret friend of the Karmidee.

Otto had recently given Sween a portable crystal communicator. It was a new model, designed by Professor Flowers, inventor and florist. It didn't just light up when someone was trying to get in touch, it made a buzzing noise.

As he skirted the edge of BlueCat Wood, climbing towards the castle where Sween lived with his father, Otto spotted a familiar figure crossing a square below. He dared to

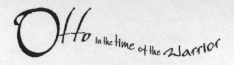

drop a little height, hiding behind orange butterflies as big as his head.

The boy crossed the square rapidly on his long legs, guitar case swinging in his hand. He had a pale face with lots of angles in it and two long, black plaits. As always he was dressed smartly, today especially so, black waistcoat over a white shirt, black breeches and buckled shoes.

Otto let go of the fringe of the mat with one hand and found his crystal communicator, a small glass sphere, in his bag. He held it to his face, grinning. 'Calling Sween Softly,' he said clearly. 'Calling Sween Softly.'

He saw Sween dart down a narrow street. The buzzing should be starting about now. He would probably start dancing about like an idiot.

Sween, however, showed no sign of receiving communication of any sort. He broke into a run, turned a corner and stopped outside a telephone box. Had he, despite emphatic instructions, actually left his communicator at home?

Suddenly Otto's communicator lit up. With a lurch of alarm he saw someone staring sternly at him. They blurred and wavered a little and then grew much bigger. Whoever it was had picked up the communicator and brought it close to their face. And it was an unfamiliar and decidedly unfriendly face.

'What on earth is this, Maxie?' asked the face. A question clearly not addressed to Otto, who prudently chose not to assist by answering.

Clumsy with panic, he tried to shove the communicator in his pocket, failed, lost a lot of height and crash-landed on a sloping roof, narrowly missing a chimney stack.

'There was a face in there!' exclaimed the person who wasn't Sween. 'I told you it was some Impossible object. It's probably been under that floor for years. Completely Not Respectable. Magico! Don't touch it! It might get out! It might bite! AAHH!'

Otto saw a glimpse of things blurring and spinning inside the communicator, it became full of blue, then green. A loud thud came from inside it . . .

'Goodbye,' he whispered, holding it away from him. He could hear what sounded to be birds singing.

He dared to look closer. It hummed. A bee flew across from one side to the other.

'Goodbye!' he hissed. These things didn't always turn off as easily as they turned on. Especially the portable ones. Mercifully the communicator went black. Just in time. Otto, his mat and his bag, were all starting to slide slowly down the roof.

He let go of the communicator and it rolled merrily ahead of him, gaining speed, starting to bounce, something

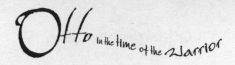

he, too, would presumably be doing in a minute.

Struggling to get the mat properly underneath him, he began to roll instead, the gutter came rapidly into view, he glimpsed something green beyond, a long way down, his mind flooded with pictures of his parents and the twins, he was in the air, lying sideways on the carpet, not hitting the ground, falling but beginning to float and then with a gentle thud, he arrived on something solid. The roof of the telephone box.

'What the skink are you doing up there, Hush?' asked Sween, smiling with the most broad and cheerful of his smile collection. Holding up Otto's communicator. 'Lost something?'

'Help me off here,' growled Otto.

'If you insist,' said Sween pleasantly. 'But there's someone in the phone box. I thought you people didn't like to be seen zipping around on your rugs.'

'Mats,' said Otto, through clenched teeth.

He passed Sween the mat in question and then swung down from the roof of the phone box, to the alarmed fascination of a woman inside.

'Suggest we leave the area,' said Sween, raising his hat to various people who were staring at them.

'Didn't you want to use the phone?'

Sween set off briskly back the way he had come.

'Not now, I was only going to call you.'

They were crossing the square. Many of the butterflies Otto had met in the sky had settled here. The branches of the trees seemed to be covered with restless orange flowers.

'My dad's got this new girlfriend,' continued Sween, striding on his long legs. 'Well I think she's a girlfriend. She certainly wants to be. Anyway she's absolutely tediously Respectable. And for various reasons I can't stand her. And she found the communicator thing you gave me when she was tidying—'

'Yes, well, that explains the fact that when I tried to communicate with you just now some total stranger answered. Plus, I think they threw it into a flower bed or something.'

Sween, no longer smiling, also stopped walking.

Otto stopped too. He was glad to, he was getting out of breath. 'I told you to keep it with you or hide it—'

'But that's what I did,' said Sween. 'That's what's so unsatisfactory about it, I did hide it, I hid it in this secret place under the floor in the kitchen and then she appeared with it just now, showing it to my dad—'

'She was tidying under the floor?'

'Apparently the board was sticking up a bit, and she tripped, at least that's what she said. But I think she was looking for the treasure.'

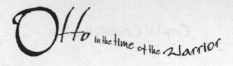

'What treasure?'

They started walking again, more slowly. Someone passed them pushing a barrow full of cherries. A green lizard was sitting on the top. 'There's this old legend thing that someone hid some treasure in our house. I thought I'd told you—'

'You mean your castle—'

'Yeah, well, small castle, anyway, it was hundreds of years ago. No one's ever found it. Some gold miner or robber or whatever lived here at some stage . . .'

They came out of the square into the shade of sand-coloured buildings and began to climb a long flight of stone steps. There were copper lampposts at intervals, green with age, with iron cats curled around the lamps.

The steps were steep and they both stopped talking.

On and on, up and up. Otto stopped to change his bag to his other shoulder and, more importantly, gasp in mouthfuls of air. He looked back and down. The City stretched away and away into afternoon haze. He really wanted a drink of water.

At last they came to the top. Here the steps met a narrow lane of much older houses that marked the margin where the trees began. These trees, many of them very old, were the real BlueCat Wood. All that was left of what must once have been a forest. Higher up among them, partly built, partly carved out of the rockface, Max Softly's castle baked and burned against the side of the Mountain.

'You came all the way down just to phone me,' said Otto, breathlessly.

'Yes. I wanted to warn you. She's visiting now. Didn't want her to overhear. She tends to snoop herself about.'

'So I gathered.'

'Dad seems to quite like her, unfortunately. And she's got this awful daughter.'

Otto grunted. Sween had told him before that Max often fell in love and that his judgement in these matters was poor. Sween's own cold-hearted mother, Marlene the Scream, the High Frequency Voice Artiste, had left a long time ago.

'It's a long way up, isn't it?' said Otto. The path to the castle disappeared up through the trees from the other side of the lane. It looked even longer than normal.

'Let's get out the rug,' said Sween, grinning again. He was a pale person, and yet he didn't look hot. How did he do this?

'OK,' said Otto.

Bibi Sargasso

They landed on the broad parapet outside the French windows. It was obvious why Max and Sween's home was known as a castle. There was a turreted tower with a pointed roof and, lower down, a parapet with a view across the City. The entrance was a narrow gate, only the size of an ordinary door, in a stone wall which blended into the rock of the mountainside. However there were no arrow slits, no places for bowmen to hide and the carvings on the walls in the courtyard were not of battles but of the Mountain Spirits, animals and trees.

The parapet was cluttered with flower pots and the air was full of scent and unusually large bees. It was reached by French windows.

'Ah,' said Sween. 'A problem.'

The French windows led into a room which Max and Sween called the music room. They were slightly open. Someone was in there now.

'You can't move the King that way. I thought you said you could play,' said a woman's voice, all warm amusement.

'It just seems a bit boring, darling—'

'Max! It's one of the oldest games there is. It involves strategy, forethought, planning . . .' She trailed off. She had started laughing quietly. There was a clink of glasses.

'And they're not *prawns*, Maxie, they're *pawns* . . .'

'Pawns, prawns, whatever, I just don't see the point. There's these Kings and Queens, why don't they just stop standing about in squares and have a party or something?'

'Oh, Maxie.' More laughter, and then, 'You're not one of *them* are you? Perhaps that glass ball thing with the face was *yours* . . .'

'One of what?'

'You know, magicos.'

'Oh, the Karmidee—'

'Yes, they don't make very good chess players, that's all. They don't have that essential something.'

'What essential something, Bibi?'

'They don't care enough about winning. Winning for its own sake. They don't have the final ruthless instinct, the

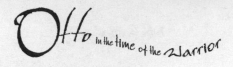

killing instinct. In fact, that's probably the reason they're a teeny bit inferior, darling.'

Out on the sunny parapet, Otto felt suddenly cold. It wasn't what this stupid woman was saying. It was the fear of what Max might reply while he was alone with her, two Citizens together. Even though Max had secretly risked prison many times to help the Karmidee, did he think they were inferior too?

He glanced at Sween, who raised his eyebrows.

There had been a short silence in the study. Then Max spoke, his voice cool. 'Perhaps we could all learn something from the Karmidee.'

'*Citizens* learn from *them*?'

'This whole City, come to think of it, is very much like your delightful chess board, Bibi . . .'

There was the scrape of a chair on a wooden floor. Max had moved. It was harder to hear him clearly. Otto and Sween sidled closer to the windows.

'When the Karmidee had it to themselves, possibly for at least a thousand years—'

'WHAT?'

'I think they must have learnt how to get along together, don't you? There are many kinds of Karmidee, Bibi. It is only a word for magical energy. The different kinds of Karmidee may not have very much in common. And yet they were all stuck here together and built this wonderful City. Then the Citizens arrived with this will to win which you are so proud of and, well, pushed them out . . .'

The woman shrieked.

Sween grinned at Otto.

'The Karmidee were *not* here first and they did *not* build the City. They were probably brought here as servants, everyone knows that, Max!'

High-heeled shoes clicking across the floor.

There was a pause. Perhaps they were really going to quarrel.

But then the woman spoke again and her voice had changed. It made Otto think of syrup. 'Well, I didn't realize that you harboured such extreme views. Max Softly, I wonder if I should really be in your house at all.'

'Really, Bibi? I thought you liked me because I'm exciting and different.'

She giggled.

Otto stepped on to the mat. He nodded to Sween. He wanted to go home.

But Sween caught his arm. Bibi had just mentioned his name. It was even harder to hear what they were saying now. Someone, almost certainly Max, was playing woeful runs of notes on the piano. Every time Bibi paused he played another one.

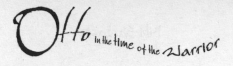

Nevertheless, she persisted.

'As a woman and a mother myself I do feel protective towards Sween. I've been meaning to mention it, I'm concerned.' Pling, pling, pling. 'This place is absolutely unique of course, but is it really suitable for him?' Pling, pling pling. 'That tower where his room is, I don't know how one gets up there, you'll have to show me around properly sometime, darling, that tower, well, the whole place really, is in need of attention. There are cracks.' A serious chord from the piano, full of big, doomy notes.

'The roof does leak here and there sometimes,' said Max. 'But we have buckets to catch the drops.' Pling, plingetty pling, plunk.

'You should have the whole place thoroughly examined. I'd be happy to supervise here while you are at your office. There may be dry rot, death watch beetle, creeping strangulation fungus, there may be many hidden dangers . . .'

Otto and Sween, straining to listen to these alarming suggestions, both failed to notice that her voice was getting nearer until the last moment. Suddenly she stepped through the floating curtains and on to the terrace.

There was no time to organize themselves in any way. They loitered uneasily next to the carpet.

Bibi was small and slender with golden skin. She wore a

knee-length black dress with a pattern of coloured circles on it, and a feathery snake thing around her shoulders. Her hair was like a neat pink hat.

'Oh, Sweenie, there you are,' she said, looking not at Sween but at Otto and his carpet. 'How ever did you get here?'

Handsome Max appeared behind her.

'Otto,' he said in his easy way. 'What a pleasant surprise. Are you coming in for a while? Bibi, this is Otto, a friend of ours.'

'But how did you get up here?' repeated Bibi.

'Bibi's daughter is Norah Sargasso, the Chess Champion, Otto,' continued Max smoothly. 'They have this ruthless instinct to win apparently. Terribly important.' He grinned, which made him look like Sween.

But Bibi could not take her eyes off Otto and the carpet.

He rolled it up. She stared.

'If you will excuse us,' said Sween, 'I need to show Otto something upstairs.'

'Upstairs!' exclaimed Max. 'What a coincidence! Bibi was just saying how she can't work out how to get up to your tower, Sween, I think she wants to examine it for leaks or something . . .'

'It's really the only part of your lovely home that I haven't seen, Sweenie,' said Bibi.

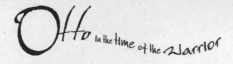

'It's a bit boring,' mumbled Sween.

'Perhaps another time,' said Max, cheerfully. 'Come and explain this business with the Knight and the Crow, Bibi—'

'Rook, Max,' said Bibi.

'So much to learn,' said Max, winking at Otto.

'And you must tell me about this wonderful carving,' persisted Bibi. She ran her hand across the worn surface of a circle of running hares, etched into a stone block in the wall. 'Do you think it means something?'

'No doubt part of some bigger picture,' said Max, soothingly. 'As you can see most of the blocks around it have been replaced. Very, very old, Bibi. Dangerously Karmidee.'

'Don't be naughty, Max. And look at these lovely little animals over the door . . .'

'Yes, we have them in all the rooms. Much too small to be really dangerous, of course. Unicorns, bears, dragons, troll-trees . . .'

'There are no such *things* as troll-trees, Max . . .'

Otto followed Sween out of the music room. Sween was pretending to be sick. They went down to the kitchen. Here they opened the door into the pantry and closed it quietly behind them. They crouched down under the lowest shelf and crawled out of sight. This was, and still is, the only way to reach the spiral staircase leading up to Sween's room.

THE *Miniature Kute*

Rosie, the pink-footed, rock-nibbling jewelled armadillo was sitting on the windowsill eating a pebble. She cheeped a greeting. Otto and Sween had rescued her from a trap during the winter. (Rock-nibbling armadillos are hunted for the little bits of gemstone in their shells. They get these because they eat rocks.)

'She's not going to get up here,' said Sween. 'And I bet she hasn't seen all the rest of it either. Dad's too clever for that. There's a tunnel that goes right down under the wood. He hides stuff down there.'

'A tunnel? Under the wood?'

'Yeah, out of the cellar. It's quite narrow. Dad thinks it's natural. A crack inside the rock. He just uses this end of it to

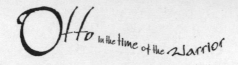

store stuff that he doesn't want other people to see.'

'And there's plenty of other nooks and crannies. Which reminds me. Remember that box I dug up in the garden, the one I was showing to you and Mab? The one that rattles?'

Otto nodded.

'Still can't get it open,' said Sween, and laughed.

Otto sat down on some cushions against one of the potentially cracked and dangerous walls. There were piles of sheet music on the floor. A large, tattered toy lion which they never discussed, was sitting next to Rosie's basket.

There was a moment of quiet except for the small but unnerving sound of the armadillo chipping bits off the pebble.

Otto knew exactly what he wanted to talk about. If he didn't talk about it soon he would go mad. It was just a question of starting.

'Anyway,' said Sween. 'Let's distract ourselves from the dreadful Bibi. I want to show you something. He lifted up the toy lion and there, underneath, was a very small musical instrument.

'Is it some sort of violin?' asked Otto knowledgeably.

'It's a lute. It's what they had before guitars. You can hold it if you like.'

Otto picked it up. It was all smooth curves. There was a pattern of inlaid shells and silver.

'Mother of Pearl,' whispered Sween. 'But that's not the point. Listen . . .'

He took the lute, it was not much longer than his hand, and plucked a string. A high note, exceptionally clear and sure.

'This was made by Domenico Nocte, the greatest lute maker who ever lived. He made it about three hundred years ago. Apparently he didn't make many. There are only three full-sized ones in existence now, made by him, I mean, and everybody knows who's got them and they're not for sale. He must have made this little one for a special present or something. My dad won it in a card game.'

'Have you ever heard anyone play one of them?' asked Otto.

'They don't play them,' said Sween bitterly. 'They keep them in bank vaults. Too expensive to play.'

Otto sighed. He guessed that if such a rare and beautiful instrument would sing for anyone it would sing for Sween.

'Imagine finding one somehow,' added Sween, dropping his voice, 'one that no one knows about. I could carry it about with me and play it whenever I liked and no one would try to steal it because they wouldn't know what it was.'

'If I see one lying around I'll let you know,' said Otto.

'Do that.' Sween held the miniature lute a moment longer. Then he put it back behind the lion.

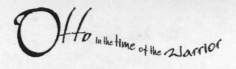

Otto cleared his throat. 'Some things have been happening. First of all this boy just appeared on the roof when I was looking at the crate nest. He was older than us. He seemed to have got there by mistake. I think it might have been something to do with the thunderstorm. I think maybe it sent him off course, or something. He disappeared again pretty much straight away.' He plunged on before Sween could ask anything. 'Anyway, there was something really strange about him. But then I met this amazing weird *girl*. And then I think I got this message from her asking for help. And I don't know what to do.'

And he described the meeting with Blue as best he could, and then he showed Sween the page of parchment that Albert had given him:

> Otto Hush, I hope you'll see this.
> Come and help me to get out. I'll be in the dome

'And you think it's from her?'

'Yes. She told me her name is Blue. She had that pattern of hares on her clothes. You know, that symbol, like hares running in a circle. She could have been named after the Blue Hare, the Mountain Spirit, couldn't she?'

'And your dad said this parchment was at the back of this hole in the wall, but they didn't find it until the morning.'

'Yes, yes. There were all these loose pages that had

come out of the book, it's sort of falling apart, and they didn't get them all until this morning, in the daylight. And so the page is three hundred years old or something, like the book, but that's just the paper and I think something happened to her after I saw her and she went and wrote the message there.'

'But how does she know your name? How did she know you would see this anyway? You could be anyone—'

'Sween! Listen. She knew my name already. She knew my dad is Albert the Quiet.'

Sween, infuriatingly, was picking up his guitar. Now he played a few notes of some slow tune.

'SWEEN! This is important!'

'I've gathered that,' said Sween, cradling the guitar. He looked thoughtfully at Otto. 'It's just that none of this is making much sense.'

'I think she's in some sort of danger,' said Otto. 'She said a lot of things about a struggle, a battle or something.'

'She seems to have been able to look after herself.'

Otto could see her so clearly in his mind. He could hear her too. *I will call for help . . . And you will save my life. You will be a hero, Otto Hush.*

'If she's trapped somewhere then how could she put the message in the hole in the wall in the library? And how come she could appear and disappear like that anyway? Is that a

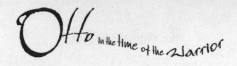

Karmidee ability? I've never heard of it.' Sween tapped his fingers lightly on the side of the guitar.

'OK,' said Otto, standing up. 'I'm going to try and find this dome. She's trapped in a *dome*. She just didn't have time to finish the message properly and tell me *where*. Are you coming or not? I don't see how it could be the Reading Room at the library, people go there all the time . . .'

He looked down at Sween and imagined grabbing him by his two long plaits and yanking him to his feet.

'It could be the Banqueting Hall,' said Sween.

'What?'

'The Banqueting Hall in the Town Hall. It's got a dome. Huge. I've been there with my dad. Although I'm not sure how whoever wrote this could be trapped in the actual dome—'

'*She* wrote it—'

'All right, all right. *She* wrote it—'

A buzzing noise had started somewhere in the room. Everyone, including Rosie, looked around.

'Hang on a minute,' muttered Otto. It was his crystal communicator and therefore very likely to be Dolores.

She was holding it upside down.

'Otto Hush. Come in Otto Hush.'

'Hello, Mum.'

No, she was upside down. She was standing on her head. Why was this?

'Are you all right, Mum?'

'Yes, I'm just doing a few . . . exercises . . . No, Hepzie!'

The communicator swung round, blurring, and then Hepzie filled it with her face.

'Hello, Ottie.'

'Hello, Hepzie, give it back to Mum now—'

Hepzie's beaming and freckled face was hidden abruptly by various fingers, small and large, squashed against the glass. Raised voices could be heard. The communicator was clearly the object of some dispute.

Then Dolores was back, the right way up, with her hair sticking out and about.

'Ottie, are you at Sween's?'

'Yes.'

'Well, can you give me a hand? I've got to get some shopping and the shops will be shut soon and I'm not sure it's a good thing to take Herzull with us. Can you come and look after her and take her out or something?'

Otto stared, wide-eyed, into the glass.

'Ottie? Are you all right?'

'Herzull's the bear cub?' whispered Otto. 'That's going to be her name?'

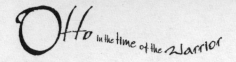

'Yes, I had the idea of calling her Herschell, after Herschell Buildings, because you found her on the roof, and the twins seem to have made it into Herzull, you know, easier for them to say. She's very young, she doesn't like being left on her own.'

A black muzzle, sniffing energetically, entered the picture from the side.

'Are you all right. Otto? You look shocked. What's the matter?'

'I'm OK, Mum,' said Otto, still whispering.

'You can tell when she's hungry,' added Dolores. 'Because she makes herself look like the fridge. And if anyone asks, just say she's a dog.'

At The  Town Hall

'It's a dog,' said Otto firmly, feeling his face go hot. Not an enthusiastic liar.

'Looks like a bear,' said the porter, peering over the top of the massive, polished reception desk. 'Bears aren't allowed. Got something spilt on him has he?'

Herzull was sitting on Sween's foot. She looked from Otto to the porter and back again and, as she did so, her fur turned a deep blue, which was the exact shade of the porter's uniform, and gold spots appeared in a row down her side. These were the same size and colour as the porter's buttons.

'Hang on a minute . . .' said the porter.

'A very rare breed,' said Sween in his most confident

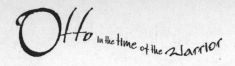

manner. He was accustomed to meeting his father's famous clients and friends.

'Is that strictly Possible?' asked the porter, gazing at Herzull, who was now, slowly but unmistakably, acquiring silver circles of fur around her eyes in the shape of his glasses.

'We're closing in fifteen minutes,' he added. 'What department do you want?'

'We just wondered if we could see the Banqueting Hall,' said Otto. He and Sween had not been able to think of a plausible reason for this request. They glanced at each other.

'Well, there's been a lot of interest,' said the porter unexpectedly. 'Especially since it's been on the radio news. I suppose I could take you up there myself . . .'

They remained silent. They had no idea what he meant.

'You'll need strong nerves,' said the porter, coming out from behind the desk. 'But I expect you know that. And this latest one,' he was talking over his shoulder now, gaining speed, 'well, this one they found today, either someone didn't like her . . .'

They plunged on past several junctions and through ferocious swinging doors and sped along the side of a cloistered courtyard, '. . . or she had a very nasty accident.'

'What's happened?' exclaimed Otto, skidding on a

corner. All the floors were covered in mosaic.

The porter, some way ahead, was greeting everyone they passed. Town Hall employees going home from work. Members of the Council . . .

'Is somebody injured?' called Otto.

But he didn't hear and Otto, feeling scared, didn't ask again.

'We'll take the lift,' said the porter cheerfully, 'because otherwise it's six hundred steps.' He had stopped outside a small door with 'Staff Only' painted on it in gold. He pressed a button in the wall. They stood still for a moment while they waited for the lift to arrive and Herzull, staring down from Sween's arms, bloomed with tiny coloured squares.

'I hope that bear isn't going to be sick in here,' said the porter. 'People are, sometimes.'

The lift, which was small and hot, shot upwards with impressive and dreadful acceleration. Herzull was slightly sick down the back of Sween's waistcoat.

'This takes us all the way up to the gallery,' continued the porter, through gritted teeth. 'I must warn you that in places the handrail is unsafe. Keep close to the wall at all times. There's one hundred and fifty porters in this Town Hall and only five of us are willing to come up here, you know.'

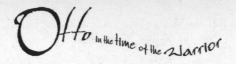

'And here we are,' he added, after another stomach-suspending minute. 'Personally I'm always pleased when members of the public express an interest in these things. Remember what I said about the handrail.' He straightened his hat and opened the door.

Otto stepped out on to a narrow wooden gallery.

He only just managed not to step straight back into the lift.

The gallery was very narrow and very high. In places it sloped away from the panelled wall towards the handrail and the dizzying chasm of the Banqueting Hall below.

Far away the great tables glittered with silverware and bowls of glass flowers. Nearby, alarmingly nearby, was the curved roof, wildly painted with clouds and dragons and other flying animals. Immense chandeliers were suspended on chains and laden with candles, each as thick as an elephant's leg.

Half closing his eyes Otto followed the carefree porter along the great sweep of the gallery. Blue was here somewhere, or had been, and something terrible had happened to her. She had believed that he would save her and she had been wrong.

The porter had stopped.

'High, isn't it?' he said. 'These are the ones that they were talking about on the radio. No one knew that they were here, you see. Then this panel came loose. Nails at the top rusted through . . .'

But already Otto wasn't listening. They had come to the first in a row of stained glass windows along the wall. He heard Sween breathe in sharply behind him.

Shapes and swirls, rainbows of light, carpeted the creaking boards of the gallery. The evening sun transformed into blues and greens, reds and browns and yellows.

'Very old, they're saying,' said the porter. 'They've been protected behind these panels, you see. Someone covered them up a very long time ago. Maybe someone thought they weren't quite Respectable enough, somewhere down the years. They need a good clean.'

Each window was at least two metres high. The first showed a boy with a rainbow round his shoulders. He had two long plaits, like Sween and a headdress of feathers. A cloud seemed to spring from his upturned hand.

Shimmering drops fell down on to a City, tiny and far below.

'Diamonds,' said the porter. 'Handsome skinker, isn't he?'

The handsome skinker was familiar to Otto and Sween and the porter and probably everyone else in the City of Trees, although he was usually represented as a grown man, not a boy, and he did not have to look handsome. He was one

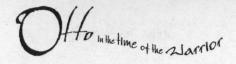

of the Mountain Spirits, the Rainmaker. And the next window, and each of the windows uncovered so far, were Mountain Spirits too, all children. Midsummer Night, dancing in a spiral of greens and golds, the full moon behind her. The Ice King, white and silver, a pale boy with a round face and very dark, straight hair with moonstones set into his clothes. TumbleMan, a clown in red and yellow.

'This is the latest,' said the porter, 'they haven't finished cleaning her yet . . .'

It was hard to make out the colours of the glass. They were very dirty and very dark. But Otto could see the figure there, ornamented with something that looked like obsidian and jet. The porter spat quietly on his handkerchief and wiped, very carefully, at the face.

'Don't,' said Otto.

The face had been attacked. The glass was still in place, but bent and crazed with cracks. They ran from a point in the middle of the forehead and spread in all directions.

It looked as if someone had hit her, just once, with something pointed and heavy.

'There,' said the porter, spitting on his handkerchief again. 'I was going to come up before I went home anyway, just to let her know she's not forgotten.'

Otto stared and stared at Blue. There was the circle of hares on the front of her shirt, the porter was cleaning it tenderly now. There, around her neck, was the diamond shaped like the head of an arrow.

He looked back at her shattered face, painted in silver lines on dark blue glass.

'Lovely, isn't she?' said the porter softly.

Quiet As A Scorpion

When Otto got home to Parry Street it was twilight. He stood under the lime trees and looked up at the fifth floor of Herschell Buildings. The Hush family flat was in darkness.

He stood there a moment longer. He had not saved Blue. Someone had attacked her picture like an assassin. He scanned the darkened windows. There was no one to tell.

He tried to raise his hat to the concierge, a gentle poetic young man, but it was a new hat recently given to him by Granny Culpepper and it wouldn't come off.

The elegant, rattling lift was just leaving, full of a family going slowly to the top floor. He walked up the faded, carpeted stairs from landing to landing, still fighting with the hat.

Although he had worked out that there was no one at home it was still a shock. The key for this rare emergency was hidden behind a loose piece of skirting board by the door. He stepped into the dark hallway and groped for the light switch. Then he went from room to room, turning every light on. Herzull followed him, yawning and muttering.

During the winter, only a few months before, Dolores had gone away. She had taken the twins. It had been a time of rows and bitterness and unspoken wrongs. Although she had returned after a short time Otto had not known where she was going or why or whether she would come back at all.

The memory of that time was always with him now. It was like a lens that he had to look through: it was always in front of his eyes.

Tonight the empty flat made him clench his fists.

Half an hour later Dolores and the twins came crashing through the front door, delayed by broken-down trams, and Albert followed, bleary-eyed from another long day at the library.

Otto was already in bed, quiet as a scorpion, armoured with sleep.

THE *Interview* AT THE *Artists' Guild*

'Do I look all right?' asked Mab, for the fifth time.

'I don't know. Fine. You look fine to me,' muttered Otto.

'She should be here by now.'

'We were early. She's not even late yet.'

They were outside the Artists' Guild near the centre of Red Moon. It was big for a stilt building. Four storeys high with pale blue shutters at the windows and carved trees framing the doorway. Large carved animals, including dragons, gazed out from the walls. They were painted in delicate shades of apricot and bronze.

Otto, who had never been here before, had just realized something. From time to time one of the animals would jump down from the front of the building and land lightly on the wooden deck and stand, vaguely transparent, sniffing the air. Then it would jump back again, taking the same place as before.

'Did you see that, Mab, look—'

'Yes I KNOW!' snapped Mab. 'They're Kinetic. I know. OK?'

In all their adventures and the dangers they had shared, he had never seen her so tense. She stood as if on guard, her face white and set. The wine-coloured dress, now finished to perfection, was beautiful, alien and frightening. It was edged with black lace from the lace makers in Water Town. Shimmering moonstones, tiny and full of blue light, had been woven into the material. They were of the best quality. Her white blonde hair, always knotted somewhere, hung as straight as light down her back.

Everything about her seemed different. Otto was seized with the fear that this was the start of a journey. That someone was going to take her away.

A clock on a nearby tower struck twelve. A giant porcupine with silver spines walked across the small square, twinkling in the sunshine. The spines banged gently together, making tiny clattering sounds.

'I'm sure it will be all right,' said Otto.

'I told you,' she hissed. 'It's not that simple.' And she

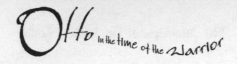

added for the first time in this whole baffling situation, 'My pictures are Flat.'

'Flat?'

'Yes.' She scanned the square restlessly, checking the shadowed alleyways. They were waiting for Genevieve.

Otto knew that many Karmidee paintings had Impossible energies. He had heard of some that you could actually walk into and stand inside, and others that spilt out into the room, or felt warm and cold. These carved animals on the front of the Artists' Guild were obviously some similar sort of thing. Mab's pictures, as far as he knew, were just pictures.

'So what?' he said now. 'Your pictures are great. Everyone says so. My dad says—'

'But they're Flat,' cried Mab. 'Oh, no, here she is . . .'

Perhaps Mab had begun to hope that Genevieve had been delayed in some mysterious way and the interview might be cancelled.

But she hadn't been. And it wasn't.

Genevieve was sombre in black and gold. Her hair was piled up and held with a comb and a flower. Her dress creaked.

'I've decided not to go in, Moth,' she said abruptly. 'It might go against you. They'll remember me. The Whispering Park—'

'NO, Gran, *please*—'

The door of the Guild swung open and a man in a grey cloak looked out into the square. He beckoned to Mab and Genevieve.

'Let's go, Mab,' said Otto. 'I'll be there.'

Nodding, staring at her grandmother, Mab turned and walked towards the the threshold. They stepped into the cool air and the shadows.

Looking back. Otto saw Genevieve staring, her hand raised. He waved back and then the doorman, or whoever he was, shut the heavy door behind them.

For a moment the darkness seemed complete. There was a smell of spices and wood polish. Then the man with the cloak led them up a sweep of staircase and in through the door of a long narrow room.

'Mab the Moth, granddaughter of Genevieve the Whisperer,' he announced. 'Mab the Moth to approach the Committee. Relatives and friends please be seated in the public area.'

Otto went over to a row of wooden chairs and sat down. He saw Mab's thin hands disappear into the folds of the dress as she lifted it a little to walk forwards alone. Her footsteps tapped and echoed in her new shoes.

She stopped in front of a large table, draped with cloth. Three men sat behind it. There were several windows along the length of the room, their shutters half closed. Mab now

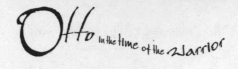

stood in a dusty beam of light. The man opposite her across the table, flanked by his two companions, was lit by another. Despite the heat he wore a thick embroidered coat. He seemed as if he was made of the same stuff as the floorboards and his huge carved chair. His face might have been chiselled from honey-coloured oak.

'Honourable greetings, Mab the Moth,' he said.

'Honourable greetings,' whispered Mab.

'These gentlemen and I are the Membership Committee of the Guild. I am the Chairman.' The two men on either side inclined their heads.

'We have looked at your work, you are clearly very talented in drawing. You also use colour exceptionally well.'

He paused.

Otto thought maybe everything was going to be all right.

But then the Chairman's face changed.

'I read on the application that your next of kin is Genevieve the Whisperer,' he said.

'My grandmother,' said Mab.

'Yes.' He gave a slight and deadly smile.

'Your grandmother. She is a sculptor like myself, of course, I remember her.'

He spoke very quietly into the ear of the man on his right, who also smiled, looking at Mab, and then spoke softly back.

'Tell me, Mab, have you ever tried to put any of your

Karmidee energy into a painting? Have you any work you can show us which can spill a little way into the room? A winter scene, for example, which, when one stands in front to view it, chills the face, leaving crystals of frost in the hair and on the eyelashes, as if one had been out on that clear and brittle day?'

The three men looked at Mab.

'No,' she whispered at last.

'Then all your work is . . . like this?'

'Yes.'

'Every painting is like this . . . excellent though they may be?'

'Yes.'

'Then your work is entirely . . . Flat?'

Otto's fists were clenched in his pockets.

'Yes,' said Mab, so quietly that one of the men leaned forward as if to hear her better. As if there was any need to hear her at all.

'Mab the Moth,' said the Chairman. 'You must understand that the purpose of our Guild is to protect the interests of those engaged in Karmidee Art. To educate them, especially those who join as children, and allow them to develop their skills. True Karmidee Art, as you may be aware, is becoming of increasing interest to the Citizens. Good prices are paid. The VeryDosh family are rumoured to

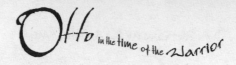

have a private collection occupying an entire floor of their house in the Heights . . .'

The two men on either side nodded yet again. One of them began to shuffle the papers on the table. Otto realized that they were Mab's paintings. He was piling them together.

'We believe that the Artists' Guild was set up over six hundred years ago, Mab the Moth, and I have no reason to think that, in all that time, any member has exclusively created art works which are indistinguishable from those of a Citizen. I am sorry to tell you that we cannot accept you into the Guild. I am surprised that your grandmother let you apply. She has reason to be aware, I believe, of our very high standards and the purity of our work. We cannot accept flat pictures, just as we cannot accept works of "art" which are essentially carnival amusements.'

Otto had shifted to the edge of his chair. There was a clunk as his bag fell off his lap on to the floor. That would be the crystal communicator.

The Chairman looked at him for the first time.

Otto stared back.

The Chairman turned his deliberate and steady gaze back to Mab.

'You must understand,' he said, 'the Guild of Artists is a Karmidee Guild. It represents the very best that our people can do.'

Otto's chair scraped on the floor as he stood up. Mab had already started gathering her work. He hurried to help her. He heard the Chairman say to his companions, 'I think some refreshment is in order, gentlemen.'

Then, laden with paintings, he and Mab were stumbling and clattering their way down the stairs. The doorman let them out, his face empty of expression. The door shut with a final, hollow sound.

'I told her,' sobbed Mab. 'I told her . . .'

Genevieve was standing in the shadows on the other side of the square. She set off towards them, walking slowly in her high-heeled shoes.

'Forgive me,' said a voice just behind Otto, who turned, expecting anything.

It was the doorman. He must have come round from some other entrance at the side of the building. In fact he must have run. He was out of breath.

'Mab the Moth,' he said speaking quickly.

'Leave her alone,' suggested Otto.

'I just wanted to say,' continued the doorman, 'that your work, the style, even the colours, although it is a different medium, greatly resembles the stained glass windows in some of the public buildings in the City. For example the new windows they have recently been uncovering in the dome of the Banqueting Hall in the Town Hall. Have you

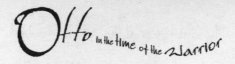

ever thought of working with glass? Windows sometimes need repair. They may even need to be replaced. And you obviously have contacts living among the Citizens . . .' He glanced at Otto.

A window creaked above them.

'Don't let this defeat you,' he said urgently. Then he raised his hat and walked rapidly away.

Back To Mab's House

'Just don't go.'

'OK, OK. But I don't see, you know, how I can—'

'Just don't go. I've never seen her like this.'

They were walking back to TigerHouse along the wooden walkways. The closer to the river the houses stood, the further they had been built off the ground. Mab and Genevieve lived very close to the water. They were nearly there now. Genevieve was marching ahead, Otto and Mab, carrying paintings, straggled along behind.

There was a midday quiet in TigerHouse, the people and animals were sheltering from the heat. A woman in the traditional green clothes of a Tree Scholar passed.

'Honourable greetings,' said Mab.

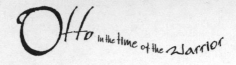

The woman smiled at them.

A moment later, Otto dropped a painting. As he bent to pick it up he saw the glistening silt below, through the cracks between the boards. The still air smelt of rotting plants. These were not called the mud towns without reason.

He stood up. The picture he had dropped was scratched along the bottom.

'It doesn't matter,' said Mab in a dull voice.

It was a picture of some people in carnival costumes. The colours melted gorgeously into each other like sweets left in the sun.

'I'm sorry,' he said.

'Everybody's sorry,' said Mab, and turned to trail after Genevieve, her beautiful dress fringed with dirt and dust.

'I've got to go out, Mab,' said Genevieve, as soon as they arrived at the house.

It was stifling in the little living room. Scraps of the costly red material lay scattered across the floor.

'Go out!' exclaimed Mab. 'Where?

Otto, at a loss, reached down to pick up a pin.

'Someone I've got to see,' muttered Genevieve.

Mab opened the window.

Genevieve shut it immediately. Then she locked the front door.

'What's *wrong?*' said Mab, more quietly. 'Why is everything so, so extreme, why does everything matter so much, *why?*'

'The Guild protects children who join them,' snapped Genevieve. 'They would have protected you. Helped you. Given you money—'

'I don't want their money,' yelled Mab. 'I don't want their protection. I've got *you.*'

Otto crouched down. He had spotted some more pins under the table. Almost underneath. He looked up from the floor. Genevieve was staring at Mab.

'What is it?' said Mab. 'Don't you want me any more?'

Genevieve didn't stop staring. She raised her hands and wrung them together, the tough, red hard-worked fingers, old faded tattoos, naked against the strange finery of the black dress and shawl.

'What is it?' asked Mab again, her voice breaking.

'Of course I want you, Moth,' whispered Genevieve.

She reached out and they held each other and both, it seemed, were crying, although Otto didn't know for sure. He just kept examining the floor for pins.

Genevieve was not in a mood to answer questions. She was going out. She might be back very late. Mab should offer Otto some food. Mab should not worry. Mab should stay

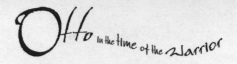

indoors until Genevieve came back. Genevieve was going somewhere on her own and Mab could not come.

'Why not?' asked Mab, full of doubts and miseries.

'Because it will be dangerous for me. And because you won't understand and having you there will make it more dangerous still. Anything might happen. You could be taken away for ever, Moth.'

'Taken away! Who by?'

'I can't talk about it now,' said Genevieve, very fierce.

At last, still wearing her black dress and the comb and the rose in her hair, she left.

'We've got to follow her,' said Mab, the instant they were alone. Otto was not surprised. He had collected sixteen pins and a reel of blood-red thread. He put them on the table.

A few minutes later they were poised at Mab's bedroom window on the mats.

Mysterious Reunion

Karmidee do not have family names in the way that Citizens do. Albert took the name Hush when he chose to live as a Citizen. The Karmidee call him Albert the Quiet. They call Genevieve 'the Whisperer' because of her ability, very rare and very powerful, to give objects the power of flight. The Whispering Park, her greatest piece of art, is full of mermaids and crate birds and other creatures, made of twisted wire, that float and circle like mobiles, but which are, in fact, neither suspended or supported in any way.

However, although she can whisper other objects into the air, Genevieve cannot fly herself.

Otto and Mab soon spotted her, walking fast and awkward in her smart shoes, making her way through the

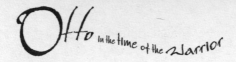

walkways and streets, out of TigerHouse and on to the edge
of the Wasteland. There she stopped, as if she were waiting
for someone.

Otto and Mab stopped too, hunched on a rooftop.

The Wasteland stretched away into the shimmer of
mirages. The City rose up, distant and beyond.

'What do you think—' began Otto.

'Look,' hissed Mab. 'There!'

Something was approaching through the haze. Something
that flew very low, skimming the ground, weaving between
the scattered, stumpy trees.

It was egg-shaped, and woven from wicker, with what
looked like a long metal bar sticking out at the front. Now
Otto could see that it had wheels. Four big metal wheels and
a small one at the end of the bar. And there was someone
sitting in it. He could just make out a pale face.

'What the—' breathed Mab.

'It's a flying chair,' whispered Otto. 'With wheels.'

'I can *see* that.'

The wicker chair came to a halt in front of Genevieve,
sending up a cloud of dust.

Genevieve leaned over into the shadowy interior where
the person inside reached out their arms. Now, clearly, she
and this stranger were embracing.

Otto and Mab were not near enough to hear what they

were saying. But they could hear the rise and fall of the voices. They could tell, without words, that this was a reunion. Down there on the dirt and sand and stones, Genevieve wiped her eyes with her shawl.

Mab looked round at Otto.

'She's getting in the chair,' he whispered. 'Get on your mat.'

Genevieve had almost disappeared under the domed roof of the chair. Her legs were still showing, her feet resting on a little shelf at the front. The person inside remained almost out of sight.

Otto realized that it must be a child.

Surely Mab had realized too. She was scrambling on to her mat, her arm round a rusting chimney to keep herself from sliding off the roof, cursing at the baking metal against her skin. She slipped. He caught her arm. She steadied herself. Without looking at him she tugged on the fringe of the mat. The chair had already taken off. It swerved around a tree and began to ascend.

Following the Chair

The wicker chair gathered speed. It was travelling towards the North West. Soon they were over Green Wood, where the sheep families were sheltering under the trees.

Then, before they reached the outskirts of the City, the wicker chair turned to the West and began to climb. Up, through the baking air and on and on towards the mountain known as the Rainmaker. Now they followed the side of the mountain, due North.

Otto had never flown here before. He could see rocks below, and solitary pine trees and great slopes of purple flowers. Then they were suddenly in the mist and they climbed again to find the sun. The wicker chair had climbed too. It bounced and sped ahead of them, its wheels a dark, spinning blur. The air smelt fresh and sweet. He looked up at the face of the mountain and glimpsed a rainbow floating over a waterfall.

They had been flying for over two hours. Otto's hands ached as he clutched the fringe of his mat.

Mab was a little ahead of him when she suddenly turned and looked over her shoulder. Something he still found it very difficult to do. She waved and pointed.

TumbleMan, the next of the great mountains, was looming up on their left. There was no mist or rain here. Boulders lay scattered and piled, as if someone had been throwing them. There were shelves of rock covered with flowers, making natural fields, some as big as the park on the Boulevard.

Otto saw a purple shape, strangely indistinct, dotted here and there with sparks of silver. This was where Mab was pointing. The wicker chair was dropping height towards it.

Otto and Mab slowed, hanging back a little in the sky.

It was a round tent. And all around it, in a sea of cream and yellow flowers, there were painted wooden caravans. The Circus.

They saw the wicker chair land. Several figures came out of one of the caravans and ran over towards it. Genevieve got out and embraced what looked like a child, although at this distance it was hard to see.

'Let's go down,' said Otto. 'They've only got to look up . . .'

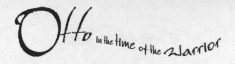

Mab didn't argue. She spiralled into the flowers and long grass and Otto drifted after her on to a slope above the tent and the caravans. He landed badly. Mab didn't laugh, pull a face, or say any of the usual things. Instead she stayed very still in the grass for a moment, watching her grandmother embracing a child dressed all in bright, shiny red. Watching her hug and hug this child, lifting her right off the ground. Then she shook hands with a man who had a silvery monkey on his shoulder. There didn't seem to be anyone else around. Maybe people had a rest in the afternoon.

'There's a lot of energy here,' whispered Mab, not taking her eyes away from Genevieve.

Otto could feel it too. As if there was something alive in the air.

The people who had gathered around Genevieve were going back into their caravan. The man with the monkey on his shoulder reached into the wicker chair and lifted someone out. It was a boy, dressed in white. The man carried him up the steps into the caravan and closed the door.

Only Genevieve was left outside. She stood there brushing at her dress, and then she brought something out of her pocket and held it up. It glinted in the sun. A little mirror. She took the carved comb from the back of her head and combed through her long silver and black hair and then wound it all up again. She held the mirror close to her face. Patted her hair.

'What now?' whispered Mab.

'Well if you want to know we're going to have to go down there,' said Otto, despite himself.

They got back on their mats and crept nearer, rippling the flowers and grass in their wake. When they reached the first caravan, surprisingly large now that they were close to it, they rolled up the mats and continued on foot.

Otto looked anxiously at each window they passed. All the shutters were closed. A dragon dozed on a doorstep. It winked a green eye.

Mab grabbed his arm. Genevieve was in sight, a little way off, picking her way in the high-heeled shoes, holding up the front of her dress. She disappeared round a corner. They followed.

Everything was very quiet and still.

Now Genevieve was walking along the side of the tent. It was a deep, velvety purple and scattered here and there with silver stars. It seemed as if it wasn't fabric at all, just an absence of light like a moonless night. As if she might be able to walk right through it.

However, there was a place where two flaps were folded a little way back. A small entrance. Genevieve stopped here.

Then she stepped into the darkness.

In The 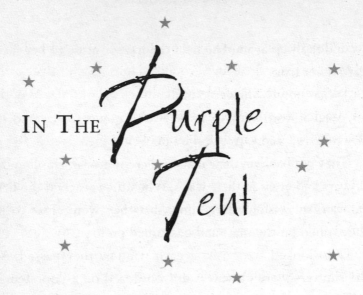 Purple Tent

Otto and Mab crept closer.

The tent seemed full of silence.

Otto peered inside. His mouth was dry. He closed his fingers around the mysterious purple fabric, unexpectedly cool in the hot sun.

Someone was standing alone, juggling in a pool of light.

As Otto grew used to the darkness he made out the banks of tiered seats around the ring. He took hold of Mab's hand and they crept underneath, into the forest of wooden beams. They were almost treading on each other. They made their way forwards until they were under the second row. There they could see into the ring easily.

The person who was juggling was a boy. Older than they

were, dressed as a clown in a bright patchwork of red and yellow. He was throwing wooden clubs, each alive with sparks. They spun up under the vaulting roof of the tent until only fragments of light could be seen.

Genevieve, stood still and straight, waiting.

The boy must have seen her.

He continued to juggle, his expression bland and unchanging, the clubs spinning faster and faster. His feet were bare on the sparkling sand which covered the floor of the ring.

He was light and graceful and dangerous,

This was the boy Otto had seen on the roof of Herschell Buildings. The one who had spun from nowhere, cursing the storm. Otto had recognized him at once. He watched him now, in fascination and fear.

'Honourable greetings, Whisperer,' said the boy, still juggling, still fixed upon the dancing clubs.

'Honourable greetings, TumbleMan,' said Genevieve, her brave voice scratchy and on the edge of some emotion.

'Seems like only yesterday,' said the boy. He caught the clubs easily, one by one. Still didn't look at her. Laughed.

'Twelve years, for me,' said Genevieve, strangely meek.

'For you, yes. I know that. I said I would give you twelve years. That is quite enough I think.' He put the pile of clubs at his feet.

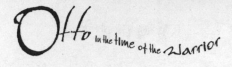

There was a silence.

Then, when Genevieve spoke, her voice sounded smaller still, horribly close to pleading.

'It doesn't seem very long. She is still very young.'

'Ha! I give you twelve years, something I have never given anyone before. That was my side of our little bargain. Now you have to return to us.'

'I still haven't found anyone else to look after her. TumbleMan—'

'Bring the brat with you then.'

'But you know why I cannot—'

'I know you have scruples, Genevieve. I don't share them. She was abandoned. You found her. By rights she should have joined us then.'

'But you know why—'

'For your own reasons you felt she should be allowed to stay. I've granted you that. Now you must leave her and come back to us. I didn't save your skin to have you wander off whenever you chose. You belong to me.'

'TumbleMan,' whispered Genevieve, and now Otto and Mab could only just hear her, 'TumbleMan, I beg you. Don't part me from her. Let me leave the Circus and stay here with her.'

He suddenly smiled. 'Are you telling me you have forgotten the other two so quickly, Whisperer? You who have always wanted to care for everyone, to gather all the little strays into your scrawny arms?'

'You have to let Cal and Morwenna stay here with me too!' cried Genevieve. '*I love them all.*'

He gave a yell of laughter. 'We are here for two days. If you do not come to us then we will come and find you.'

Now. Most dreadful of all. Genevieve hunched over in her shawl. The sound of sobs.

Mab was hunched too. She had pulled her hand free from Otto's grip only to seize his arm, clutching on to him, rigid, staring at her grandmother.

'It really would be much better for you if you came with us,' continued the boy, casually. 'I don't think I ever mentioned to you but everything here is very fragile. I'm planning to go back a long, long way, and change things. And you know how that sort of thing goes. Once you change one thing everything changes.' He sighed. 'Such responsibility.' And he pretended to wipe his forehead.

Maybe Genevieve was about to speak but he crossed the ring and the beam of light travelled with him. He reached out and took hold of Genevieve's face in his hand, spanning her cheekbones, and he put his head on one side. He pretended to look at her from different angles. A pantomime. A clown making up his mind . . .

'Your precious twelve years have made their mark. You

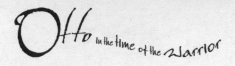

were old already and now you are weak. You are like an old
sheep scrabbling on the roadside, trying to feed some orphan
lambs. Myself, I am bored with you, Whisperer. But you
belong to me and you are useful. Whisperers are very rare.'
He let go of her face at last. Pushed her away.

Otto felt Mab's body become tense as a bow string. She
suddenly moved, as if to lunge out, and he clamped his arm
around her. She stamped at his feet. He wouldn't let go. She
bit his arm. He hung on. Despite everything he could still
think. He could still hear Genevieve's voice. 'You don't
understand . . . having you there would make it more
dangerous still. You could be taken away for ever.' Mab was
kicking at his legs. She hissed like a snake into his ear. '*Let me
go, you coward*.'

But he still hung on to her, gritting his teeth in pain. And
then Genevieve turned and walked away and the boy
followed her, grinning, spinning a single gold club on the tip
of his finger.

Otto and Mab crept behind him in the shadows.

The boy stopped where the dark of the tent met the blaze
of sun outside.

'Don't forget who I am, Whisperer. Nobody walks away
from me unless *I* let them.'

Genevieve must have kept on walking. He went outside.
They heard her shout back. 'I've forgotten nothing,

TumbleMan!' Her voice was stronger now.

'I'll swap you!' he shouted. Jeering now. 'Let the brat join us and you can go free!'

Otto and Mab, in the entrance, saw her spit on the ground where she stood.

The boy laughed. He threw his hands up in the air and a shower of tiny stones fell all around him.

'See you soon,' he called, still laughing, and he stamped his foot and the ground cracked open and the crack snaked after Genevieve, chasing her. She screamed, kicked off her shoes and began to hobble and run. Otto let go of Mab.

Caravan shutters and doors were flying open everywhere. Now people were shouting and waving and hurrying down their flights of wooden steps. Otto and Mab rushed in among them, trying to see Genevieve, following the cracked ground, deep as a house—

There she was, still managing to run—

And there, suddenly, was the wicker chair, swooping out of the air, and she was grabbing on to it and it was carrying her up, her legs kicking, clear of the caravans, up, higher, and she was scrambling inside.

Mab, screaming, threw her mat down.

Otto did the same.

'Stay away from me!' she yelled, jumping on her mat. 'I would have killed him! You stopped me! I would have broken

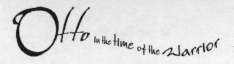

his stupid face with one of his stupid clubs! Don't follow me! You stopped me! *You are a coward!*' Her face was white. Her voice was shaking. She snatched at the fringe of her mat and dragged on it as if she meant to rip it off in her hands and the mat shot upwards.

He jumped on his own mat. Went to reach for the fringe.

Someone grabbed him from behind and pulled him, rolling, into shadows. His mouth was full of grass.

Morwenna

'Honourable greetings,' said a voice in his ear. 'Keep out of sight.'

It was the girl in the red satin clothes who had been hugging Genevieve. She had thick black hair, pale skin and slanting brown eyes. Just now these eyes were so close, he could hardly focus on them. He was crammed up close to her, she had pulled him under a caravan. She put her finger to her lips and pointed behind him. He turned awkwardly and saw steam rising from the jagged crack in the ground. Then he recognized the boy's brightly patched trousers as he paced slowly past.

Otto looked back at the girl and she grinned. 'He can get grumpy,' she whispered.

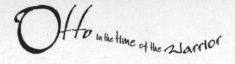

This wasn't the word Otto would have chosen.

'My name's Morwenna,' she added, holding out her small hand.

'Otto,' he said. 'I'm Otto.' They shook hands, which felt strange given that they were both lying down.

'I didn't hear you properly,' said Morwenna.

He was mumbling, of course, as if this would disguise his Citizen's accent.

'Otto,' he repeated, his heart sinking. But accents didn't seem to interest her. She nodded, smiling again. There was something very serious in her eyes, as if her smile was just painted on. She started pulling at a bolt on the bottom of the caravan. Now she was freeing another. There was a trap door. She pushed it up out of sight.

'Come on,' she said.

Otto hesitated, then wriggled after her.

The air inside the caravan was hot and dry and dark and smelt of painted wood after a long day in the sunshine. It smelt of something else too. Something familiar that he couldn't place.

Morwenna went from one window to another pulling chords, and gradually the light streamed in between the slats, until everything, including their faces, was striped with gold.

There was a kitchen at one end, a sink, a small stove and

some cupboards. The foot of a staircase. The trap door had brought them up beside a table. There were books there. And paints. Spread about.

'Were you just having a look around?' asked Morwenna, standing on tiptoe to get a large tin off a shelf. 'It would be all right normally. Just looking. Not talking though. We're not supposed to do that. But I think it's lonely not to talk. I like meeting new people. Me and my brother, we put the posters up. We have to go down in the chair just when it's getting light and—'

'In the chair?' interrupted Otto. Rudely but he couldn't help it.

She had brought the biscuit tin to the table and was struggling with the lid. A band of light fell across her pale hands. Another lit her eyes. Otto noticed that she had smudges of colour around them. Make-up. Not properly washed off. Her hands kept slipping on the tin. When she wasn't looking at him she frowned and bit her lip.

'In the chair?' said Otto again.

'Granny Jenny made it for him,' said Morwenna. 'Because he can't walk. She's been away since yesterday but we've come to get her now. We really missed her. It was only a day but it seemed like years . . .' Her voice trailed off.

'Granny Jenny,' said Otto.

'Why do you keep saying back what I say?' She had finally

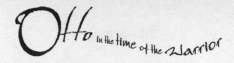

opened the biscuit tin. She looked at him over the top of it.

'I'm, I'm just wondering . . . Is your Granny called Genevieve the Whisperer?'

'Yes. Except we always call her Jenny because when I was little I couldn't say Genevieve. And Jenny is nicer. Except she's not really our granny. She found us when we were living with these really bad people. She looks after us . . .' She had stopped again. She looked at him. 'How did you know her name?'

He took a biscuit. Trying to think.

'Do you know her? Is that why you came to look at the Circus. You must know her. That means you must know her *here*. Do you know the other little baby she's been looking after? The one here? Except she's not a baby now, she's big. Bigger than me. Your sort of age. We've never met her. Me or Cal. So we wonder what she's like . . .'

Otto felt as if the caravan was getting smaller. He put the biscuit down.

'This is Granny Jenny's caravan,' said Morwenna, more quietly.

'*Her* caravan?'

She nodded. She wasn't grinning at all now. She seemed to be winding down like a clockwork toy. 'Is she very pretty? I thought Jenny might like her better than me. I thought she might have forgotten us. But that's silly, isn't it. I saw her just now and she looked different. Her hair's not all black any more.'

She stared at him intently. She reminded him of Hepzie or Zeb when they were upset. She was older than them of course. But not so very much older.

'Do you think she still loves us?' she whispered, searching his face.

He was trying to make sense of everything she had said. Somehow, Genevieve had had this other family all the time. She had looked after them. Here.

He looked around in the stripes of light and saw a bowl of dried flower heads on the table. Lavender. Genevieve's favourite. That was the scent he had recognized.

'TumbleMan was angry with her just now,' said Morwenna. She was starting to cry. Otto stood up. It was like a jigsaw. Somehow the pieces must fit. He just couldn't work out how. And he had to get home. Now. He thought of Genevieve, pleading with this TumbleMan. *You have to let Cal and Morwenna stay here with me too,* she had said. *I love them all.*

'I'm sure she still loves you,' he said firmly. 'I heard her say so.'

Fridge Magnets

There had been no chance to talk to anybody about what had happened. At least not for more than a moment. Albert was working late and then, it seemed, an outing had been arranged. They were going to the Circus with Granny and Grandpa Culpepper. They would meet Albert there. Sween and his father were going too. Otto tried to speak to Sween but Sween's crystal communicator still seemed to be in a flowerbed. Dolores was rather distracted by the twins. They were perfecting various new ways of floating.

'Look at that, Ottie,' she exclaimed as he walked back into the flat.

Hepzie and Zeb, holding hands and looking solemn, were

promenading slowly through the air about ten centimetres off the ground.

'Goody and evenings,' said Hepzie when she saw him. 'Mummy let us wear bongles and beadles and bings.' They wheeled away, arm in arm, taking small steps exactly in time with one another. They were both festooned with Dolores's jewellery.

'I'm going to start giving dance classes again,' said Dolores, pouring orange juice. 'Just for a couple of months. I was up at the House of Dance this morning. I'll be doing two afternoons a week. Granny and the twins will be coming too. She'll look after them and play the piano. Can you imagine what people will think if the girls don't stay on the floor?'

'You could just say they've got wind,' suggested Otto. The thought of Granny Culpepper assaulting some long-suffering piano almost made him smile. She was a very ferocious musician. However smiling was difficult.

'There's something else I want to talk to you about.' added Dolores.

'Mab failed her interview for the Artists' Guild,' said Otto.

'Well I can't imagine why,' said Dolores. 'Her pictures are so lovely—'

'I know, Mum. Then Genevieve went to the Circus.

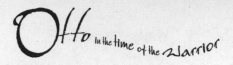

Something really strange has been going on. And there's this really evil person who works there, he runs the whole thing, I think—'

Dolores looked at him sharply. 'You've been to the Circus already? What do you mean, an evil person?'

'He didn't see us. He was talking to Genevieve—'

'HEPPIE!' exclaimed Dolores. 'What on earth—'

Hepzibah, and now Zeborah, had appeared, floating, in the kitchen doorway. They were still arm in arm and fully dressed and both drenched in water. Even their clouds of hair, usually so full of air and light, had been transformed into dark red curtains, dripping everywhere and almost completely hiding their faces. 'Mum and Ottie come in shower,' invited Zebbie politely. 'Nice and cold for the health.'

Otto sat a little while longer at the kitchen table. Herzull was asleep in her corner, surrounded by banana skins. Now he realized what Dolores had meant the other day when she had said that the bear cub looked like a fridge when she was hungry. Furry versions of the Hush family fridge magnets, mainly letters of the alphabet, were displayed along her back. However they were fading, leaving only the silver-blue colour of the fridge itself and a recognizable outline of the handle on the back of her head. What was her real colour? Did she have one?

'We'll have to go,' said Dolores, carrying wet clothes. 'It'll take a good two hours to get there. Three different trams. And then there'll be a walk at the end, up to TumbleMan's Field. Are you going like that? Or do you want to change? You've got grass stains all over that shirt . . .'

He stood up. Just hearing TumbleMan's name was bad enough. What had he done? Named himself after the mountain?

'Hepzie! That bear doesn't want a shower!'

Otto strode across the room and picked up Herzull. 'I don't need to get changed,' he said. 'No one will notice a few grass stains.'

This proved not to be the case.

Night AT THE Circus

Otto had Herzull inside his thin summer coat and was holding tightly on to Zeborah with his free hand. She bounced hopefully up to his elbow. Dolores frowned at him. He put his hand on top of his sister's head and tried to push her gently down again. She didn't move. It was like pushing gently down on the top of a tree stump.

Circus people walked to and fro, giving away paper lanterns filled with moonlight and paper bags of crystallized raspberries. The grass and flowers underfoot, already much trampled, smelt warm and sweet.

Albert, just in front of Otto, was talking quietly to Max Softly and Bibi. Bibi's daughter, apparently, was at a chess tournament. Everyone knew this because Bibi kept telling them. Sween was next to Dolores. Each time she spoke to him he started grinning.

The twins were bored. It was a long queue and they had already been in it a long time. Hepzie, now waving a lantern, had been confined to the buggy after an incident involving the hat worn by the woman standing in front of her. It had real cherries on it, although fewer than there had been before the Hush family arrived. Grandpa Culpepper had soothed the situation by offering the woman the golden daisy from his button hole. He was skilled in matters of diplomacy. Granny Culpepper, who owned a hat shop, had invited her to visit and pick out a new hat free of charge. Hepzie had eaten the cherries.

In order to try and entertain the twins, Otto had had his face painted while they were waiting in the queue. It was excellently and Impossibly done and he looked like a lion. Unfortunately he looked so like a lion that instead of being entertained the twins had been frightened.

He made this an excuse to look away from everyone as much as he could. The truth was that he was full of misery.

Blue had looked for him on the roof of Herschell Buildings. She had told him that he would save her life. Then she had sent him a message, calling to him for help. Somehow he had failed her. Somehow he should have protected her. Somehow the shattered face in the stained

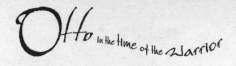

glass window in the Banqueting Hall was his fault.

Now today, Mab had screamed at him to go away, not to follow her.

She had called him a coward. A *coward*.

And she and Genevieve were in some sort of terrible trouble.

'Nearly there,' said Dolores. She wore a simple cream dress and a slim bangle the colour of coral. Other mothers as far as the eye could see looked wrapped up and clumsy.

At last they filed through the curtains (which were fluttering, although there was no breeze) and into the cavernous heart of the purple tent.

The Hush family and their friends settled themselves. All was dark. Soon the chattering turned to whispering. Fireflies flickered over the ring.

A single pipe began to play a slow wistful tune. The audience, Citizens and Karmidee alike, were held as one in a breath of expectation.

Then a beam of light shone towards the roof and there was the wicker chair so familiar to Otto. This time he could see the boy sitting in it with his legs crossed in front of him. This must be Morwenna's brother. He wore white make-up, a white baggy suit with big furry buttons and a small cone-shaped hat. He was playing a wooden flute. A musical clown.

There was a great sigh from the audience as the chair circled. The tune was like a bird.

Otto saw something shift in the deeper darkness at the edge of the ring. A figure in a top hat stepped forward, barely visible, and the boy and the chair and the birdlike tune soared up and were gone.

'Ladies and gentlemen!' cried a voice, the voice of a young man. 'Allow me to introduce myself. I am TumbleMan. And this is my Travelling Circus!'

A blast of light lit him up like a flame, all in yellow and red, his top hat spinning on his hand. He smiled his unforgiving smile and snapped his fingers sending up a crackle of sparks and small silver dragons which flew, whirring and dipping, over the heads of the audience.

'I told you it wasn't going to be Respectable,' a woman muttered behind Otto.

'It's just entertainment,' a man hissed back. 'They can't do us any harm.'

'We are a Circus of defiance, ladies and gentlemen,' continued TumbleMan in a softer voice. 'For your entertainment and our pleasure, we will defy the laws that tie up your little lives.'

He turned slowly as he spoke, looking at them all, and a wave of unease rippled around the tent. Herzull, on Otto's knee, ducked her head down into his coat. Otto, however,

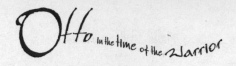

had nowhere to hide. He wondered, as TumbleMan's pale eyes swept past him, just how clearly he could be seen from the ring, and whether TumbleMan had noticed him that afternoon, before Morwenna had pulled him under the caravan. Then he remembered that his face was expertly and magically painted to look like a lion.

'We will defy gravity, that weighs you down in your little button boots, ladies and gentlemen. The gravity that drags the flesh down your faces and makes you grow old.'

TumbleMan threw his top hat into the air, it spun up and up and disappeared somewhere. It didn't come back.

'We will defy belief,' he said. One or two people started to clap. Then stopped. Something about his manner did not invite applause.

'And we will defy time,' said TumbleMan.

He suddenly threw himself forwards on to his hands and began to cartwheel around the ring. Faster and faster, a blur of yellow and red, bare feet, red gold hair, faster, faster . . . Then in a crash of cymbals and a flash of blue light, he vanished.

The drums kept up a steady, insistent rhythm. The whole ring was lit and empty.

'It's harmless,' whispered the man behind Otto, firmly. 'Just a bit of fun.'

The drums seemed to be speeding up. Otto saw the

intent, fixed expressions of the people opposite him, staring ahead.

Then he sensed the panic that was beginning to flicker around the tent.

The panic magnified. It fed off itself. The drums pounded like a frightened heart beat. One or two people stood up. Now everyone kept darting their eyes to the exits and up into the darkness and at the glittering curtains which concealed the performers' entrance.

Then suddenly, with another explosion of sound and blue light, TumbleMan reappeared in the spot where they had last seen him, still cartwheeling just as fast, just as blurred. He bounced back on to his feet and bowed deeply, his face flushed, turning and sweeping his arm to include everyone.

And now, it seemed, people felt it was right and expected to applaud. And a moment later everything went dark, orange light bathed the tent and clowns and tumblers and dancing dogs came running into the ring. Fast music started playing. Hepzie, on Grandpa Culpepper's knee, began jiggling Impossibly high and yelling with excitement.

Otto saw Morwenna standing on someone's shoulders in her red satin suit, juggling with a stream of sparkling balls.

The wicker chair came floating over the ring and a very colourful clown tried to reach it by climbing a ladder leaning on nothing at all, and then threw buckets of water at it, and

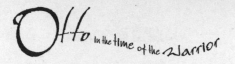

then threw a great many other things, like apples and spoons and flying monkeys, which he had hidden in his clothes.

But the boy in the chair was very skilled in the art of steering and nothing ever hit him and the audience cheered and clapped and the colourful clown threw sweets at them. Then they were distracted as he hurried away because the ring was filling with water and the water was rippling with green and sapphire-blue water snakes.

Then the ring was forgotten because tightrope walkers started dancing along the high wire and one man went spinning right off into the dark above the audience. Everyone started screaming. A moment later, astonishingly, he came down somersaulting through the air, and landed on his feet on an empty seat in the third row.

There was a woman whose clothes changed each time she clapped her hands, a strong man who picked up six people from the front row at once, a fire-eater and a sword-swallower who, to gasps of amazement, seemed to completely swallow a number of swords.

A little girl came into the ring on her own. She ran round throwing handfuls of what looked like coloured sand into the air, smiling and waving at everyone. When she was gone there was only the warm, velvet darkness and the soothing summer smell of the lavender.

Otto heard the flute again and looked up to see the

musical clown in his chair, drifting in a silver haze.

And now ice cool beams of light picked out figures floating over the heads of the audience. Sculpted figures, made of metal and wire. Women in long dresses, unicorns, hares that leapt, slowly, slowly through the air.

Even the twins were quiet and still.

Otto had only seen figures like this once before, they were designed and made to fly by Genevieve and they were in the Whispering Park.

TumbleMan strolled throught the fluttering curtains again. He was not alone. A shoal of silver metal fish swam in the air beside him. The Citizens in the audience were already pointing and marvelling at the metal women and animals. Now they gasped to see the fish leap through the air, away from TumbleMan, and fly across the ring and on, until they were over the audience itself.

The Karmidee, including Otto, guessed that these fish were much more than they seemed. A very similar shoal had a purpose in the Whispering Park.

It seemed to the Karmidee that TumbleMan was sharing a private joke with them. And perhaps he was.

The fish began to flicker over the audience, close to their heads, only just out of reach. They did not follow the same sedate path as the woman and the unicorns. They glided forward in a straight line, over upturned, curious faces,

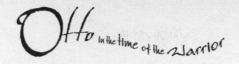

shimmering in the spotlight. Then suddenly the shoal would turn as one. Sometimes only a little, sometimes back the way they had come. Crossing and recrossing the ring.

Now suddenly they were directly above Otto.

For the first time they spun completely through a full circle, through 360 degrees. The spotlight immediately darted down on to Otto's face, revealed, cringing behind Herzull. Someone in the audience gave a whoop, there was a mutter of approval, brief scattered clapping.

Otto looked across at TumbleMan.

Their eyes met. TumbleMan was staring straight at him.

The Karmidee, including Otto, knew that the fish were measuring the Karmidee energy of the people below them. A turn right through 360 degrees was rare.

TumbleMan, in the bright ring of sand, inclined his head in a bow of recognition, still keeping his eyes on Otto's face.

The shoal swam off again, flicking and turning.

Then they suddenly dived away from the audience and sped towards TumbleMan himself. They stopped just above his head and began to tremble.

He grinned at everyone, not looking up.

The fish turned through 180 degrees, on through 360, on again, 540, and on yet again to reach 1080. They turned again. They turned and turned and Otto lost count. The Karmidee in the audience were much outnumbered by

Citizens, who understandably thought this was some harmless finale. However, when the fish were still at last, it was the shocked silence of the Karmidee that seemed to fill the tent.

Otto watched as TumbleMan waved his hand lazily in the air and the fish, the unicorns, the hares and the women with flowing hair, glided away through the flickering curtains. What ability did he have, with such great magical energy? Something unknown?

'And now we bid you farewell,' said TumbleMan, his cloak billowing. He seemed to be looking at each and everyone in the audience in turn. The darkness was full of sudden gasps and shrieks. Now he was looking towards the stand where the Hush family were sitting. Herzull jammed her head into Otto's armpit—

It was no longer the grinning boy looking out from under the tall hat. It was a skull.

'Sadly, for you, I think this is our last visit. I have something I have to do soon. Far away from here. And when I have done it, well, let's just say nothing will be quite the same again. Perhaps we will come back. But if we do, and I look into our esteemed audience as I am looking now, I will see other faces looking back at me. Once we change one thing, ladies and gentlemen, we change everything.'

Otto felt the fear surge through the audience. No one

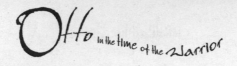

was able, it seemed, to turn away from the stark and pitiless skull.

Then TumbleMan gave a burst of laughter, the whole tent was bright with red and orange light, his face was restored and smiling as if it had all been a joke and the wild music began again. A clown ran into the ring throwing toys.

'Honourable greetings!' yelled TumbleMan. 'And good night!'

Otto glanced down the row at Albert, who was starting to stand up and, in the same moment, Herzull leapt off Otto's knee and scurried out of sight under the seat in front.

Otto looked round wildly. Now everyone was collecting themselves and shuffling towards the aisles.

'I'll see you outside,' he said to Grandpa Culpepper. 'By the gates. Herzull's run off.'

'Is that her?' said his grandfather calmly.

It was. Crossing the ring. Heading for the far side.

Otto clambered and stumbled his way over the backs of the seats and fell on to the sand. She had already disappeared.

'Hey, Threesixty,' called a voice. Not beside him. Above him.

He looked up. It was the boy in the wicker chair, the musical clown, Morwenna's brother.

The boy winked.

'I saw where your bear went,' he said, pointing. 'Get out under the tent. I'll see you out there.'

Otto ran between the banks of seats, apologizing and muttering his way between the people who were filing towards the exits. As soon as he reached the side of the tent he bent down and tugged and found he could lift it far enough to worm his way underneath.

A Handful of Rings

Otto was out in the moonlight between the looming caravans. He could smell the woodsmoke from their chimneys. Windows lit and glowing.

Herzull had been terrified. Had she finally managed to make herself invisible?

He shouted for her.

The chair came swerving into sight.

'I can see her, Threesixty,' called the clown. 'Stay where you are.'

He shot past, the wheels of the chair spinning, and Otto, locked in hesitation, didn't know whether to chase after him or not, and then someone wandered out of the shadows between the caravans, carrying a bag.

'MAB! I've sent the beetle about a hundred times! What's going on?'

'Oh, Otto, I didn't recognize you. I've left,' said Mab. Standing still.

'Left!'

'Yes. Look. Since you're here you can take these.'

One by one she took off her silver rings, three from one hand and two from the other. Never, ever, had he seen her remove those rings.

'But I thought your gran gave you these . . .'

'Yes.' She stared at the rings where they lay empty in the palm of his hand.

'Yes, she did. Put them somewhere safe. If you ever need money for anything you can sell them.'

Otto couldn't speak.

Just beside them, through the wooden side of a caravan, he could hear someone washing up.

'Oh stop standing there with your mouth open,' said Mab. 'I'm not a proper Karmidee Artist. I can't be in the Guild because my pictures are Flat. I don't belong. I'm not like everyone else.'

'*Nobody is like everyone else,*' whispered Otto.

'And for your information Genevieve isn't my grandmother. She was in some sort of trouble with the police or somebody, and TumbleMan saved her by letting her

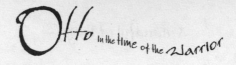

join the Circus. He wanted her because she's a Whisperer.
She's useful for the show. When I was a baby she went for a
walk in the mud towns one day and she found me.
Abandoned. Under a tree.

'TumbleMan let her be away from the Circus for twelve
years. Now he's come back for her. That's why she was so
desperate for me to join the Guild. So they would look after
me if she had to leave. He's frightening, Otto. He doesn't
like anyone to leave once they've joined. He owns them, he
says. And there are secrets, things only the Circus people
know. But I'm taking her place—'

'You're *what?*'

'Taking her place, swapping, he's agreed.'

'Does Genevieve know you're doing this?'

'No, of course not.'

Otto stared at her. 'I think you should talk to her about
this, Mab,' he said slowly. 'Let's go and see her.'

'She'll understand,' said Mab.

'I'm not sure she will,' said Otto. He even seemed to be
thinking slowly.

'*I've* had to understand lots of things,' said Mab. 'I've had
to understand that she's not really my grandmother. There
are a lot of things she didn't tell me, Otto. A lot.

'My parents, who I thought were dead, could be anyone
and they abandoned me. Even Demetrius isn't really my

cousin. He's just someone my Gran tried to look after once when he'd come out of prison and had nowhere to go.'

The thought of her thieving cousin made Otto grin. 'Well that's good anyway,' he said, terrified.

'I don't know who I am, Otto,' added Mab.

There were noises all around them now. Voices, laughter, doors shutting. The Circus people going back to their caravans.

'I didn't mean to be a coward,' he whispered.

A creaking sound, getting closer, maybe someone pushing a cart, about to come round a corner and into view.

Mab looked at him. 'Perhaps you'll see the girl you met on the roof soon,' she said softly. 'The one you said was incredible . . .' Then, very quickly and quietly, she walked away.

And here, immediately, came the wicker chair, rolling and lurching, the big iron wheels sinking into the carpet of crushed grass. The clown leant forward slightly from inside the dark interior. The moonlight caught his face, the chalk-white make-up and the single black tear painted on his cheekbone. He was holding Herzull.

'Thank you,' said Otto, talking quickly. 'Thank you.' He took Herzull and held her tightly. 'When are you leaving? On the posters it says there's another show tomorrow.'

'We're going tonight. As soon as everyone has gone home.'

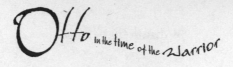

'Tonight!'

'TumbleMan's like that, Threesixty, he changes his mind. Gets an idea, gets another idea, he only came back here to collect my gran. She should be here very soon. Someone's chasing TumbleMan. To tell you the truth he's got something that doesn't belong to him. He's had it for a long time. But now he's planning to put it back where it should be. Or so he says.'

'What time tonight? How long does it take to pack everything up and everything?' Otto pointed at the silhouette of the tent, towering over the caravans behind him.

'Pack?' repeated the clown, as if this puzzled him. Then he seemed to suddenly realize something. 'Oh, yes, of course, *pack*, yes. Not long. No. Not long.'

Otto was thinking frantically. If Mab would not come back to talk to Genevieve than he would go and fetch Genevieve and bring her to the Circus again to talk to Mab. He must do this now, at once.

'You know Jenny, don't you,' said the clown. 'I saw you when you were going home after TumbleMan got in such a rage, after Morwenna hid you in our caravan. I recognize those grass stains on your clothes. And your hair.

'Why was he so angry with Jenny? Do you know? She does still want to be with us doesn't she?'

'Yes,' said Otto quickly. This boy in the white clothes and

Morwenna were somehow to do with Genevieve too. Genevieve had brought them all up.

'It's so strange,' continued the clown, 'to think of her being here all that time.'

There was a sound of voices, the clown raised his hand in warning and, her small eyes very round, Herzull began to get the shape of a skull across her back.

'It's him,' whispered the clown. 'He'll come round checking everything's OK now. You should go, Threesixty. In case he wants you to stay—'

'To stay?' echoed Otto, clutching Herzull.

'That's why he sends the fish round. Looking for people with powerful energy. Sometimes he asks them to stay. He might have been looking for you already in the queue, when all the people were going through the gates. I was going to tell you to go out another way.'

'My ability is only heartsight,' gabbled Otto. 'Threesixty's not so much. He's got more energy than most Karmidee I know put together.' He was pulling his mat out of his bag.

'Well he's different, isn't he?' said the clown, whispering now. 'He's one of the first children. Can't really compare.'

'First children?'

'Good luck, Threesixty.' The chair was beginning to creep forwards. 'I've got to go. I'll wait for Jenny in the caravan. He doesn't like us being outside just before we move on. You

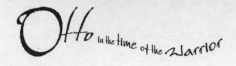

go too. Keep out of his sight. You've got a family haven't you?'

Otto stood back to let the chair go past.

'Wait!' he exclaimed. And then forced himself to whisper too, although he wanted to shout. 'Tell me where you're going to be next.'

He grabbed the side of the chair. It travelled on at exactly the same speed, pulling him with it so that he was almost running. He saw the clown's face, now full of fear, and began to feel truly terrified himself.

'Where are you going to be next?' he gasped. 'Whereabouts in the City. I need to know.'

The chair came to a halt.

'Let go of the chair and promise me you'll run for it,' whispered the clown.

'I'll do better than run for it,' said Otto. He let go of the chair.

He could recognize TumbleMan's voice now. Saying something about small creatures being harder to catch.

The chair creaked forward.

'Where in the City will you be doing your next show?' he hissed, desperate now.

'Here,' said the clown.

And the chair shot forward and he caught a glimpse of a pale hand, raised in farewell.

Invitation

Otto threw his mat on the grass and Herzull jumped down on to it. They would go to the entrance, land outside, and then walk back and try and see where his family were waiting. Maybe he would even ask Albert or Dolores, or his grandfather or all of them, what he should do.

He couldn't hear any voices now. The only sound was coming from Herzull. She was making a very small chattering noise. A cloud covered the moon and everything went very dark.

Then a hand clamped on to his shoulder and the fingers dug into his skin through his coat. 'Got you,' said a voice. A horribly familiar voice.

Otto turned round. As far as he could.

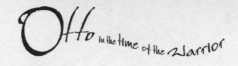

Faint moonlight returned, growing brighter.

It was him, of course, still wearing his bright costume and the billowing cloak and his top hat tilted on to the back of his head.

'You're the Threesixty, aren't you?' said TumbleMan, letting go. 'I saw you in the audience when the fish found you. There's a few kids in here tonight with the lion mask but you've also got very distinctive stains all over your clothes. Makes you easy to recognize.'

'I've got to go,' said Otto, stepping on to the mat, without looking down.

TumbleMan, moving closer, stepped on it too. Just one corner. Just under one foot. Enough.

'Interesting face paint. Did you enjoy our little entertainment?' he asked.

'Yes, thanks,' said Otto.

'How does your energy manifest? Something quite powerful by your standards, I imagine. Whispering? Counterfeiting? Or is it heartsight, the springing open of memories, the ones that are secret, lost . . . Hidden deep in our hearts?'

'It's nothing much,' said Otto. 'It's just about useless. Nothing like anything you had going on tonight.'

'But that's good. I like variety. So how does it manifest?'

Otto's mind was racing like a rabbit.

'I just get a few colours around me. When I'm upset.'

'Colours round you when you're upset! I don't think that can be the whole story, Threesixty. I think you're missing something out . . .'

The night was drowsy and clinging and full of scents and smells and heat, but TumbleMan seemed to have his own air around him, very clean and fresh. Unhurried now, smiling, he took something dark and gleaming out of his pocket. He balanced it on the tip of his finger and it began to spin. It was the sphere of obsidian. The one Otto had seen him throw into the air on the roof of Herschell Buildings, and catch so neatly, as if it were a part of him.

'I think you should come with us,' he said. 'I'm sure we'll find that you have some rather extraordinary abilities by and by. And anyway. I'd advise you not to stay here. The future is disturbingly uncertain.'

The spinning sphere was very close to Otto's face. He was beginning to feel as if the ground was tilting. All around them, everything was starting to blur.

TumbleMan, bright in the moonlight, seemed made of many details. His skin was light and dotted with freckles which, Otto realized, were shaped like tiny stars. There was a down of bronze hair on his upper lip.

'Don't try to run,' said TumbleMan softly. 'It's too late.'

Otto looked at the sphere and it seemed to be

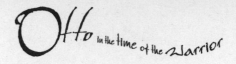

completely still. It was the Circus, the caravans, everything else, that was spinning all around them. He felt as if he were going to fall, he felt terribly, terribly strange.

Then, summoning his strength before it left him completely, he shoved TumbleMan as hard as he could with both hands. TumbleMan staggered backwards. Otto was on the mat, then he almost fell off it again because Herzull, who had already positioned herself, pulled at the fringe with her teeth and the mat lurched up before he had time to sit down. Then, finally, they were huddled together and shot into the air.

And up. through the centre of the swirling shapes of the caravans.

Into the calm night above.

He looked down at last and saw the dim shape of TumbleMan in a patch of shadow. He must have dropped the sphere when Otto pushed him. Now he was looking for it down there in the dark. Whatever it was.

Otto peered to see whether his family were waiting for him at the bottom of the path. There only seemed to be one person there. He let the mat drop towards them.

Telling Genevieve

'I've got to go and see Genevieve,' gabbled Otto.

Sween was sitting on a rock. He had obviously been playing his guitar. It was on his knee.

'Hepzie was sick. Your mum says it was just excitement. But they thought they ought to take her home. I said I'd wait to tell you because I reasoned that you could take me home on your rug. Plus I wanted more time away from Bibi the Pain. Your Mum says she hopes you found Herzull. Did you know that your grandad can play the guitar?'

'Sween,' said Otto, trying to breathe and talk, which suddenly seemed difficult, 'go after them and tell them I've got to see Genevieve. Tell them I'll be home later. That Ring Master person, TumbleMan, tried to put some

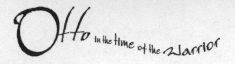

sort of spell on me, I think, it was really bad—'

'A spell?'

'Yes. It was really horrible.'

'Is he a widge? Does he have a cat amplifying for him?'

'No, no, I don't think he's a widge, the point is, he was trying to stop me leaving. He wanted me to join the Circus. He's got huge magical energy, Sween. And I saw Mab, Sween. And now I *must* see Genevieve.'

'Mab was there?'

'Yes. There's no time to explain—'

'I'll come with you.'

'No, look, please, you go and tell them, or they'll worry and I haven't got my communicator, *hurry*, Sween—'

Sween nodded, watching Otto closely. He stood up and put the guitar in its case. 'Have no fear,' he said. 'Just make sure you tell me what's going on. I'm away for two weeks now, playing at the Heights Hydro—'

'Yes, yes, yes,' cried Otto, already starting to take off.

'And be careful, you mat-flying maniac.'

It was well after midnight now, but TigerHouse was busy. Otto heard singing as he circled down over Mab's house. Men and women, dazed out on bloodberry juice, swayed along the walkways. Someone threw something, or possibly somebody, into the river, high with black water, crowded with barges moored for the night. Splashes, laughter, shouting.

Otto, with difficulty, steered down on to the veranda outside Mab's door. A light glowed through the shell curtain.

He took Herzull out from inside his coat and put her down on the wooden floor.

Then he knocked.

The house seemed full to the roof with silence.

Otto knocked again.

Then he pushed the door and it swung open and, his heart thumping, he called Genevieve's name.

Herzull, perhaps to comfort herself during the flight, had taken on the colour of the porter's uniform at the Town Hall. She looked up at Otto now, her eyes anxious inside the ghost of the steel-rimmed glasses.

'It's OK,' he whispered.

'Otto?'

He spun round. Genevieve was behind him. She must have come up the ladder.

'Honourable greetings,' he said quickly. 'I thought you should know I've just been to the Circus and I saw Mab there—'

'At the Circus?'

Genevieve, he realized, was still wearing the long black dress with the lace shawl.

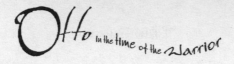

'At the Circus?' she repeated. Her voice sounded vague, she seemed almost to be looking through him, everything about her, including the dress, looked dirty.

'Is she coming home now?'

Why oh why had he come here by himself?

'Genevieve,' he said, his voice faltering, 'she seems very upset. I thought you should know—'

'Yes, I know, I know, she's so upset, my little moth . . .' Tears started in Genevieve's eyes, already swollen and bloodshot. 'My little moth . . . she's my life, you see, Otto, she's everything to me, they all are, all three of them—' She broke off, staring around her.

'I think you should go there, Genevieve.'

'I am. I am. I was just coming back for my bag. It's all packed . . . I've got to go with them you see. And I couldn't find anyone to look after her. I'm going to ask the King to give her his protection. Your father. He's a good man. Because she must stay here, you see. I'll tell him that. I'll tell him why. I've kept it secret all this time but I'll tell him now . . .' She was patting Otto's arm while she was talking. Now she held on to him. Was she going to fall over? Should he call out for help?

A fight seemed to have started somewhere below. Yells and crashes. Splintering wood.

'I'm sure if you see each other everything will be all right,' he heard himself saying. 'I'll take you there on my mat.

But we must hurry. They said they were leaving tonight. Not tomorrow. Tonight.'

Genevieve was transformed. Her face broke into a scream. Soundless.

Then she spoke so quietly he could barely hear her.

'Tonight?'

'Yes . . .' He was sweating with panic. He swayed back, supporting her. She had doubled forward as if someone had punched her in the stomach.

'*But it will be too late,*' she whispered. 'They will be gone by the time we get there. It's so late. They will be gone by *now* . . . Oh, Otto,' she was sobbing. 'My little moth has taken my place. I have lost them *all* . . .'

'We'll find the Circus,' said Otto, terrified. 'They must have gone somewhere, somewhere far off, like Harm's Way, maybe, or—'

Somehow Genevieve had grabbed him by the shoulders. She suddenly screamed right down into his face.

'We will never find them, Otto. *Not even if we look for the rest of our lives.*'

And she pushed him away from her, so that he stumbled, and she scrambled down the ladder, and ran off, her feet echoing and thudding along the walkways.

And Otto was left by the half open door, under the bloodless moon.

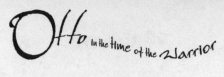

* * *

After a moment, or maybe longer, he felt something press against his foot. Herzull. He picked her up. In the rectangle of light from the abandoned house he saw that she had relinquished the porter's uniform. Instead she was the colour of the Circus tent, the fathomless purple, and a skull grinned and glowed on her back.

Norah AND Albert

'Can I help you, Miss Sargasso?' asked the library man, wringing his hands enthusiastically. 'You *are* a regular visitor these days . . .'

They were in the T section. Norah stared thoughtfully along the nearest bookshelf. At once the books started to rearrange themselves in her imagination. By their size, their colour, their subject, the number of letters in the title . . . She sighed.

'Are you looking for a book on a particular subject?' asked Mr Paxton, full of purpose. 'The T section is exceptionally good at the moment. We are also rather proud of the Ms and the Bs. Now, if it is X or Z which you have in mind, the choice may be easier because the number of texts

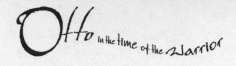

is smaller, though not, if I say so myself,' he paused briefly to breathe, 'in any way inferior.'

'I want to find out about time travel,' said Norah. Someone at a nearby table looked up from his reading. Mr Paxton's neat eyebrows shot up his forehead.

'Time travel, Miss Sargasso? Are you sure that is Respectable?'

'I don't know,' said Norah.

'I really don't think we have information about anything like that,' said Mr Paxton, firmly.

'There's a time machine in the Amaze,' persisted Norah.

'That is a fairground amusement,' said Mr Paxton. 'No one goes any further than two weeks, always backwards, and passengers can't get out of their seats. I took my nephews on it last summer. It would not surprise me in the least if mirrors are involved. All we saw was the same piece of hedge and a man with a green beard feeding a rabbit. In addition to which it was raining in the past. We got very wet and had not worn suitable clothing. I almost asked for my money back.'

'Oh,' said Norah.

'I would advise you to confine your interests to matters which are Possible, Respectable and Normal,' said Mr Paxton, perhaps trying to sound kindly. 'That's the best for all of us, you know.'

Norah nodded.

Evening light was turning the gilded glass dome of the Reading Room from white to amber. Floors creaked with the peaceable tread of readers going home.

'Thanks,' she said, walking away from Mr Paxton and opening the first door she saw. The Department of Ancient Documents.

This was a smaller room with glass-fronted bookcases around the walls. Two rows of cabinets ran down the middle, their tops also glass, and Norah could see rolls of parchment inside, faded and cracked with age.

A man with yellow-brown hair was sitting at a desk, reading something in a pool of light.

Norah remained still. So did everything else in this quiet room. A good sign.

She walked slowly over to the desk, dreading the chance that this man might have an interest in chess, and recognize her and ask for her autograph or, worst of all, challenge her there and then to a game.

But Albert Hush just looked up slowly and closed his book, which had a shiny stone cover.

He smiled.

'Can I help you?' he asked.

And his courtesy was such that Norah had no way of knowing whether he recognized her or not.

THE Notes IN THE Margin

Otto was sitting on a wooden seat on the roof garden. There were more flowers, fruit and insects than ever. He could see the crate bird nest, now finished – if a crate bird nest can ever really be said to be finished – and towering over the end of the garden, topped with a cluster of umbrellas and parasols and a lightning conductor. The female was sitting in there now, dozing. The male had recently brought her some bananas. There were three striped eggs, each as big as a large melon. Otto had seen them the day before.

But none of this was a comfort.

It was two weeks since the night of the Circus. Two weeks, therefore, since Mab had disappeared. Nobody, anywhere, had seen them. Genevieve, who surely knew something of great importance, probably several things, had become mute. She was being cared for by the Tree Scholars. Otto was not to go bothering her.

Mab had run away with the Circus. She had not told Otto where she was going or if she was ever coming back. He would have cheered her up if she hadn't run away. He would have found out what this story was about Genevieve not being her grandmother. He would have spoken to Max Softly about Mab's paintings. Max wouldn't have minded that they were flat. He would have been able to sell them for her. Max knew everybody.

But Otto could do none of these things. She had said goodbye and given him her rings.

A week had passed. Then another.

Albert had asked that every Karmidee, in the City, in the mud towns, wherever they were, should send him word immediately if they saw or heard anything of the Circus. There had been no news. The Circus, somehow, had completely disappeared.

The summer seethed and swarmed. Otto had nightmares every time he slept. The Circus dissolved into mist. All the faces became grinning skulls. Mab's face became a skull. The Circus melted like carved ice. It collapsed into the ground and was gone.

In the daytime he wandered the City. Albert was very

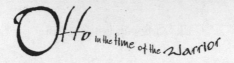

busy at the Library, making a record of the pictures in the obsidian book. Dolores had begun the dance classes and was always tired. Sween had been away playing with a Karmidee band in the Heights Hydro Cellar Lounge.

Each morning Otto woke up and realized, as if for the first time, that Mab had left and that she had chosen to leave. He would jump out of bed to try and leave this truth behind. The truth would follow him.

Now he turned the pages of one of Albert's encyclopaedias, distracting himself from one misery by thinking about another.

He ran his finger down the page.

There was no entry under 'first children'. No suggestion, under 'TumbleMan', that TumbleMan was anything more than a legend, named after a mountain.

Otto shuddered. He tried another page.

Blue Hare: The Blue Hare is an ancient mythical figure representing the spirit of BlueRemembered Mountain. Otherwise, origin is unknown. Symbol, a circle of three hares running, can be seen in various places in the City often in association with pictures of the full moon.

Otto stared at this entry.

It told him absolutely nothing that he did not already know. Then, as he started to close the book, he noticed a scribble of writing down one side of the opposite page, where there was more room. It was in pencil. This was Albert's encyclopaedia. If he was going to write in a book at all it would be in pencil.

Blue — this colour of great importance to the Karmidee? Also, yellow and red.

Very helpful, thought Otto.

The encyclopaedias, like most such books, had been written by Citizens. He flicked through a few pages and saw other handwritten notes. His father, trying to record what little the Karmidee knew about their own history.

The Warrior — Karmidee King, reputed to be fearless, saved by a mysterious traveller, a giant and forest spirits from ambush by Citizen possibly known as the Crow.

Nothing new there.

TumbleMan: Western Mountain. Ancient meaning of this name now unknown. Although this mountain known for its rockfalls. TumbleMan as mountain spirit, sometimes represented as clown. See other mountain names viz., Rainmaker, CrabFace, Midsummer Night, Ice King etc.

Otto closed the heavy book, brushed a ladybird off his nose and stood up. He had had an idea.

Mook's Famous Family Woolshop

'Mook's Famous Family WoolShop,' said a husky voice on the other end of the telephone, recognizable immediately as Roxie Lightning Needles Mook.

'Wait a moment please,' (much rustling of paper) 'now, oh, no, yes, here we are . . . In much addition to our magnificient range of wools unrivalled in the City now or at any other time in history, we also offers an ad-ee-vising service for all your knitting problems on Tuesdays and late night opening on Thursdays. Next Friday week niece child Mattie Merryweather Mook will be giving a demonstration of—'

'Roxie?'

'Yes,' growled the voice, suspiciously.

'Roxie, it's me, Otto Hush.'

There was a cackle that made Otto hold the phone away from his ear.

'Otto, friend of the Mooks and the Bandits, how are you keeping yourself? Do you have anyone that is getting on your nerve ends?'

'No, no,' exclaimed Otto. Roxie and Mattie were skilled in the art of combat knitting.

'Are you sure?' persisted Roxie. 'All is well here, but,' she lowered her voice, 'between you and me, Otto, it can be a bit *quiet* and the niece child keeps making me have baths. I could do with some hand to hand battle if you have one available.'

'NO, no, it's all right, please, I just wondered if I could ask you something, you and Mattie, I wondered if you have any information about the colour blue. You know, like the Blue Hare?'

The Mook family have run their Woolshop for many generations. Every shade and mixture has a name. Some wools, Otto had discovered during the winter, have extraordinary and Impossible properties. (It was the Mooks who made Mayor Crumb's flying jacket.)

'You'll be wanting to speak to Mattie,' said Roxie. 'She's the one with the scientific brain . . .' Mattie, presumably, was serving the customers. Roxie served customers too but

had the tendency to become frustrated and use bad language if they didn't make their minds up quickly.

Otto heard voices and footsteps. The phone, he knew, was in the little parlour behind the shop. Here was Mattie now, her voice soft and thoughtful. He told her about the written entry in the margin of the encyclopaedia.

There was a pause.

He imagined her round rosy face and her solemn frown. She was very, very serious about any matter concerning wool.

'I think I know what that might be about, Otto,' she said. 'It's about colour. It comes before the wool.'

Otto narrowed his eyes into the phone. His chosen expression when he thought he wasn't going to understand what people were about to tell him.

'It's in my book *Wool: Colour, Texture and Cosmic Energy*. There's the Three Beginnings. Red, blue and yellow. Red is . . . um . . . red is the . . . matter . . .'

There was a silence.

'What's the matter with it?' prompted Otto.

'Red is the matter, the thing everything is made of . . . and yellow is the energy, yes, that's it, red is matter and yellow is energy, or you know, light, the energy that's in everything . . .'

'What about blue?' asked Otto.

'Blue is the third one, Otto. Blue is the colour of time.'

Another Message

'The Tree Scholars are looking after her?'

'Yes,' said Otto. 'They live in the forest. Especially up on BlueRemembered. They think about things and stuff. It's to do with the trees.'

Sween nodded thoughtfully.

'Trees are very important to the Karmidee,' mumbled Otto.

'I know that,' said Sween. 'That's why there's so many of them here.'

He shoved the box of tangerines with his foot and it wrinkled the faded rug on its way to Otto. The tangerines sparkled inside, being wrapped in gold and silver paper. Otto took one and gave it to Herzull.

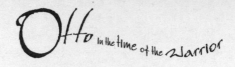

'She's in a terrible state. She's stopped speaking. She's stopped eating. My mum and dad have been to see her a few times . . .' Otto sighed. The thought of Genevieve made him feel horrible.

Herzull, having examined the tangerine, rolled over on to her back and started peeling it with her front paws.

'Perhaps the Circus just stops being a Circus sometimes,' said Sween. 'You know, they might have a sort of holiday. They all go home for a while. That would explain no one being able to find it.'

'Perhaps,' said Otto. 'But nothing really explains these other children, does it? Somehow Genevieve was looking after these two children and she'd never mentioned them to Mab or anybody. Which seems really, well, hard to understand. And *when* did she look after them? How did she look after Mab and look after them at the same time?'

He had tried to send the beetle to find Mab, of course. For the first time ever it had refused to come out of its box.

'If only I hadn't just *left* her at the Circus. If only I'd just, you know, *insisted*. *Made* her go back with me to see Genevieve . . .'

'I can't imagine anyone making Mab do anything,' said Sween.

Neither could Otto. But it didn't help.

It was a relief to be here at Sween's, though, sitting in the cool of his potentially dangerous tower room, while the sun baked the City below. There were two small arched windows and as he sat there on the pile of ancient cushions he could see the sky through the one near Sween's bed. He had flown in through this window about an hour before and bounced off the bed on to the floor. Bibi and her daughter were visiting downstairs, apparently.

'It was my fault,' he added. 'I was the only one who could do something and I didn't do the right thing. Like Blue, the girl in the stained glass window, she needed me to help her . . .'

He looked up and found Sween staring at him.

'Whatever's going on between Mab and Genevieve is not your fault,' he said flatly. 'And you are more than somewhat getting big ideas about your own importance if you think you could have stopped someone breaking a window three hundred years ago, plus it was only a window, not a person, that got broken.'

Otto didn't speak. For a bad moment he thought he was going to cry. He looked down and saw that Herzull was turning from tangerine and silver to a dramatic violet blue. The colour of Sween's stare.

'There's a reason I'm saying this,' added Sween in a quieter voice. 'I just think you can take this responsibility thing too far, that's all. Otherwise, the state you're in,

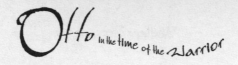

you could end up being looked after by the Tree Scholars yourself—'

'What do you mean?'

'I want you to remain calm and unruffled. Hush. Either someone's playing a not very funny joke on us or I've found another clue to your mystery—

'What? Which mystery?'

'I mean Blue. The Mystery Girl. The one whose portrait got damaged. The one you think you should have helped. Remember that old box I showed you and Mab? The one that I dug up in the little garden and couldn't get open? Well I got it open last night and this was inside. Nothing else, just this.'

He pulled something out of the inside pocket of his waistcoat. It was a piece of flat red glass, smoothed round the edges. He handed it to Otto.

There was a picture, and some writing. It all looked as if it had been scratched there: it was made up of tiny little lines, as if someone had been scratching for a long time.

The picture looked like a bicycle. The person had had difficulty making the wheels look round. If anything they looked hairy.

Underneath it said, in slightly hairy letters:

SWEEN TELL OTTO TO PLEASE GET ME
TIME OF THE WARRIOR RED MOON
THE AMAZE

Otto yelped. He dropped the piece of glass. Then he grabbed it up again.

The words seemed to be shouting at him. He ran his finger over the picture of the bicycle. There was a date too. Part of a date anyway. A year.

'There's not much you can scratch glass with,' added Sween. 'Except maybe a diamond.'

Otto looking up at last, barely saw Sween at all, being ambushed by the memory of Blue's face as she spoke to him, and the glitter of tiny stones on her skin, like bright clear sand. She had worn a diamond around her neck.

'Any idea what it means?' asked Sween.

'Not much,' said Otto. 'The Time of the Warrior is what the Karmidee call the time that began after Araminta the Tiger built the Gates that sealed the City. She disappeared a couple of years later. Then there was a Karmidee King called the Warrior.'

Sween nodded, looking serious. Unlike almost every other Citizen in the City, he knew about the Gates and their purpose.

'The Amaze is that massive maze over in Cloudy Town,' added Otto.

Sween nodded again. 'Do people ride bicycles round it?'

'I don't think so. I've never heard of it if they do.'

Otto stared at the picture. Sween brought the box from

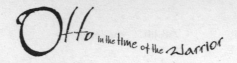

underneath his bed. It was small and made out of some dark wood. There were two gold letters inlaid on the lid. It was still dirty, of course, and the letters were very twirly and complicated, but they looked like a J and an S. The box had little brass feet shaped like paws.

'Do you think it means we should go to the Amaze *on* a bicycle?' asked Sween.

'Probably not,' said Otto.

'I thought you would understand the whole thing in an immediate and impressive fashion,' said Sween. 'You haven't thanked me yet. Rosie nearly ate it this morning.'

'Thanks,' said Otto, and took a nervous breath before rushing on. 'Apparently there's this sort of tradition that blue is, well, that it's the colour of time.'

He waited for Sween to crack a joke. Meanwhile, seeking an appearance of nonchalance, he peeled a tangerine, put a segment in his mouth and began chewing casually.

'That makes sense,' said Sween after a moment.

Otto almost choked on the tangerine. 'It does?'

'Yes. If you're going to start spitting things everywhere I suggest leaning out of the window. Have you ever noticed how the mountains go blue in the distance? They might be behind you, in the past. Or you might be going towards them, they might be the future. Or they might just be, you know, there. Somewhere where you're not. The only place that isn't blue is where you are now. The present.'

'I think Blue can travel through time, from one time to another,' Otto blurted out, before he could stop himself.

Sween flicked his plaits over his shoulders and picked up the beloved guitar.

'Sure,' he said. 'Why not? The question is, how?'

The Unexpected Visitor

In the silence that followed, Herzull and Rosie both stopped eating (a tangerine and a piece of brick) and looked at the door.

Otto and Sween, seeing this, looked too. There was a creak out there on the stairs. Then, definitely, another. Sween jumped up and flung the door back.

Norah Sargasso was standing on the threshold, holding Sween's crystal communicator with little bits of flowerbed still stuck to it.

'How long have you been listening?' asked Sween, savagely.

Norah didn't answer.

Otto stood up, which established, if nothing else, that he was the shortest of the three.

'Before you go,' added Sween. 'You appear to have something of mine.'

'It was in the garden,' said Norah. 'That's why I'm here. My mum told me she'd found something and thrown it out of the window. I saw it just now when I was out there. In that little garden with walls all around it. I thought it might have been something important, when she said it had been hidden under the floorboards.'

She held it out to Sween. It was smeared with fingerprints and soil. When he didn't take it immediately she began rubbing at the surface with the sleeve of her dress. Watched by four pairs of suspicious eyes.

'How did you get up here?' said Sween. 'How did you find this room?'

'I did hear something just then,' said Norah. 'I was going to knock. I heard you say something about travelling in time. I'm very interested in that myself. Hello,' she added, nodding to Otto.

Otto nodded back, curt and tense out of loyalty to Sween.

'Why?' he asked, curtly and tensely.

She looked at them both, then glanced behind her as if someone might be coming. Then, very strangely, she shielded her eyes with her hand for a moment, as if a bright light was coming from the muddled pile of things on Sween's bed.

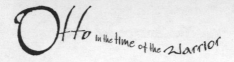

'I think I can do it.'

'You! Travel in time!' exclaimed Otto.

'I found a message I had written to myself. I wrote it three hundred years ago,' said Norah, simply. 'And it seems that there is a story that there was once a type of magico who could travel. Although it might just be a story. It probably is just a story. But there is a story. A man in the library told me. In the Department of Ancient Documents—'

'A man. In the Library. In the Department of Ancient Documents,' said Otto hoarsely.

'Yes. They were called hares. They could leap through time.'

'Hares!' exclaimed Otto, unable to contain himself. 'I can't believe it! Are you sure?'

'Yes, but it's a legend. They've just discovered this book with a lot of pictures in it. The man in the library said there were some pictures of them in there. They were people who could turn into hares.'

Sween yawned as if all this was boring and flopped down on his bed among the books and piles of sheet music.

'Haven't you heard of them, Otto?' he said. 'And you're such an expert on our Karmidee brothers and sisters. You met one once, didn't you? A Karmidee, I mean.'

Otto ignored him. This chess girl with the ignorant mother knew more about all this than he did and had even spoken to Albert on the matter, something he himself had tried and failed to do. This sort of thing always seemed to be happening.

'Well, apparently there is this legend, but if it's a magico thing—'

'KAR-MID-EE,' corrected Otto.

'Yes. So it's not surprising none of us have heard of it. Because we're Citizens, aren't we? And it's not easy to *meet* magicos, is it?'

'Incredibly difficult,' agreed Sween, picking up his guitar. 'Not to mention dangerous. Who knows what we might catch.'

Otto glared at him.

Then he, too, sat down. Herzull turned a sort of golden brown. This was the colour of Sween's guitar. Narrow black stripes ran from her nose to her tail. These were the strings.

'Is that a bear?' asked Norah. 'Are they allowed?'

'It's a DOG,' snarled Otto.

'Let's be calm, fellow Citizens,' said Sween. 'You have so recently burst into our humble lives, Norah, and here you are telling us you have travelled in time. Just when we were talking about it. Just when you have been eavesdropping. It's a coincidence, isn't it?'

'I might have done it,' said Norah, quietly. 'Or I might still be going to do it.'

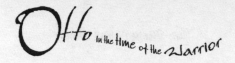

Otto tried to roll his eyes the way Mab did. Hurt himself somehow. Blinked a bit.

'You see, I don't remember writing this note,' she persisted. 'So maybe I haven't written it yet. Maybe, in the future, I'm going to go back into the past and I'll write it then. I want to find a real magico, Karmidee, that I can trust, to ask them about it. I never meet any because they're no good at chess—'

'How did you find this room, which can only be reached by steecut scares?' demanded Otto stridently.

'*Stairs*,' said Sween, '*secret stairs*.'

Norah looked at the floor.

Otto disapproved of her face. Her eyebrows were too thick, her lips were too thin. Her skin was too sallow. Her plaits of hair looked like greasy ropes. Her eyes were small and hard to understand. Couldn't she tell that they didn't like her?

'The man in the library said that the Blue Hare, you know, the Mountain Spirit, probably represents one of the Karmidee who could travel in time. There's that symbol, a hare running in a circle—'

'NORRAAH!'

'Sounds like your mum,' said Sween. 'You'd better be tripping along—'

'No!' exclaimed Otto. 'No. Don't. What else did he say?'

'NORRAAH, hurry up, sweetie. Timc to go home. You know that journalist is coming to interview you about you next tourn-a-ment. Mustn't be la-ate!'

Bibi, by the sound of it, was standing on the parapet far below and shouting up at the window. However Norah dropped her voice as if she might be coming up the stairs at any minute. 'Nothing. He didn't say anything else. But he was very nice.'

'So how *did* you find this room?' asked Sween.

'I looked at the outside and the inside of the building, calculated the liklihood of a number of possibilities and worked it out,' said Norah. 'I've got to go now. The Chief Librarian told me that there is a time machine in the Amaze. But he says it only goes back a few days and he thinks mirrors are involved and it might not really go anywhere at all.'

And she disappeared through the doorway and they heard the boards creak as she set off back down the tower.

'How on *earth* did she find thc way up here?' whispered Sween immediately. 'What does she mean, "worked it out"?' He looked anxiously around the small stone room as if Norah might appear again at any moment, possibly from inside a cupboard.

But Otto had sprung to his feet. 'We're going to the Amaze tomorrow,' he said. 'I knew about the time machine. I can't believe I didn't remember.'

Bibi AND Norah go home

Later, when it was almost dark, Norah and her mother set off back to their house in their chauffeur-driven steam car. They had not rushed straight home to meet a journalist. This had been a lie. Instead they had visited a number of shops selling medical supplies and specialist foods and they had collected a great pile of sheets from a laundry.

Now the car was chugging through Pig Street Hill.

Norah held the curtain away from the window. Not very far. Just enough to see the busy pavements and the people gathered around long tables in the squares, eating and drinking together. She saw a man sitting on a low wall playing an accordion. The window was open at the top and the warm air reached her face.

'Close the curtains, Norah,' said Bibi. 'We are both public figures.'

There was a great scraping and banging from the front of the car. The chauffeur, still steering with one hand, was throwing wood into the fire box with the other.

'And shut the window,' added Bibi. 'Smoke's coming in.'

Norah pushed the window up. The steam car was all black and gold at the front where the engine and the boiler and the chimney and the chauffeur were. The passenger compartment was wooden. The window rattled in its frame.

'Are you making friends with Sween?' asked Bibi, looking for something in her handbag.

'A bit,' said Norah.

'Where did you go off to earlier, did you find a way up to the tower?'

'I was just looking around,' said Norah.

'I'm counting on you to find out how to get up there,' continued Bibi. 'I'm quite sure he's not going to tell *me*. I'm counting on you to make friends, find the way up and search the place thoroughly.'

'I know,' said Norah quietly.

'Remember we're looking for secret panels in the walls, trap doors, uneven floorboards, anything like that. Everyone knows there is treasure in that place. Legendary treasure,

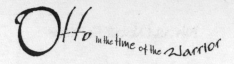

that's been there for hundreds of years. We're a team, remember. It's not stealing. You are the direct descendant of Jack Sargasso, the first Mayor of the City. He built that castle. It's in the history books.'

'I know,' said Norah.

She still held the edge of the velvet curtain between her fingers. Once she had seen a fight through the window. A man had blood on his face and down his shirt. She had seen wolves running in the dark under the street lamps, a moth as big as a man resting in the moonlight on the side of a house. Once, as they passed the corner of a lonely square she had been quite certain that she had seen a tree walking along, very slowly.

'You do realize this could be our big chance,' added her mother, in a different voice.

Norah looked around. Bibi had finished with the handbag. She sat back in her chair looking tired and older. The fabric of her dress was decorated with blue and green circles of various sizes and now these rearranged themselves as Norah looked. According to size, to colour, then making new patterns of their own. Diamonds, squares. Rows.

'Maybe our last chance,' said Bibi softly.

'I know, Mother,' said Norah.

They looked at each other wearily. The steam car thudded to a halt and the chauffeur jumped down from his footplate and opened the door. He was hired by the hour. Bibi paid him out of the handbag.

Then he blew the whistle and ground off down the road.

They were in a quiet street. The houses did not have gardens in front, as they do in some parts of the City. Nor were they joined in long rows, or crowded with balconies. Instead, here in Casa Rosa it was hard to see the houses at all. Walls ran the length of the street on both sides. Every now and then, unevenly spaced, there was a wooden door or, in some places, wrought iron gates.

The steam car had finally gone out of earshot. The quiet was broken by the faint sound of water splashing. Bibi unlocked the nearest door and she and Norah entered the shadows in the courtyard of their home. There was a lemon tree, an orange tree and a small tiled fountain. The sun would have shown stonework stained with lichens and walls painted in peeling ochre and cream. But it was night. All colours were hushed and whispering in the moonlight. The balcony and the shuttered windows were in darkness.

Bibi and her daughter went into their kitchen. All was dark here too. except by the stove, where a man was sitting, wrapped in a blanket despite the warm night. He wore long sleeves and had cotton gloves on his hands. Only his face was uncovered. His skin was glistening. A sheen of sweat. But that was nothing. Something moved on his cheekbones and his

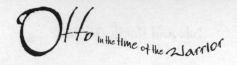

forehead, under the stubble on his jaw. Across the bridge of his hooked nose.

Bibi shuddered, as she always did.

But Norah hurried forward and hugged him around the shoulders and kissed his face. Even though, it was clear now, there were little creeping creatures, like bands of light, coiling and winding on his skin. Or perhaps the surface of his skin had become transparent and they were living there, moving, just underneath.

'Any news?' said the man, in his faint voice, as he always did, scratching fretfully at the back of his hands, at his wrists, at his neck.

'We are getting closer every day,' said Bibi.

'You keep saying that,' said the man. He looked up at them and, at that moment, the burning wood in the stove flared and sparked.

It lit the strange blanket that covered him, woven with threads and nuggets of gold.

It lit his face.

Bibi stumbled as if someone had pushed her. Norah wrung her hands together, her calm expression rigid as a mask.

'What is it?' asked the man, frightened. 'What's wrong?'

'It's all right, Father,' whispered Norah.

'Why are you both looking at me like that? You've seen it all before . . .'

Norah forced herself to smile and to keep her voice steady, but it was hard. She could see them clearly now. Luminous and writhing. They had reached his eyes.

'I keep seeing shadows,' he said. 'All day today. Winding . . .' he waved his arm, 'winding wherever I look. Big dark shadows. I want Norah to stay with me—'

'I needed her today,' said Bibi. She had turned her face away and was tugging at the pink confection of her hair. It came off in one piece, a wig. Underneath her own hair was short and grey.

'We have heard of another doctor,' she said. 'And we will take you to him soon. Norah won the Cloudy Town Supreme Championship last week, remember. The prize money is all in the bank.'

'*Another* doctor?' he said quietly, 'You think *another* doctor will know what to do? You think I want you to spend any more money? You have already spent everything we had, I think . . . And all the time, while you're out there finding the next person who will not be able to help me, *I am a prisoner*, no one knows what has become of me, I cannot bear anyone to see me, I cannot bear to see myself—'

'Somebody must know,' said Norah, fiercely. 'Someone must know what to do and we *will* find them, I promise you.'

'You and your passionate heart,' said the man, leaning

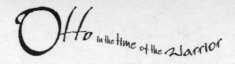

back and closing his eyes. 'It has been two years now. If there is an answer for me it lies in the mud towns.'

'No!' exclaimed Bibi and Norah together.

Bibi was lighting lamps. She put down her taper and wiped her forehead with the back of her hand. 'We are Citizens, Gregor. We buy carnival costumes from them. Not medicine. Who knows what poison they might sell us.'

Norah pulled a small table over to his chair. She began to arrange a chess set. Then she fetched a chair for herself. She tucked her father's golden blanket around him.

But tonight he would not be comforted. He picked up the golden Queen and rubbed the cool metal across his cheek. The silvery worms followed it back and forth, rippling under his skin like waves on water.

'So they might sell me poison,' he said. 'That would be a solution, don't you think?'

THE Glass Bicycle

'Mind those ones by the door, Otto, they're really getting quite *vicious*.'

Otto and Sween both ducked. Professor Flowers, florist and inventor, threatened the plants with a walking stick. His small shop had become like a jungle.

'Go on, go on . . . oh dear, I'm afraid that keeps happening. It's since the end of the winter, you know. Some of these species have, well, *undergone* something of a *change*, allow me . . .'

A sprouting, uncurling tendril had swung down from the roof of the shop and grabbed Otto's hat. Another patted Sween on the head.

'Drop that,' said Professor Flowers. He was wearing a hat

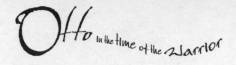

himself, a green one that exactly matched his hair, eyebrows and beard. Several tendrils, some bearing pink spiky fruit, came creeping towards it and then withdrew, squeaking their leaves together softly, menaced by the stick. Otto's hat was being passed around the ceiling. Finally it was released and landed on top of Herzull.

'Let's go straight through to the machine,' said the Professor, snatching the hat. 'And I'll try to answer any questions you have once we're there.'

He shouldered his way through the dense thicket of flowers at the back of the shop, swatting at wandering tendrils as he went.

Otto and Sween and Herzull followed.

They went through a small door with a panel of striped glass and into what rapidly became a tunnel. Otto knew that the Professor and the widge Madame Doriel lived underneath the Amaze. However he had never been into their home before.

The tunnel was carpeted, and to Otto's surprise, brightly illuminated by electricity. Bookshelves, laden with books, piles of magazines and wooden boxes with brass corners lined the walls all the way along.

'Bit of a long way, I'm afraid,' called the Professor. 'Ah, that's my Inventing Room. Nothing about time in there though, I'm working on a new sort of fastener to go down the front of coats instead of buttons, little tiny *hooks*, all made out of plastic, you see, that, ah, hook on to little tiny, ah, *loops*.' (The City of Trees, of course, has been isolated from the Outside for over three hundred years. Scientific discoveries have taken place there, together with changes in art and fashion. However these things have occurred at their own pace.)

'And that's our living room, the kitchen's on the other side . . . now, if we *continue* . . .'

They continued. Professor Flowers, generally cheerful, did not seem quite himself. As they climbed the vertical ladder which led up to the Amaze he sighed deeply. 'I don't get many enquiries.' He opened the trap door. 'People are not generally interested in how things work.'

He stopped, as if there was a possibility that they might decide that they, too, were not interested in the Time Machine.

Then everyone climbed the ladder, except Herzull, who was carried.

The Amaze had only just closed for the day. The trap door the Professor had chosen led them directly into the centre. A pleasant place with various attractions, including a mulberry tree which bore fruit all year round. There was a battered park bench some distance away and a sign which read *Time Machine*.

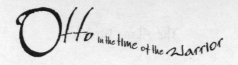

'The visitors sit here. And then when they put their money in here,' the Professor indicated an iron box with a slot on top, 'it rings a bell downstairs and I come up and operate it.'

'Has it been here a long time?' asked Otto.

'It has been here quite a while, I believe. Yes.'

'Is that it?' said Sween. 'Just the bench? How does—'

'It is not just the bench, Sween,' said the Professor, almost sternly. 'Observe the harnesses, very important.'

He stopped and stood there as if there was nothing more to say.

Otto and Sween exchanged glances.

'We just wondered, you know, how it's powered, and how you, you know, make sure it goes where you want it to go,' said Otto.

'It travels back two weeks, stays three minutes and returns,' said the Professor.

'Is that all it can do?' said Sween.

Otto frowned at him.

The Professor also frowned. He was standing with his back to a small wooden shed near the mulberry tree. The sort of shed which normally contains compost, pots and a lawnmower. There was a sign on the door saying *No Admittance – Staff Only*.

'Tell me. Otto,' he said. 'Is it fashionable to wear shapeless floppy suits among persons of your age, at present?'

'I don't think so,' said Otto, who didn't really notice such things.

'No,' said Sween, who did.

'And do you have a friend, a girl, who sometimes wears a shiny jewel in her nose?'

'No' said Otto. Sween shook his head.

'Everyone looked at the ground.

'Could it go further back than two weeks, if you wanted it to?' asked Otto.

The Professor didn't reply. He gave another thoughtful sigh and pulled some keys out of his pocket. Then he turned towards the shed and Otto and Sween followed him. Puzzled.

A moment later they were too astounded to speak.

Inside, the shed was alive with soft, silvery blue light.

There was a bicycle in the middle, leaning on nothing, standing a few centimetres above the ground. It was made entirely of glass. Every spoke of its wheels, fine as a spider's web. The frame, the saddle, the handlebars. All bright glass. It looked like the ghost of a bicycle. Like something drawn on a cloud. Like something that wasn't there.

'This bicycle is made of blackglass, of obsidian,' said the Professor quietly. 'A substance which, as you know, can hold magical energy. The obsidian from which this bicycle is made

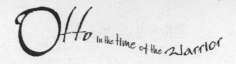

was, we, er, think, filled with magical energy, using a combination of widge spells, caver assistance and scientific deduction.' He paused. 'The amount of magical energy in the fabric of this machine is too great to measure.'

'But how—' began Otto.

'The basic theory of time travel,' continued the Professor, 'is closely linked with Impossibility Logic and Models of Immense Energy Maintenance. This bicycle, as you can see, is extremely fragile. Anyone trying to climb on to the saddle would break it. It is illogical. It is a bicycle and yet it cannot travel in space. It cannot take the rightful place of a bicycle in the world. Nevertheless it exists. It must go somewhere. It therefore takes the only option left to it. It travels in time.'

'Somebody rides it?' asked Otto, who had not quite followed all this.

'Nobody rides it,' said the Professor. 'If someone could ride it it wouldn't be able to travel in time. It would be far too logical for that.'

Sween sneezed.

'Now,' said the Professor. 'As you can see the bicycle is hovering just above this section of wooden floor. This is actually part of a small circular track, most of which is concealed under the ground. I wind this handle,' he indicated a large brass handle attached to a box. 'And it tightens up the *mechanism*. Very simple, cogs, you see, in this box.'

'Like a clock?' asked Otto, who knew what a clock was.

'No, well, a little. But more like a clockwork toy. When I've done that I lower the bicycle, very gently, on to the floor. Now everything is wound up, you see. The floor which is part of my, er, track, which is round, will start to move in a few seconds' time. If I was planning to go on a little ride myself, which I am *not*,' he coughed briefly, 'it would give me time to rush over and get on to the bench and do up the harness. Very important. Anyway, then the track begins to move, and so, of course, do the bicycle wheels. They go backwards. The bicycle travels backwards in time, about two weeks, just a short ride taking the bench with it. Then the spring, part of the *mechanism*, springs back and the track revolves the other way and there you are, they're back. The distance travelled, two weeks, is determined by setting this dial here.'

'More than somewhat,' said Sween.

'I try to set it so that people visit a time two weeks before, in the evening, when the Amaze is closed. I should have said that the bench is *linked* to the bicycle and travels *with* it.'

'But the bicycle is here in the shed and the bench is outside over there,' said Otto.

'A magical line of time synchronization and local energy flux maintenance runs underground. It starts under

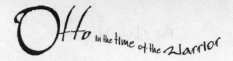

the bicycle and it ends under the bench. It is conducted by copper wire, protected from corrosion by a layer of gold,' said the Professor, slowly and clearly, as if there was a possibility that they would have any idea what he was talking about.

Sween and Otto both nodded.

'So does it only go as far as two weeks?' asked Sween. 'Do you think it could go any further?'

'Time travel is dangerous,' said the Professor. 'It takes place on the very edge of Impossibility. We do not understand it fully. But, since you ask, yes.'

'So it can go back as far as it has existed,' exclaimed Sween. 'If you set the dial and wound it up and everything – ow!'

Otto had stood on his foot.

'Well,' said the Professor mildly, 'in *theory* . . .'

'But of course, even if someone did want to try and do that it wouldn't be all that useful,' said Otto. 'Because they would still come back after only a few minutes in the past.'

There was a pause. Herzull, sitting by the door, changed slowly from leaf-green to bicycle-blue.

'Ah, now, that's very interesting, you know, I've shown this machine to one or two persons over the years and no one has ever raised that point,' said the Professor. 'There are several other dials, not immediately obvious, well not obvious at all really . . .' He pressed a lever at the side of the first dial and another smaller one swung out from underneath it on a short metal arm. 'This one can be set for a certain period of time, *as it were*, so, in theory, a traveller could go back to their chosen, ah, point, and then, well, I'm assuming that they would wish to return . . .'

He looked up. Otto and Sween were staring at him like owls watching a pottering mouse.

'I'm assuming that they would wish to return,' he said again.

'Oh yes,' said Sween.

'In that event they would need to set this dial here to give them the amount of time they needed. Then it would be a matter of making absolutely sure that they were back here, in their seats, before that time ran out. If they were not here in time then the machine would leave without them.'

Otto cleared his throat. 'Couldn't they get it back again?'

'No. This machine travels backwards in time from its starting point and returns to its starting point. It can't travel forwards from its starting point. The mechanism would need to be the other way around.'

The Professor seemed in the last moments to have become an older and sadder version of himself.

'Well, anyway,' he opened the door of the shed, 'that is how it works, you see. It is really just a plaything now.'

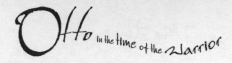

'Now?' said Sween.

Otto was pulling him by the arm.

The Professor locked the door behind them as if they had been visiting a tomb.

'A plaything,' he repeated. 'For Citizens who have never known anything and Karmidee who have forgotten what they knew.'

Sween Insists

They were out in the busy street. Herzull was green again. The rather lovely green of Professor Flowers' beard. Otto had bought a pot plant for Dolores. The Professor had assured him that it would not grow taller than two metres. It had grown a few centimetres already while they were walking along.

'This is my idea,' said Otto, breathlessly. 'We go to the Amaze at night. Use the bicycle. Go back to the Time of the Warrior, have a look in Red Moon, see if Blue's there. Because it says Time of the Warrior and Red Moon on your piece of glass. If she's not there, go to the dome in the Town Hall where the stained glass picture is. Then, whatever, you know, happens, come back, on the bicycle, well on

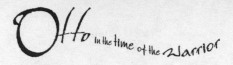

the bench, you know what I mean, so that we haven't been away for any time at all. From here.' He stopped and looked at Sween.

'You're joking,' said Sween

'No!'

'You're serious?'

'Yes.'

Sween nodded. 'Your well thought-out plan is that we go to one of the most dangerous times in the history of the City, with not much idea about how people talk or behave or whatever, on a time machine which only usually travels a distance of two weeks, to rescue a girl, older than us, with exceptional powers, who can bounce across the centuries without any need of a machine at all, who may or may not be in danger, at an unspecified location which we don't know. And come back.'

'Yes,' said Otto. If Sween wouldn't come he'd do it on his own.

'She is also involved in a battle or struggle, about which we know nothing, but that's all right because it is only to do with unimportant things like the past, present and future of the City. That's all. No danger.'

'Yes,' said Otto. 'We could try and find your lute maker. Get you a Domino Socktee—'

'A *Domenico Nocte*. I had thought of that, Hush. I'm just

not sure I want to risk my life to get one. If I come it's because you aren't safe to go on your own. And I have one condition.'

'Name it.'

'Norah Sargasso comes too.'

'WHAT?'

'She found a message she'd written to herself. She must have travelled safely. One way at least.'

Otto only just managed to stop himself from throwing the plant somewhere. Against the nearest wall, for example.

'But we don't *like* her. You don't like her. I don't like her. She creeps about, she thinks the Karmidee are *inferior*, Sween.'

'She's a chess champion,' said Sween, unmoved. 'She worked out where the secret entrance is to the tower. She's clever. That could be useful. She's ignorant at the moment. She'll soon learn that she's wrong about the Karmidee.'

A knight in a suit of armour dodged round Herzull and stood on Otto's foot.

'Ow!' shouted Otto.

'Forgive me,' said the knight. He walked off, lurching around a lamppost. *Follow Me For Bargain Cookware*, it said on his back. *Stan's the Man when you Need A Pan*.

'Norah is absolutely definitely not coming with us,' said Otto.

Herzull AT THE Window

It was too hot to sleep.

Otto lay on his back trying to think relaxing thoughts. His spiders and dragons mobile threw its familiar shadows across the ceiling, lit by the street lamps below.

Albert was working late. Apparently Mr Paxton had asked everyone to help with a complicated new library ticket filing system, or something. Dolores, on finally hearing the beginning of the story of meeting Blue, had interrupted Otto to make him promise to come downstairs immediately if anyone suddenly appeared out of nowhere on the roof again.

He sat up against his pillows and saw that Herzull was on the floor in front of the window.

It was a sash window and, tonight, was open at both the top and bottom. The curtains were also open to let in a non-existent breeze. He thought of calling to her but then something about the way she was sitting made him curious. She was very still and she was staring out across the street, towards the gardens on top of Owen Mansions.

Otto stared that way too. There were lantern trees directly opposite, a new addition to the gardens, laden, like all the trees at the moment, with fruit and flowers, and, in this case, with the papery lantern blooms which shed a soft orange light, attracting moths.

He could see a number of moths fluttering there now. And, something else, just beside the tree on top of the parapet. Dark shapes. What?

Herzull made a cooing sound.

She put her front paws on the windowsill and, to Otto's alarm, heaved herself up so that she was partly standing on the other windowsill, the stone one on the outside of the building.

He jumped off the bed on to the rug his grandparents had recently given him. Then, afraid of startling her, he stood still, his heart thumping. She could fall at any moment . . . now, for some reason, she had manoeuvred herself so that she was standing sideways.

He crept forwards. Now it was easier to understand

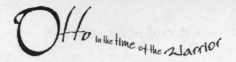

the shapes on the parapet of Owen Mansions. They were bears. Not as small as Herzull. Full grown perhaps, nearly as big as wolves.

Herzull's fur was beginning to change. The brass buttoned uniform of the porter in the Town Hall, the scattered stars of the Circus tent and then, horribly, TumbleMan's grinning skull . . . The bears across the street gave grunts of concern. Then the skull faded and she became a single shade all over. Possibly the rust-red of the twins' hair, it was hard to see the colour in the dark. Then he recognized the strings of Sween's guitar and, finally and impressively, curves and lines which brightened and became luminous. The glass bicycle. Herzull shuffled about on the windowsill. Presumably she was showing them the whole of it.

The watching bears muttered. Then, slowly, all but one of them seemed to fade where they stood.

Otto breathed in sharply; he had just seen them make themselves invisible.

The lower branches of the lantern tree swayed as they went past, then other bushes further along . . . until everything was still again.

Only one bear was left now.

This bear shuffled along the parapet until she was in the brightest patch of lantern light. Then skilfully and slowly she shimmered with stars, which became broad shifting leaves, and the stripes where sunshine reaches into the forest.

Herzull gave a tiny mournful cry.

Otto, an uncomfortable intruder, crept back on to his bed. From there he could just make out the other bear, he was sure it must be Herzull's mother, suddenly lighten and become covered with fruit. Dietary advice, no doubt.

Then the two bears stayed, unmoving and unchanging, separated only by the midnight street and the lime trees and the sultry air. It was Otto, worrying, who fell asleep.

Breakfast Puzzle

Dolores never used her magical abilities except in an emergency. This morning, however, she was trying to use them to help her with the washing up. Wishtacka, her cat, sat sternly on the fridge, ready to amplify. Widges cast spells with the assistance of their cats. The widge stares the spell at the cat, who empties his or her mind, thereby allowing the spell room to amplify. (Only cats can empty their minds in this way.) The cat then stares the amplified spell out again.

Wishtacka had no difficulty with any of this. Dolores did.

'Wouldn't it be quicker to just do it the usual way, Mum?' asked Otto, skidding in a pool of orange juice. The marmalade jar was emptying itself into the toaster. The taps had tied themselves in a knot.

'Keep out of here,' he added to the twins. 'Dangerous.'

'It is *not* dangerous,' exclaimed Dolores. 'I need to practice my skills. I never know when they might be needed.'

'I just meant—'

'I know what you meant,' she ducked as the marmalade jar returned itself smartly to the shelf. 'The question is, Otto, do *you* know what *I* mean?'

He goggled at her. She was covered in blobs of food. He had no idea what she meant at all.

'I just thought it was a bit, you know dangerous, I mean, I nearly fell over, the tea towel is on fire—'

She gave the tea towel a mouthful of words that would undoubtedly have intimidated a much larger one, a bath towel for example. Wishtacka fixed her relentless eyes on the sink. The tea towel jumped into it.

'This is not dangerous, Otto,' said Dolores, sounding angry and awful. 'This is not dangerous. There are much, much more dangerous things than this. For example . . .'

She stopped. She was staring at the door. Albert was there. He had already left very early for work once and now here he was, back again. They looked at each other.

Otto felt as if he were invisible.

'I thought you might like these, Dolores,' said Albert. He held out a bunch of fresh flowers, wrapped in the paper from

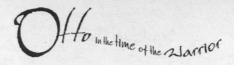

Professor Flowers' shop. They were all different shades of red. Shades and tones which could only be described using words Otto didn't know. Carmine, cinnabar, damask, vermilion, carnelian, the colours of blood and fire . . .

Dolores took them and clutched them tightly. Tears in her eyes.

Night Flight

Three days of tense preparation were at an end.

It was late at night.

Otto Hush and Sween Softly, cramped and anxious, had flown across to Cloudy Town on the carpet. They were accompanied by Rosie the armadillo, Herzull, two large bags of useful things, which belonged to Sween, and a small compact sensibly-sized bag which belonged to Otto.

The luggage contained a change of clothes for Sween based on the small stained glass fragment in the window in Albert's office at the Library. On this fragment the legendary traveller who had saved the Warrior was shown wearing what appeared to be a striped suit. The change of clothes consisted of pyjamas. Otto was already wearing his.

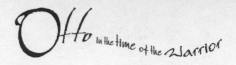

'It will be really important not to look noticeable,' he had explained.

Sween, whose clothes were always in excellent taste, had sighed and finally agreed to change into his pyjamas after they arrived.

There were other important items as well. The two crystal communicators. The remarkable hat Granny Culpepper had given Otto during the winter, which had saved him from an angry mob on the top of a tram. Bananas for Herzull and to Otto's annoyance, pebbles for Rosie.

'I'm sure they had pebbles in the past, Sween,' he said, testing the weight of the bag.

'You can't be too careful,' said Sween. 'These are hand-picked, granite for strength. And these,' he held up a handful of small deep blue fragments, 'these are a little treat, lapis lazuli, she's very fond of them.'

A single piece of the blue stone slipped from his hand and on to the floor. Otto, muttering, picked it up and put it in his own pocket and forgot about it.

In addition to everything else, of course, Sween had his guitar.

They landed heavily outside the steamy window of Professor Flowers' shop. A plant waved to them.

A moment later Norah Sargasso came up the cobbled

street. Otto gritted his teeth. He couldn't believe he had given in. But he had.

She had dressed as if they were going on some kind of walking holiday. Thick, sensible dress. Boots. A small, neat bag with, Otto now noticed, an equally neat luggage label tied to the handle.

This was the first time he had seen her since they had met in Sween's room.

'Could you remind me,' he whispered. 'Why exactly you want to come with us?'

She nodded politely. Did she never get angry?

'There's something important I have to do for my family,' she said.

'I think we should go now,' said Sween.

When it was quite clear that there was no one coming from either direction Sween unpicked the lock of the small, humble door which opens on to the Amaze. This is the public entrance, labelled with the opening hours in faded gold letters. The Amaze, of course, is enormous, but fits into a small space between Professor Flowers' shop on one side and a boot and shoemaker's on the other.

'My dad taught me,' said Sween to Norah, who was looking shocked. 'He's very versatile.'

He opened the door and they went inside. He closed it carefully behind them. They climbed over the brass turnstile.

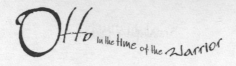

Now they were at the start of the maze. The mighty hedges towered above them. It was at this early stage of their intended journey that they met with their first difficulty. The time machine is in the centre of the maze and the centre, as is only to be expected, is very hard to find.

'Do we have a map?' asked Norah.

'Not exactly,' said Otto briskly. 'But I'm sure we'll be OK.' He glanced at Sween, who raised his eyebrows, grinning.

'You mean we're just going to wander about in there?' said Norah. 'It could be daylight before we find the centre. We might not find it at all.'

'She's got a point,' said Sween.

'I'll use the carpet,' said Otto, not looking at Norah. 'Flying's the quickest way. When I've worked out where it is, I'll come back and fetch you one at a time.'

'You'll fly!' exclaimed Norah. 'On a carpet. But isn't that a magico—'

'KARM-ID-EE,' groaned Otto. This would all have been so much easier, better and happier and better, if it were just him and Sween.

He unrolled the carpet and Herzull, sleepy and miserable, stepped on to it and sat down.

'Stand clear,' said Sween. 'Anything could happen.'

Otto gave him a murderous look and took off.

Everything was very quiet. Down below, the maze was lit along its many corridors and crossroads by iron lamps like those in the street.

It was just a question of finding the centre . . .

Otto gasped, causing Herzull to cover her eyes with her paws.

He had just seen the entire maze. It was a picture. A picture made of lights and the dim walls and the hedges. And the centre, with the mulberry tree and the time machine, was not actually in the middle at all. It was between the front paws of a leaping hare. And the hare was one of three leaping in a circle.

He banked round and flew back towards the entrance.

'Do we ride that?' whispered Norah.

'No,' said Sween and Otto both at once.

Sween had just picked the lock of the little shed. They were standing at the door, bathed in the ice-blue light which held the luminous, ghostly bicycle in its heart.

They crept nearer, until they reached the brass dial and the winding handle.

'We wind it up here,' explained Otto, despite himself. 'And there's another dial here.' He pulled the small lever, as he had seen the Professor do, and the second smaller dial swung out. He had not been able to see it clearly

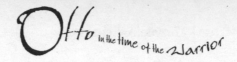

before. Now he was much closer. It was marked out with little pictures of circles, some shaded in, some empty. And there were more dials inside the circumference of the first, so that they could all be turned and lined up in different configurations.

Otto had expected numbers. So had Sween. They had planned to try and set the dial for the year scratched on the red glass message from Blue. They stared at each other.

Norah meanwhile, narrowed her eyes in concentration.

Otto began to speak. Sween nudged him.

'Eclipses,' said Norah, finally. 'It's a calendar of eclipses of the sun and moon. There's going to be an eclipse of the moon here soon. Next week, I think. These lines must be the years—'

'Can you tell which is three hundred years ago?' asked Sween.

'It's all been on the television,' said Norah. 'And in the papers. The eclipse next week will be one where the moon looks red—'

'So can you tell where three hundred years ago would be?'

Norah began counting the lines.

'Red Moon,' whispered Otto. 'That's what it says on the piece of glass. I thought it meant, you know, the town.'

'About here,' said Norah, pressing the square end of her finger on the dial. 'There was the same sort of eclipse here too. See? Here's the moon, all red. Is that the day you want to go to?'

Otto and Sween looked at each other.

'Before the eclipse,' said Sween. 'Say three days before. We're looking for someone. We thought they might be in the town, in Red Moon. But if red moon is the date then we'll have to look for them somewhere else, so, well . . .' he trailed off.

Norah was already clicking the dials into position. She swung the dial back in postion and another one appeared with gold letters on it.

'This is called the chronometric adjuster,' she said. 'It says *danger* on it. I'm not sure what it does. I suggest we leave it as it is.'

No one argued.

Now followed much tightening of straps on bags and checking of fastenings. Herzull was to go on Otto's lap, inside the safety harness. Rosie was concealed in Sween's pocket. No one was speaking. Otto felt fear beginning to spread through him like cold water in his bones. It seemed to him that the flat on Parry Street, and his family, were already far away. And travelling in time was suddenly the most frightening thing he could imagine.

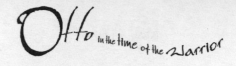

He stood absolutely still.

Sween and Norah were standing still too.

The light that surrounded the bicycle lit the three of them in different shades of blue.

Otto took a deep breath. 'Perhaps we—'

'I have to do this,' said Norah. 'If you don't want to come I'll go on my own. I've written a note to my parents.' She took an envelope out of her pocket and put it carefully on the floor by the wall. 'If I don't come back tonight, someone will find it and give it to them.'

Otto and Sween stared at her with eyes like saucers.

'I have to go,' she repeated. 'I have to try.'

'I think I'll write something too,' said Sween. 'Although I'm sure everything will be OK.'

He had a pen and some paper in his bag.

'Hang on,' said Otto.

Sween hung on.

Otto glanced at Norah, who was staring at him. If he could just speak to Sween on his own, for a moment.

'I'll just say I'll find some other way back,' said Sween. 'Perhaps you should do one too, Otto. Your dad told Norah that there used to be Karmidee who could travel in time. There must have been some around three hundred years ago. Probably lots. We'll get a lift.'

He handed Otto the piece of paper and the pen.

Otto turned away from the others and fixed his eyes on the stark page. Tried to think.

Behind him he heard clunking as someone began to wind the handle. *You will save my life . . . You will be a hero, Otto Hush . . . You don't have something secret that I entrusted to you? . . . There are two in this struggle . . . I am one of them. The other is someone who has the power to sweep all this away . . .* What on earth had she been talking about? Was she even real?

He held the paper flat against the wall and wrote. *Dear Mum and Dad . . .*

The handle ground relentlessly. When Dolores left in the winter with the twins she hadn't explained anything. People shouldn't do things like that, especially not mothers. Or fathers.

'Ready?' said Sween, quietly, right next to him.

So it was Norah winding up the time machine.

'I'm really worried,' whispered Otto. 'What if we can't come back? I hadn't thought of it like that before. Not properly.'

'We can still not go,' said Sween. 'If we decide, you know, that we don't want to—'

Otto put his finger to his lips.

They were close to the door of the shed. He could hear voices. Distinctly. Professor Flowers and his wife, Madame Doriel.

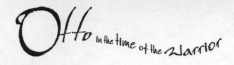

'Finished!' said Norah.

Otto pushed the door wider and looked out. There was the bench, of course. With room for three.

'I'm wondering if it is something to do with that new fertilizer,' said the Professor, somewhere near, through a hedge.

'. . . didn't expect it to burst throught the roof like that . . .' replied Doriel.

Norah was already on the bench, doing up her harness. The blue light of the bicycle was getting brighter and brighter. The wheels began to shimmer. Powerful energy. The logic of Impossiblity. It had to go somewhere. Now. Otto jammed the unfinished letter down the front of his coat.

'. . . overwatering,' concluded the Professor thoughtfully, very close, surely only one hedge away.

'. . . maybe less camel dung,' said Doriel.

Sween and Otto grabbed on to each other, ran outside and jumped at the bench. They were both pulling bags on to their knees. Sween tried to push the strap of his harness through the handle of his guitar case. Herzull was wriggling and kicking. Otto struggled to buckle his harness over her, her wet nose collided with his face.

They were engulfed in devastating blue light.

He screwed up his eyes.

Otto In The Forest

A moment later, or was it even as long as a moment, the light had gone.

Otto looked around, expecting to see Sween and the bench and the shed and the Amaze. And, because there was no choice, Norah. Maybe the hedges of the Amaze would be very small, maybe they had only just been planted.

However there was no sign of the hedges, or the shed or the bench. Or Sween. Or anyone. And he was sitting on the ground. Just him. No bags. No Herzull. He was on a path of stones and pebbles and there was only the moonlight and he was completely alone.

He stood up. Breathing fast. There was a breeze blowing. In the gloom to one side of the path, looking

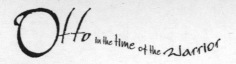

like a cliff, he recognized the silhouettes of vast trees. He heard the familiar sound of the wind moving through the branches.

'Sween!' he shouted. 'Herzull!'

He walked a few paces, looking all around, shouting their names at the top of his voice, over and over, so fiercely and desperately, his throat began to hurt . . .

His eyes were taking time to adjust. Now he could see that the path stretched away in front of him, along the edge of a forest. And, stopping his shouting to catch his breath, he heard a secretive, intimate sound. The sound of the river when it is not too fast, shallow on the rocks close to the bank, like voices muttering.

His sat down again on the edge of the path with the forest on one side and the river on the other. If he waited here a little while Sween and Herzull and Norah would find him. Obviously the time machine hadn't worked. Probably had never worked. Although that didn't explain how he came to be here now.

He hugged his arms around his chest and felt the crackle of paper. It was the letter he had started writing to Albert and Dolores. He whispered the start. 'Dear Mum and Dad.'

A bird flew past and became part of the dark bulk of the forest. There were bats too. He heard an owl call. Then there was a crunch on the path further up the river and he heard voices, growing nearer.

He stood up. Two people were coming along the path with lanterns.

For a moment he thought he would hurry to meet them but then, suddenly, he jumped into the deeper darkness between the trees, stumbled, and climbed up among tree roots. There he stopped, hidden, watching.

The voices and the footsteps grew louder. If he stepped into view and spoke to them he was sure these people would tell him where he was and how to get home.

But panic was creeping and whispering and growing inside him. He stayed still and out of sight. Perhaps he was not so sure after all.

The men walked past. Very close. They were dragging something very heavy, tied to wooden poles. He waited, without moving, until they had gone a long way up the path and he couldn't see or hear them any more. Then he reached for the bag he had brought with him and remembered, in the same moment, that it wasn't there. It had contained among other things, his mat, his crystal communicator, a supply of food, and his magic hat. It didn't matter. Any minute now he'd find the others. They would come down the path. They'd step out of the forest.

Perhaps he would follow the path himself. The men had

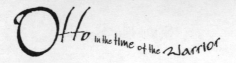

been going upstream, towards the City. He would go downstream. Eventually he'd come to the stilt houses.

And so Otto set off along the path with the forest sighing on one side and the river on the other. Beyond the far bank lay the black emptiness of the Wasteland, and beyond that he could make out the familiar shapes of the Western mountains far, far away. He would reach Red Moon very soon.

Once he was sure that he heard rustling and creaking. He stopped and stared and thought he saw several pairs of eyes.

'Herzull?'

But then the eyes were suddenly gone and everything was quiet and after a moment he set off again. He was still calling her, but since he had seen the men struggling with their burden along the path, his voice had dropped, almost to a whisper, and it was lost in the shadows and the trees.

And then the path faltered. It became little more than a track a bear or a wolf might have made. And then it was gone.

Nevertheless, climbing over rocks, pushing through bracken, he began looking down the river for the lights of the stilt houses. He would find someone to help him in Red Moon. If not, he knew two other mat flyers, friends of Mab, who lived in TigerHouse. They would give him a ride home. Then he'd make sure Sween had got home all right too. Then tomorrow they would come and find Herzull.

No boats or barges came past on the black water. Instead he saw wolves on the far bank, and several times he looked up and saw dragons, high up in the sky, crossing the face of the moon.

And still there was no sign of the familiar lights. And no smell of woodsmoke. And he turned the last bend in the river and stopped absolutely still.

Red Moon wasn't there.

He recognized the shapes of the rocky islands. There were two oak trees. He and Mab had tried to climb one of them.

There they were.

But the jetty that joined their island to the bank, and the houses that should be standing just behind them were missing.

Otto crept into the very edge of the forest again and leant against a tree.

Now, finally, he allowed himself to know the truth. He had realized, of course, when he had seen the men on the path. They had worn chain mail and strange helmets. One of them had carried a crossbow. They had been dragging the body of a caver on a pallet of woven rushes. This scene could not have happened in the city he knew. The cavers lived secretly and safely in their mountain fastness. No one wore

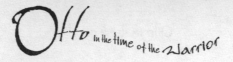

armour. Poor Citizens and Karmidee might hunt for rabbits but not with crossbows designed to kill a man.

The time machine had worked. He was in the far away past.

Everyone he knew was lost to him.

THE Warrior

After a little while Otto set off again. Even if Red Moon had not been built yet he might still find TigerHouse. All he had to do was keep walking. He had an idea that TigerHouse had been built first. He would speak to someone there. He would get help to go back to the Amaze and the Time Machine. He would get help.

Otto's mind scurried on in this manner, busy with ideas, like someone frantically throwing sticks on a tiny fire while all around is cold, creeping dark.

He walked for a long time, still calling Herzull, until he recognized Rose Island.

This was normally to be found in the middle of the river in the heart of TigerHouse. Now it was just in the middle of

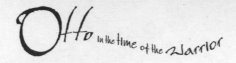

the river. Water birds drifted among the reeds, muttering at him as he stood on the bank.

Then suddenly he heard a scrabbling, slithering sound behind him. He turned quickly just in time to see a small shape, indistinct against a background of bushes, apparently fighting to climb out of the river.

'Herzull!' he yelled. He ran towards the scene of the drama, shouting encouragement, and arrived just as Herzull splashed down into the water, bobbing and coughing.

Otto looked frantically around them. In his own time the river was dangerous enough. Swamp dragons still lived in deep places. The bank here was steep and crumbling. He ran on, skirted some rocks and found a stony beach.

'Herzull!' he yelled. 'This way! Quick!'

A cloud drifted across the moon, leaving only the faintest starlight. He stumbled and river pebbles crunched under his feet. A few terrible moments later he heard an animal shake itself, felt the fine, cold spray of water on his face.

'Herzull!' he gasped. 'Herzull, I can't believe it, I was so worried . . .'

The cloud moved away from the moon.

It was not Herzull looking up at him. It was a dog. This dog now shook himself again, emphatically, and Otto took a step back.

'Don't move!' said a voice behind him. And then added,

rather hesitantly, 'Turn around slowly and put down your warpon.'

Otto looked at the dog a moment longer. It definitely wasn't Herzull. It really was a dog. Then, expecting anything, he turned round.

There was only one person standing there. A girl holding a warpon of her own, a frying pan. She seemed to be dressed in sacks. She stared at him. The dog ambled past her and Otto saw a strange-looking tent where the scrubby grass met the shingle, a camp fire, something that looked like a washing line.

'I haven't got a weapon,' he said, suddenly feeling exhausted. 'I haven't got anything.'

She put the frying pan down.

'I thought your dog was my bear,' he added. 'But he wasn't.'

She went on staring.

He decided to take a chance. Surely this was not a Citizen, so far from the City.

'Honourable greetings, sister,' he said, sounding stern by mistake. 'Greetings to your family. May the trees shade you and guard you and bring you strength.' He swallowed, wishing he had listened when Albert had talked about the art of Karmidee courtesy.

'Honourable greetings, brother,' she said. 'Greetings

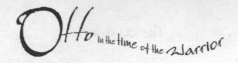

to your family. May the forest offer you sanctuary and touch you with wisdom. Thank you for helping my companion, he can't see very well . . . You have a strange way of speaking, I can't understand everything, you have lost your boar?'

'Bear. I've lost my bear.' This, although true, didn't seem to cover the situation. He took a step sideways for some reason and slipped. She grabbed his arm. They swayed. She steered him towards the makeshift tent and the glow of the fire. 'You need to rest, brother,' she said. 'You must have walked a long way.'

'I was wondering if this is the Time of the Warrior,' Otto blurted out. A mad, mad question, like asking the year. 'I've been travelling,' he added, firmly.

Her serious face cracked into a smile. Some bits of tooth missing.

'Not *Warrior*,' she said, starting to laugh. 'Not *Warrior*. I wish it *was*.'

He gaped at her. Terrified.

'Not Warrior,' she added, laughing, hooting in fact, and having to sit down.

'*Worrier*.'

'Woo-ree-er?'

Screech of mirth.

'No. *Worrier*, the person who *worries*.'

'The Worrier?'

'Yes. Delilah the Worrier.'

'The King is called—'

'Queen, Queen . . .' She was wiping her eyes. It was as if she hadn't laughed for years. She crossed her legs in front of her and showed him the sole of her foot in the firelight.

'Delilah the Worrier,' she said. 'That's me.'

There was the butterfly, the birthmark of the Karmidee Kings and Queens.

'You?' whispered Otto.

'Yes.' The laughing was finished. 'I expect you are disappointed. Everyone else is. I've only just, you know, started. Araminta the Tiger disappeared, you probably know that. Then there was a big fuss, of course, looking for the next one. Even the Normos realized something was going on. I wasn't extremely clean, but they persuaded me. And it is a question of honour.'

'Do you have to be clean?'

'KEEN.'

'My parents are in prison on CrabFace. Debtors Prison. They owe the Normos foul smelling money, you know how it is. So I've got to do everything myself. It's only been a couple of weeks. But it's very hard and I wish I was addled.'

'You wish what?'

'You know, grown up. Knew more things. Soup?'

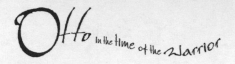

She began ladling something into a wooden bowl. He took it trying not to scrutinize the surface. No, surely not a fish head . . .

'You haven't told me your name, stranger,' she said.

Of course he hadn't and this was rude. Think fast.

'Forgive me, my name is Otto,' he said carefully.

She waited patiently, staring at him. Her eyes were dark, bright with interest. After all, a Karmidee should have a full name and that name should mean something, say something about them. He looked down into the soup and met the baleful eye of the fish. No inspiration there. Mab would probably suggest *Otto the Clueless* . . . have suggested . . .

'Otto the Stranger,' he said.

'The Stranger?'

'Yes.'

She looked at him for a moment longer and then smiled. 'Stranger than what?'

He grinned back.

THE *Rings* FROM THE *Past*

The soup was finished. (The dog had eaten the fish head.)

Otto and Delilah, Queen of the Karmidee, sat beside the fire which flared and rustled in its ring of stones.

Delilah wound her hands together as she talked, something Otto had seen his mother do frequently ever since his sisters had started floating about.

'There's been so much fighting. So many people have had to move out. Outsiders just kept arriving and arriving. There are far more of them than there are of us. At first all they wanted was gold and jewel stones and such rubbish that means nothing to us. But they always want more, more of everything. And then, you know, we have all these different groups and chiefs and things. The Artists' Guild, the

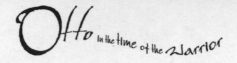

dammerung, ice-makers, fire-makers, multiples, lamp-eyes, troll-trees, even counterfeiters . . . all sorts of Karmidee with all sorts of ideas about what we should do. Some of them sign treaties, some of them try to fight. There's been so much fighting . . . So they've told me that I've got to have a plan, and they will follow, because I have the mark.'

She shuddered as if she were cold.

Otto jumped to his feet with a yell.

A rat, a *bright red rat*, was sitting on the ground beside him. It had orange eyes. It looked at him, bared its teeth and sprouted feathery black wings . . .

'Just ignore it,' said Delilah, starting to rock backwards and forwards. 'It's me, I'm an Artist, this sort of thing always happens where I'm worried.'

The rat disappeared.

'More than somewhat,' whispered Otto, staring at the place where it had been sitting. Slowly sitting down again himself.

'Haven't you ever met an Artist before?'

'Did you do that on purpose?'

'No. I *can* make pictures like that on purpose but I just said, it happens when I'm worried or upset. Or even if I'm very happy and relieved or something except it's been so long since I was happy or relieved that I can't really remember. Anyway, I do have a plan. Because I must.

Because I am the Karmidee Queen. I am going to tell our
people to build themselves their own places. Here, along the
river, where the floods come. Houses with long legs. Like
water birds, herons, egrets . . . We will build our own
towns on land they don't want.'

She sighed and looked at him sadly. 'Are you a spy?'

He recoiled as if she had hit him.

'There are many Citizen chiefs,' she added, throwing
a fir cone on to the fire. 'But the most powerful is the
Rook. He knows about me, I think. He doesn't understand
much but he would like to get rid of me. He cares for no
one but himself. He lives in the castle in the Forest of the
Blue Hare—'

'The *Blue Hare*—' exclaimed Otto, despite himself.

'Oh, yes. That is our name, the old name. That castle in
the forest was her castle, in the beginning. We believe
she still visits there, you see. We think the Citizens must
have seen her in among the trees. But they only saw her
in the distance, so they gave it their own kind of name . . .
perhaps you know it, they call it BlueCat Wood.' Delilah
had her eyes fixed on the fir cone as it started to glow in
among the flames.

'Well, yes . . .' but realized at once that he had made
a mistake.

She nodded, still not looking at him. 'That's what the

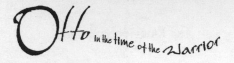

Citizens call it.' Yellow and gold spiders came from nowhere and danced on the grass all around them. 'But I will always call it the Forest of the Blue Hare, because she has a good heart.'

'I'm not a spy,' said Otto, trying to ignore the spiders. 'I, I swear to you——' He was about to start the sacred oath of the Mountain, the most serious and solemn oath in the City of Trees. So serious, in fact, that he had only used it once before in his life. But she interrupted him.

'You are not from here,' she said softly. 'If I don't speak slowly you don't understand me. You speak in a different way, some of your words I have never heard. And I have heard many, many accents and ways of talking. The Outsiders brought many languages with them. You know that? All melting and merging into one another——'

'I'm not a spy,' said Otto, carefully. 'I am a traveller. I have travelled in time.'

'You are a hare?'

'No, no. I used . . . another means. A time machine. But it must have gone wrong . . .' And he told her how he had found himself in the forest and how Sween, Norah and Herzull had disappeared.

'I am a Karmidee, from a different time. My father is the King, in the time I come from, his name is Albert the Quiet. My mother is a widge. Her father is a Citizen. My best friend for a long time was called Mab the Moth.' Why was he telling her all this? 'I've got her rings here.' He pulled Mab's rings out of his pocket on their grubby piece of string.

Delilah looked at them. She turned them over in her small hands. She too wore rings, although hers were set with moonstones. The snakes writhed and faded in the grass.

'Why do you have her rings? Is she dead?'

'No!' exclaimed Otto. 'She ran away.'

'The Karmidee make these rings,' said Delilah, still examining them. 'They are to mark particular events. These two, see, they fit together, each one has one half of the stone. They celebrate something.'

'Araminta's Gates,' guessed Otto.

'Yes.' She sighed. 'You know about the Gates. How far away is your time from now?'

'I'm not sure. I think about three hundred years, if the time machine worked. About three hundred years in the future.'

'Are you sure?'

She frowned. Then he noticed that something was taking shape in the air above her head. A spiralling cloud of bats.

'Yes,' he whispered.

'Then I must ask you to leave me now. I cannot be sure who you are.'

'No! NO! I'm NOT a spy, you've got to believe me, I—'

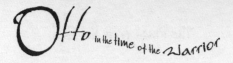

'You are saying that these rings belonged to someone who lives three hundred years in the future. But they are hardly worn. See the mark here? The mark of the person who made them? Silver wears with time. My father was a silversmith before they came. I've seen lots and lots of silver things. These are hardly worn at all. They should be three hundred years old. It is a year since the Gates were finished—'

'Her grandmother gave them to her,' exclaimed Otto, desperately. 'Genevieve the Whisperer. Well, she thought she was her grandmother—'

'The WHISPERER?'

The dog had woken up. The bats changed into huge menacing birds.

'Genevieve the Whisperer is famous. Ask any Karmidee. They still talk about her. She was an Artist who made things fly. She became Head of the Guild. Then, after the Citizens came, she rescued these two children from a Citizen family. Slaves. Bought from a Foundling Shop. The boy was a musician, I think. The Citizen family were very powerful. They were looking for the Whisperer and the children everywhere. Then they all disappeared. There is even a little street named after her.'

'But it's true!' cried Otto. They were all standing up now. The dog bared his teeth. 'All the things I've told you are absolutely *true*, and she *does* have two children, as well as Mab, I mean—'

Delilah shook her head. 'You must go now, whoever you are.'

Everything about her was skinny and sharp except her eyes. Large and dark and starting to fill with tears.

'I'll tell you something that's true, Otto the Strange, being the Karmidee Queen is the loneliest job in the world.'

Night In The Forest

Otto kept walking. After a while he looked back and saw the small orange glow above the fire, although the fire itself and the tent were hidden down by the water. He thought he saw a bird circling, but it faded and then became something that looked like a sword. Other shapes, too small and far away to understand, drifted around the column of smoke.

He walked on for a long time. He came to the place where Red Moon should have been. He found the end of the path and estimated that it would take him until well into the morning before he reached the edge of the City.

He was very, very tired.

The sound of his own jagged breath frightened him.

Slowly, wearily, he turned into the edge of the forest and

climbed into a tree, almost falling, barely able to see away from the moonlight. He tied himself into the fork of a branch with the belt of his coat.

Then he wound the string of silver rings around his wrist. He wriggled around, trying to make himself comfortable, and the unfinished letter down the front of his shirt rustled. Albert had said that there had once been many different sorts of chameleon animals in the forest. What sort of animals could climb trees anyway? Bears, he was sure. Snakes, presumably. Lions, tigers, all those sorts of things.

He would start walking again as soon as it was light. He would go to the castle. That was where they had found the last message from Blue. And the real name was the Forest of the Blue Hare. And somehow or other it was supposed to have been her castle. And she was probably trapped there, in the castle, right now, by this awful Citizen, the Rook.

Norah IN THE Amaze

The blue light had gone. Norah found herself quite alone, sitting neatly in the middle of the bench, still wearing her safety harness and holding her bag. On one side lay Sween Softly's harness, torn in two. The other boy didn't appear to have fastened his at all. Both halves were still there, unbuckled.

She blinked. Her eyes felt dry and sore. She observed that the great hedges of the Amaze were all around her, just as tall as when she and Otto and Sween had sat down.

However, other things were not the same. Now the moon was almost full. And the night air was much colder. Frost glittered.

She unbuckled her safety harness and stood up.

She would go into the shed and examine the dials on the Time Machine.

She walked slowly. Her legs felt strange. She reached the door and found it partly open and went inside.

And there she stood for some time in the blue light of the bicycle staring at the array of dials and symbols in front of her. She was used to remaining calm during long and difficult chess tournaments. For some years now chess commentators and journalists had been calling her Frost Face. She remained calm now.

'Excuse me,' said a soft voice. 'Can I help you?'

A boy was standing in the doorway of the shed, holding a lantern. He had a woollen hat pulled down almost to his eyebrows. He didn't come any closer. He stared at her as if she was some rare and shy animal.

'Don't be frightened,' he said, in his strange accent. 'I saw the bench, something's happened to the harnesses. Please don't go . . . you've, you've travelled in time haven't you? You *must* have travelled! And you must have come *from* the future. You can't have come from the past.' He grinned. 'I wanted it to go into the future, but I put the mechanism in the wrong way round. I'm the one who built it, you see, with a bit of help. My first attempt. Only just finished.'

He took the few steps to where she was standing and looked at the dials. 'It's set for you to go back, of course,

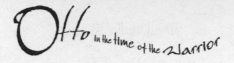

don't worry, I won't let anyone in, I'll keep everything safe
in here. The maze is closed anyway. That's why I put it here.
No one comes in here but me . . . but was there an
accident? Did someone fall off?'

Norah imagined possibilities and calculated odds. Then,
having decided that this boy was probably not dangerous, she
nodded, stiffly.

'You've come three hundred years!' he exclaimed. 'But
these are terrible times. Why would you want to come here
now? Are you a Karmidee?'

'Certainly not,' said Norah.

His gentle face seemed sad for a moment, he raised
his eyebrows.

'Are there any Karmidee left where you come from?'

'Yes, yes, of course. I'm just not one of them, that's all. I
don't really know any. People like me don't meet them, you
see. I only meet very clever people, usually.'

'Ah, yes . . . I see.' He put his hand to his jaw, cupped his
chin. Thinking.

'People will take you for a Karmidee, though. You do
know that, don't you? You have history books?'

'No. Why? Why will they take me for a magico? Do you
mean the way I talk?'

'Unless you've got yours in your bag there. I always wear
mine because I'm so scared of losing the wretched thing.'

'My what? Got what in my bag?'

He suddenly put his finger to his lips. Someone was shouting. A deep angry voice coming from quite far away.

'You've got to get out,' whispered the boy. 'You must get out now. That's my boss. I'm supposed to be working. Well, I *was* working and then I saw the blue flash. Incredible.'

He paused and handed her something rolled up which he had been carrying under his arm. 'I think you might need this, did you drop it? I found it a little way away . . . I don't know why you're here but I think you should, well, if you don't have the—'

'Foundling! Where have you crept off to now? Get back to work! And be quick about it! Do you want me to take you back to the shop, you lazy scrap of bones?'

'If you don't have lodestones you might be better off if you pretend to be a Karmidee. Otherwise you could be arrested. Or worse. You're not too big to be sold in a Foundling Shop yourself.' He looked at her intently. 'These are very dangerous times, do you understand me? Can you understand what I'm saying?'

'Yes,' said Norah. 'But I'm sure no one would sell me in a shop. I am a chess champion.'

'Do they have Foundling Shops in your time?'

'Well, no, I've never heard of anything—'

More shouting in the background.

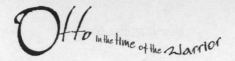
Otto In the time of the Warrior

The boy jiggled from foot to foot. 'Citizens like entertainment just as much as they like servants,' he said quickly. 'Being a chess champion might make you more valuable.'

'But I'm a Citizen—' exclaimed Norah.

'I can see that you are outraged, I wish I could ask you many, many questions about your time, but we are in danger here. You must trust me. Of course it is easier to be a Citizen, but it is not so safe as you seem to expect. I was sold in a Foundling Shop when I was nine years old. And I am a Citizen.'

He hustled her out of the shed and closed the door. 'Don't worry, nobody comes to this part except me. He can't even find it. He's only just bought this place. Well, not bought, it was owned by Karmidee, anyway he's opening the bit round the entrance, as a sort of *tea garden*. But he thinks the actual maze is some sort of *dangerous magic*. Very ignorant, of course. Big rush to get it all ready. I'm the one doing it all. Night and day . . .' He pushed her towards an opening in the hedge. 'May the trees shelter you, as our brothers and sisters say.'

'What are lodestones?' hissed Norah.

But he was already hurrying off, agile for someone in heavy clothes, lantern swinging. She decided to hurry too, and set off down the wide corridor between the hedges, pushing her way through frosty grass grown long with neglect.

There were lamps here, just as there had been in her own time, but they were not lit. Out of the moonlight it was horribly dark. She heard voices again, or thought she did, and unrolled the carpet. It was useful, even though it was not at all Respectable.

The question was, how did Otto make it fly?

She had seen him pull on the fringe at the front to steer. She pulled. Unbidden and unwanted, her mind bustled into calculation. It was not Possible for this piece of material (she observed that it had been repaired, in places, with *knitting*), it was not Possible for this piece of partially *knitted* material to suddenly leave the ground. With or without the presence of a girl and a sensibly packed bag of essentials. She knew all the reasons why it was not Possible. They paraded insistently through her imagination.

The carpet remained absolutely still.

Norah guessed that the logical strategy would be to abandon all logic. With a huge effort she forced all the carefully deduced conclusions out of her mind. The space that was left was frightening. She tried to fill it with the possibility of the Impossible.

A minute or two later, wild-eyed and silently screaming, she was bouncing over the hedges, colliding with the topiary

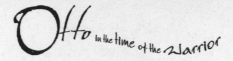

animals, dipping, diving and reeling and then, still clutching her precious bag, she shot backwards over the roof of what would one day be Professor Flowers' shop and crashed into a pile of rubbish in the street.

She stood up. She brushed orange peel off her coat. She thought of the very different way Otto had flown the carpet. Perhaps it was not logical to think of the Karmidee as inferior in every respect.

Then Norah began to walk cautiously down the quiet, cold street, thinking about what she had to do.

Somehow, she was going to obtain treasure. Then, somehow, she was going to get inside the castle in BlueCat Wood, the castle that would one day belong to Max Softly. She was going to hide the treasure in the castle, and leave herself a message about it inside a guide book. This same guide book would survive for the next three hundred years. Waiting for her in the City Central Library.

And this treasure, whatever it was, wherever she would find it, would one day pay for her father's treatment.

And he would be well again.

THE *Beast*

'Calling Otto Hush. Calling Otto Hush.'

Nothing was happening inside the crystal communicator.

'Be quiet, Rosie,' hissed Sween. Very wound up. Rosie put down her pebble. Perhaps it was disappointing anyway, the best ones had been in the bag.

'Where the skink *is* he,' muttered Sween. 'Why doesn't he *answer*?'

They were sitting in the early morning sunshine on the roof garden of a large building on the Boulevard. There had been a more than somewhat bright blue flash of light and then, instantly, they had found themselves here, on this roof in the night and had stayed, huddled, until dawn. All attempts to contact Otto with the communicator had failed.

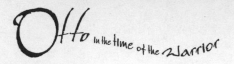

Now the City was starting to wake up. Sween put the communicator back in his pocket. Rosie picked up her pebble.

Sween went and looked down on to the Boulevard. There were many trees there and many more stumps where others had been cut down. Trails of sawdust. Piles of logs. Trees grew right down the middle of the road where the trams should be.

There were no trams now of course. No tram lines. No steam cars. All the familiar sounds were missing.

A man walked past leading a donkey. Sween heard the thud of his clogs on the ground. No cobbles. No paving stones. The air was fresh and warm. It smelt sweet.

Then, slowly, Sween began to recognize some of the buildings opposite. The shapes of the bay windows, the carved pillars on each side of the door. Fozzard's Ice Cream Soda Bar was directly in front of him, with five storeys of round windows piled above it. They were round. Max had assured him when he was very small, on account of the bubbles in the soda. Well, it wasn't a soda bar this morning, it was a jeweller's shop. There was a sign, just above the door, saying *Citizens Only*, and a picture of a K with a line through it.

Someone unlocked the door and pulled down the awning to shade the window. A man with a large hat with an even larger feather, strange stockings on his legs, what was that called, a doublet? And a scabbard on his hip which undoubtedly held a sword. The man lit candles in the bay window of what should be Fozzard's Ice Cream Soda Bar. He laid out sparkling things. Just another morning for him.

On the roof opposite, Sween Softly watched in a terrified fascination.

Then he leant over the parapet and looked up the Boulevard. There was the Karmidee Tower, soaring into the sky as always. A great dark pinnacle of carved wooden animals. The elephants at the bottom, as big as trams, except there were no trams. And the tower was not dark. Sween was used to it being the many shades of ancient wood, weathered, stained and sombre. Now it was brightly and beautifully painted. The elephants were green. The tigers striped with blue and gold.

He looked away, fighting yet another surge of panic. He would go to BlueCat Wood. No, madness, it wasn't his home, nowhere here was his home, there was no point in looking for Otto in Parry Street, or for Albert in the City Central Library, or rushing to the offices of Max Softly, Theatrical Agent.

He would go to the Amaze. The time machine. Maybe Otto and Norah would be there.

He picked Rosie up and put her in his pocket, seized his

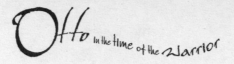

guitar case, the only luggage he hadn't lost, and began to creep across the garden, between beds of roses and sunflowers. What if someone saw him here?

A moment later someone did. Just as he reached a door, which he was hoping led downstairs, a woman came out through it. There was a sizeable pile of logs partially hidden by a sheet of canvas. She bent down, pulled out a log and perched it on her hip. The log was as long as he was tall. He could barely have reached his arms around it. This had to be the strongest woman he had ever seen.

She looked up and saw him. There was a swirl of tattoos across the back of her knuckles, like black lace on her pale skin. Another tattoo, in the shape of a comet, spanned the breadth of her forehead. Its starry tail swept over her cheekbone, right down to the corner of her mouth.

Sween smiled.

She didn't.

No time to worry about his accent. Think what Hush would do. She must be a Karmidee, surely, with tattoos like that.

'Honourable greetings, sister,' he said. And added, because Karmidee generally seemed to greet each other for a long time, 'Well met on this bright morning.' This didn't sound quite right.

'Honourable greetings,' she said in an accent he had never

heard before, and coming extremely close to him. 'The boss told me to report anyone trespassing up here to the guards. The Boulevard is all under the protection of the Rook. His guards are the worst . . .'

She stared. Her eyes were deep set under neat, thick brows, 'Unless you're the man coming to see to the tusks. Are you?'

'That's me,' said Sween promptly.

'Forgive me.' She was looking him up and down. 'Only you're so young. I thought there'd be at least two of you. Big men. It's a very big beast.'

Sween nodded.

'Well, you'd better come down then. The boss is still getting himself all poshed and perfumed ready to open up the shop. He wants the beast looking good today. He likes showing off his possessions and he's got some important guests coming. Well, customers really, it's all business . . . everything's business with them, isn't it?'

Sween nodded again. *Tusks . . . The beast ready.* Just what exactly might this involve?

'You came over the roof walks,' she continued, leading the way to a door. 'There's been some robberies on the gardens recently. There's robberies everywhere these days, isn't there? You should be careful, in those clothes.'

Of course. His clothes. Obviously he should be wearing

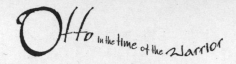

his pyjamas. Lost with all the other things in his bag.

'It's Citizens Only in the shop, but then I've no doubt you're familiar with all the new laws. Is that why you didn't want to wait in the street? I don't blame you.'

They were climbing down a narrow stairway, similar to the one at the top of Herschell Buildings. She turned on the landing at the bottom, expertly swinging the log, and he followed her past carved doors, all closed, and then down further, the stairs getting wider with each floor they left behind, until they were in a monstrous tiled hallway with mirrors and mosaics and gleaming chandeliers. Here was the front door on to the Boulevard, alarmingly locked with bolts and padlocks, and another, standing half open.

'The shop,' she whispered. 'But you'll not want to go in there, will you? Your work is waiting outside.'

Rosie had stuck her head out of Sween's pocket.

The woman's eyes widened. 'Is that a rock-nibbler?'

Sween nodded. It seemed to be his main form of communication.

'Don't let him see that, will you, they're only for Citizens, didn't you know that? Karmidee are forbidden to have any, on account of the jewels, wherever did you get it from?'

'She was injured,' said Sween. 'I rescued her.'

The woman glanced back up the stairwell. Someone had

coughed. She rolled her eyes at him as if they both understood things about bosses. Sween tried to look both worldly wise and sympathetic in return, tripped over his own feet and stumbled, almost dropping his guitar case. He followed her into a large kitchen with an open fire, what seemed to be grass on the floor, various metal pots and pans hanging on the walls and a scrubbed wooden table with a number of chairs grouped around it.

'You're brave for such a young man,' she said, almost pleasantly. 'You'd have to be, I suppose, yours is not a job for the faint-hearted, is it?'

He shook his head, clenching his jaw in panic.

'Sit there, brother, and I'll get you a bowl of pottage, since I expect you've had a long walk since your breakfast. You've time to eat it. I was told not to expect you until nearer noon.'

Good. At least that must mean that the real person or persons coming about the beast with tusks were not about to knock on the door at any moment.

She let the log fall with a spectacular crash beside the fireplace.

'You're a bit young, aren't you? All skin and bone and long shanks. Still, children have to do all sorts of jobs these days. I'd stay to watch only I've got to go and get the monkeys' trousers, they're being embroidered, at the

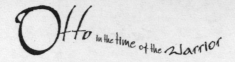

tailors. Nothing but gold thread for his greediness.'

The monkeys' trousers. What monkeys? What trousers?

'Oh, and an extra sort of necklace thing for the beast,' she added brightly, putting a bowl of greyish brown stuff in front of him.

She opened the top half of another wooden door and sunlight poured in, gilding the straw on the floor and her oiled skin and her scraped back, yellow hair. There seemed to be a yard out there. Sween heard sounds of snuffling, grunting and snorting.

'My name's Loveday,' said the woman.

She looked at him, waiting. Her arms, now folded across her chest, looked like someone else's legs.

Sween's mind emptied like an upended bucket.

'What's your name, brother?' she added.

'Herzull,' said Sween. 'Herzull Crumb.'

He took a spoonful of the pottage and swallowed with difficulty.

'Oh,' she said, 'You've taken up their habit of a family name, have you? I'm just Loveday the Strong, and that's good enough for me. I used to work on a timber barge. Throwing logs.' She looked at him coldly.

'Herzull *the* Crumb,' said Sween. 'I used to work in a bakery. Sweeping crumbs.'

Not long after this, when he had managed a few more

mouthfuls of the pottage stuff, she went out of the kitchen, back through the door into the hall, and Sween immediately hurried over to look out into the yard.

And there was the beast. And it was big. It was one of those very, very big and dangerous pigs. What did they call them? Boars. It was a boar. It had very sharp curved tusks, brown bristles all over and it stood at least as tall as his shoulder. This was easy to measure because it was standing very close to the door at the moment, and therefore very close to him. Their eyes met. The boar's eyes were small and ruthless and cunning. Sween's were quite possibly as large as they had ever been.

The boar was wearing a collar studded with rubies and emeralds. The ring in his nose was gold.

Beyond this alarming spectacle Sween saw a small cage containing two downcast monkeys, both dressed in little suits of embroidered cloth and with hats tied on to their heads.

He rushed back to the table, grabbed his breakfast and poured it in front of the boar. Then, sweating, he went and sat down.

Loveday came back, carrying a basket piled with folded cloth.

'You'll be wanting to sharpen your implements,' she said, sitting down at the table.

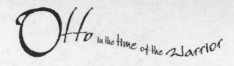

'That's all right,' said Sween. His throat tightened. He coughed.

'They're in there, are they? I've never seen a bag that shape before . . .' She was looking at his guitar case.

'Oh, er, yes.' He glanced down at the case, which was canvas and, he now realized, had several stickers on the side, including one which said, *I was brave at the dentist's today*, and had a smiling dragon in the middle with a lot of teeth. Hush must have stuck it there. He slid his hand down now to cover it up.

'Well then, I've got to go, Herzull the Crumb. The boss will be down at any moment. Shop opens at eight.'

'What does he sell?' asked Sween, mainly out of panic.

'Oh, they're all jewellers along here. Fussing over little bits of stone. You know what Normos are like. Jackdaws. Only not innocent and harmless.'

She picked up two empty baskets from among the great many other things by the fireplace and with a smiling, 'Honourable greetings, brother,' she opened the studded door into the hall and Sween followed her, very interested to see the way out.

'How do you catch him?' she asked, unlocking a massive lock with a massive key and then starting on a number of massive bolts. 'If it was me I wouldn't use any fancy stuff. I'd pick him up under one arm and saw the tusks off with my free hand. That way he'd have no chance of ripping my guts open. But that's just me. You're the professional.'

'Lasso,' said Sween, and added, when she frowned, 'And I also have a boomerang, in my bag.'

A moment later the professional was standing alone in the hallway. The key turned in the lock outside.

'I'll be down to give you some assistance in a moment, my good man,' called a deep voice from upstairs.

Sween stared wildly around him. He glimpsed himself, white-faced in a large mirror, sped back into the kitchen and grabbed his guitar case. He could hear the deep voice starting on more conversation, muffled but definitely coming towards him down the stairs.

He vaulted over the lower half of the door into the yard. There was the boar, who had presumably been waiting, small eyes alert, tusks at the ready. Sween ran to the monkeys' cage and opened it. The monkeys tumbled out, chattering excitedly. He spotted a door in the wall at the bottom of the yard. Flung himself towards it. It was bolted. The boar charged at him. Sween, yelping with terror, jumped as high as he could. He landed on top of the boar.

'OI! YOU!' shouted the voice. 'Where are you off to?'

'Just going to fetch some extra equipment,' gasped Sween, hauling on the bolt, still standing on the boar's back all muscle and bone, lurching and snorting.

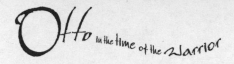

'What the devil are you doing?'

Sween pirouetted on one leg, dragging on the door with all his weight, this must be the heaviest door ever made, the boar stepped neatly out of the way, the door opened inwards and the boar trotted briskly out of the yard.

'You come here! Thief! Stop thief!' bellowed the voice.

'Back in a moment!' shouted Sween, turning and seeing a giant of a man, all beard and belly, advancing towards him across the very very small yard and brandishing a spade in the air.

There was a terrible split second or two when it seemed that the boar was in no particular hurry to go anywhere, then he suddenly set off up the alleyway, gaining speed rapidly with Sween now lying along his back, trying to grab his ears, still clinging on to the guitar case.

'Neighbours!' yelled the jeweller, pounding into the yard, 'I'm being robbed. After him! Stop!'

But the boar had no intention of stopping. With the monkeys dancing along the tops of the walls, squeaking and whooping, the boar and Sween swung around a corner, down another alley and on and on past the cluttered backs of shop after shop, yards, storerooms, a well, several ruined buildings . . .

Sween had managed to scramble up so that he was sitting,

sideways, but at least sitting, with Rosie screaming in his ear, hanging on to one of his plaits.

They hurtled down an even narrower, darker alleyway and shot out on to the Boulevard. The boar made a skidding turn to the right, towards the Karmidee Tower. Sween and Rosie skidded with him.

The Boulevard was busier now and, from Sween's perspective, blurred and full of people jumping and cursing.

'Magico filth!' shouted a man on stilts, cleaning windows. There was a nasty part of the journey when the boar had this man's bucket stuck on his face, but Sween managed to kick it free and the Karmidee Tower rushed towards them. They reached it and the boar thundered underneath.

There, under the archways, in the cool shade of the elephants, the boar stopped, breathing like a steam car, and Sween slid on to the paved stone floor.

For a moment he thought he saw shocked faces. He definitely heard shouts of surprise. Then the faces, if they were faces, disappeared into the shadows.

The boar looked back the way they had come. Then, grunting as he passed, his collar jingling, he set off down the Boulevard again at a crisp trot. He seemed very sure where he was going.

The base of the Karmidee Tower consists of mighty elephants. Their legs are pillars. In the middle, underneath,

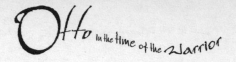

it is possible to look up and see the narrowing space as the carved animals grow smaller and smaller, until the sides touch one another and it is no longer hollow. Sween was used to the tower being dark and dank. Now, gasping for breath, he looked up and saw uneven ladders of light. The tower was clean, sunshine was filtering between wooden paws and feathers and spines.

As he grew more used to the shadows he saw that the animals were painted on the inside too.

And then he saw something else.

There were cats all around him, standing staring.

Eyes like glass, gold, green, amber. Backs arched. And among them, also standing, there was a boy.

The boy whispered something. The cats moved closer to Sween.

THE Cats

Sween Softly, surrounded by menacing cats, had decided to stay where he was for a moment. Trying to seem unconcerned he checked on Rosie, who had climbed head first back into his pocket, brushed down his coat and removed his one remaining shoe.

His hat had been a present from Otto's grandmother. It had not fallen off, despite the ride on the boar. It never fell off, she had undoubtedly made it like that, with the aid of her cat Shinnabac, an excellent widge's cat, skilled in the matter of amplification. In fact the hat was quite hard to take off at all, despite being a little too large. He tugged it upwards by the brim and it made a tiny popping noise, like a cork coming out of a bottle. There was a puff of green smoke.

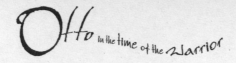

The boy laughed quietly.

Sween brushed his hat.

The boy leaned forward into a patch of light. He had absolutely white skin, as white as the painted face of the clown in the flying chair at the Circus. His lips were a pale lilac. His thick hair stood up on his head. It was black. His eyes were the colour of lemons.

'Honourable greetings,' he said.

'Honourable greetings,' mumbled Sween.

The boy stepped towards Sween and held out a chalk-white hand. Short pointed finger nails. The cats sat soundless and staring.

'I've never seen anyone ride a boar before,' he said. 'Do you have an ability with animals?'

'Only falling off,' said Sween.

The boy laughed again. Nodding. All the time watching.

'I'm looking for my friends,' added Sween. 'I'm looking for a boy with brown skin and white hair, with a very colourful small bear companion, and a pinkish girl, with brown hair in plaits, like mine, but brown, and she plays chess and we've got separated—'

'Plays chess,' said the boy. 'Did you say plays chess, brother?'

'Yes,' said Sween. 'Have you seen her?'

The boy had become very alert, like an animal hunting.

'My name is Tiler of the Rooftops,' he said. 'I think we can help you find your friend. Do you play the chess game too?'

Sween moved towards the sunlight outside the Tower and the cats rippled and rearranged around him.

Rubbing against his legs. Blocking his way.

'I am a musician,' said Sween. Trying to keep his voice steady. Smiling slightly as if he were not afraid.

'Musician, is it? I know of someone who appreciates a little musical entertainment, and he is a great lover of the chess game. We will find your friend and you can both come and meet him.'

'I don't see how you're going to find her so easily,' said Sween, still managing the smile. 'She could be anywhere.'

He realized, as he spoke, that apart from the fact that she played chess he knew almost nothing about Norah. Everything else she kept secret. Then he thought of something else. The woman at the jeweller's, and now this boy, had both assumed he was a Karmidee like them. Norah, he was sure, would be insisting that she was a Citizen, even if it meant being arrested.

'You're not from this part of the City, brother,' said Tiler. 'You have a strange way of speaking. It's not my business. We are all trying to find a home these days. Does your friend dress in fine clothes and ride dangerous creatures like you do? Does she speak the way you speak?'

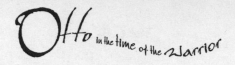

It seemed to Sween that all the cats were waiting for his reply.

'These are my friends,' said Tiler, winking, assuming, apparently, that Sween understood something. 'We can find her.'

'It's not just her,' began Sween. 'My other friend, with the bear—'

'Does the bear do tricks?' interrupted Tiler. 'Is it an entertainer?'

'A bit,' said Sween. 'But not on purpose. And she's not for sale. It's not like that.'

'We know many, many people,' said Tiler. 'Our people. We can go secretly. We can listen. Watch. The Citizens never know we are there. And when we have found your friends, you will help us in return. Yes? What is your name?'

'Sween,' said Sween, without giving himself time to worry about it. 'Sween the Tuneful.'

Rosie wriggled in Sween's pocket. Did cats eat miniature armadillos?

'They may have been sold as foundlings, Sween. You know what I mean. Sold to be servants until they grow up. They may be living in the markets, sleeping in the tents and the ruins, we will find out, we go everywhere, over roofs, over walls . . .'

Tiler stepped out of the shadow of the tower and into the

bright day. His eyes suddenly changed. The pupils, which had been large and dark in their yellow rings, shrank in an instant to long black slits. Cat's eyes.

Of course. He must be a dammerung. A Karmidee with the ability to turn into another creature. In Tiler's case, a cat. Their name comes from a word for twilight. Not quite day, not quite night. And that describes them well. As a human, Tiler would still be little like a cat. And if Tiler was a dammerung then all the cats who streamed after them now, must be dammerung too. How many were there? Fifteen? Twenty? Cats who were ready, at a sign from him, to turn into children.

Tiler walked lightly, looking around. Reacting to sounds with a darting look from his pale yellow eyes.

'I can't go that way,' said Sween. 'A Citizen was chasing me.'

But they were leaving the Boulevard. They turned down a narrow lane. And down more lanes, and across squares, and even across the river along a bridge Sween had never seen before. Frequently there were ruined buildings, overgrown and abandoned. He saw Citizens, some on ponies, or riding in litters, or rickshaws, or surrounded by men who were surely there to protect them. They were laden with gold chains and, like the recently rescued monkeys, they wore clothes embroidered with gold thread. All, it seemed, wore

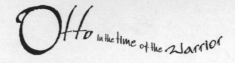

necklaces of gold nuggets strung together. Even children.

A girl walked past Sween. She was with her family and several guards who wore chain mail over their shirts and carried short-handled axes. She was dressed in a haze of white and gold.

Their eyes met. Sween felt his face fumble into a smile.

In return she did more than disdain or ignore him. It was if he wasn't there. As if nothing he could do, or say, or shout or scream could make him exist as she walked by.

'Keep moving,' whispered Tiler. 'Don't stare like that. I've got a boss who'll look after me, but he's a busy man.'

'A boss?'

'The Citizens have their own warriors and chiefs. They fight amongst themselves. You know that.'

Sween nodded.

'Well, round here everyone works for a Citizen called Jack Sargasso, goes by the name of the Rook. He's going to end up running the place. Not that I'm bothered about that.' He looked sideways, away from Sween. Cats, of course, cannot blush. 'We've got to survive, haven't we, brother? I do things for him. If I'm in trouble he'll get me out. Better than starving.'

They had come to the edge of a market place. Tiler finally stopped walking. He stepped back and leant against the wall of a high, painted building. Five storeys of windows rose above them, garlanded with pictures of creepers and tigers and trees. In front of them, a great clutter of tents and stalls.

'Anyway,' he said, lowering his voice, 'this isn't going to go on for ever, you know.'

His eyes, as he looked on to the square, were black needles on gold.

'Did you see the Circus last winter?'

'The Circus . . .' began Sween, cautiously.

'TumbleMan's Circus. It really is *him*, you know. *The* TumbleMan. One of the first children. The ones who came here in the beginning and founded the City. He's a hare. A time traveller. As well as being the greatest clown, the greatest tumbler. He has more magical energy than a hundred of us put together.'

'I've seen him,' said Sween.

'He goes about from one time to another, doing his shows. Just like you and me might go from HighNoon to PasturesGreen and back again. He travels in time and he takes the Circus with him. If he finds someone with unusual abilities, he sometimes lets them join.'

Sween thought of the shimmering purple tent on the Mountainside. Then, as if someone had hit him, he thought of Mab. 'Is the Circus coming back here soon?'

'I think it might be back now. I've heard there's been posters. Anyway,' Tiler had started to whisper, 'TumbleMan

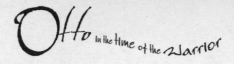

loves his Circus, just like I love my brothers and sisters that are searching for your friends . . . he loves his Circus and he loves us too, the Karmidee, all of them, his people. He knows he did wrong and he's going to make up for it.'

'What's he done?' exclaimed Sween.

'And then,' added Tiler, his face softening, 'we shall have our City all to ourselves. *And it will be as if they never came.*'

He had moved so that his back was to the sun. Sween looked at him. He saw his own shocked face reflected in Tiler's eyes. Now round and black and fathomless.

'So long as the evil, cunning Blue Hare doesn't stop him,' spat Tiler suddenly. 'She with her lies and trickery. Leading people into danger.'

Finding the Champion

An orange and white cat slipped into the shadows by Tiler's feet. Sween looked down and saw a blurring, as if the darkness had become full of mist. Then there was a girl standing there with red hair and bands of freckles like stripes on her cheeks.

'We think we have found her, brother,' she said to Tiler. 'Under the third Tower. A Karmidee, a street girl, playing chess for money. People taking bets. She has been there for at least a week.'

'Good,' said Tiler.

'A *week*,' exclaimed Sween. 'It can't be her. Definitely not. And I can't imagine her doing anything like that.'

'Let us go and see,' said Tiler. 'There are not many

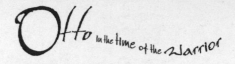

Karmidee interested in this game with the little men. They are too busy for games, I think, trying to stay alive.'

'This one is staying alive,' said the girl with the red hair. 'They are saying no one has beaten her yet.'

Sween stopped himself from saying anything else.

'You see,' said Tiler, as they started across the square, 'you are very, very fortunate that you have met me.'

But Sween did not feel fortunate. He was trying to think how he would get away from them when they had all seen this girl and it wasn't Norah. And he kept seeing things that made him even more worried about Otto. A covered cart creaked past with *Foundling Shop* written on the side and children's faces, blank and bleak, peering out through a tear in the canvas.

Then suddenly he heard a horrible scream. He swung round and saw men scrabbling and fighting in a doorway. They had hold of someone. They were dragging him. He was writhing and kicking and punching and the air around him was filling with particles of ice, and he and the men who were hauling him away were all appearing and reappearing through a savage, sparkling cloud. These men were Citizens. They snarled and shivered and cursed but they did not let go. They wore the necklace of gold stones around their necks and some sort of uniform. A picture of a bird was embroidered on their shirts under the chain mail.

'Those are the Rook's men,' said Tiler. 'That is his emblem,'

'Where are they taking him?' cried Sween. 'Can't we help him?'

'Are you mad? Shut up and keep walking.'

'But what are they *doing*, are they some sort of police?'

Sween doubled back. There was a crowd now, shifting and growing, a few Karmidee among the Citizens. Suddenly a ragged old man fell into the space around the Rook's men, on to the newly frozen ground. He scrambled to his feet, bent and limping, and for a moment it seemed all an accident, and that he was trying to get away, and then Sween glimpsed his scarred face set with desperate determination.

The Rook's men were ignoring him. He staggered into one of them. Sparks flared up. Tiny terrible fingers of flame clawed at the clothes of the attackers. The old man threw back his head and gave a shout of rage and heat shimmered around him, seeming to melt the air itself.

The Rook's men were screaming. Their clothes were on fire. They flung themselves on the ground and rolled to crush the flames and the crowd surged away from them.

Sween felt Tiler's grip on his arm tighten. All around them Karmidee and Citizens alike were shouting and tumbling to escape. The old man roared again, hobbling

forwards, but the Rook's men had already let go of their victim. Smoke filled the air now. Shouts and more smoke. Tiler and the girl with red hair were dragging Sween backwards. Sparks spat and died on his guitar case. Two of the Rook's men staggered to their feet. Sween looked for the old man but could only see the ice-maker, the man they had been trying to take, stumbling into the crowd, bleeding and doubled forwards. Three Karmidee seized him. No one tried to stop them carrying him away.

One of the Rook's men raised his axe. He stood scorched and bloody, glowering at anyone who dared to look.

The girl with red hair had been knocked over. She leapt to her feet. She and Tiler pushed Sween into an alleyway. Then they all ran, and did not stop until they came to a quiet, empty street.

'Well, well,' said Tiler, softly. 'Who'd have thought it? I don't think I've ever seen anyone escape before.' And there was a hint of pride in his voice, which Sween suspected he was trying to hide.

'Why doesn't everybody fight?' he asked quickly.

Tiler's face became extremely cat-like in its stillness.

'You think we have not fought? Where have you been?'

Sween breathed in slowly, snatching time to think.

'Forgive me my ignorance, brother,' he said, very carefully. 'But I have been as far away from here as it is was possible for me to be. It has not been my choice that I am ignorant of the fate of my brothers and sisters.'

'Sounds like he's been in the mountains,' said the girl. 'Some families sent their children there in the beginning, remember. Hoping they'd be safer there. Cavers looked after them.'

'Cavers have got their own problems now,' said Tiler. 'Their skins are worth twice their weight in gold, so they say.' He had not taken his eyes off Sween. 'There were those of us who fought, although we do not have their weapons or their readiness to hurt and kill. We are many different kinds. We did not always agree. The Outsiders kept arriving. Many, many, many. Ruthless. Arrogant. My father died. You think I would choose to live on the streets?'

'I'm sorry,' said Sween.

'They are very many,' said the girl, almost too quiet to hear. 'And nothing is sacred to them except gold.'

And they walked on. Past fruit stalls and bread stalls and stalls piled with wooden cages full of chickens and lizards and large spiders. They dodged around towers of baskets and rolls of carpet and bundles of crate bird tail feathers. Sween saw a pile of wolf skins. He saw bear skins. He saw a little Karmidee boy, surely only as old as Hepzie and Zeborah, spinning in the air, while another child, not much older, collected money in a hat.

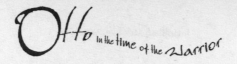

Down lanes and alleys and under archways of grinning carved faces and they were suddenly on the Boulevard again.

And there, where it should not be, was the Karmidee Tower again.

'Here?' whispered Sween, as people pushed past them on either side. A woman leading a leopard with a golden collar. A man carrying a basket of giant glowing eggs. 'Isn't this where we started?'

'The third Tower,' said Tiler. 'This is the second. You dismounted from the boar under the first. Do you know nothing about this City at all?'

A boy came hurrying towards them. Another dammerung, Sween realized. His hair was grey. His skin pale and scattered with freckles the colour of burnt paper. He stopped when he saw Sween.

'How does your energy manifest, brother?' asked Tiler quietly. 'Forgive me, I intrude by asking, but it would reassure me to know.' His language and his manner had suddenly become very formal.

Sween tried to smile. Just about managed it.

'It is indeed a personal question,' he said, playing yet again for time. 'But since we are companions today . . .' He paused. He had decided to pretend to have some rare ability that no one would have heard of; now he couldn't think of one.

'My music,' he said, tapping the guitar case. 'My ability manifests when I play.'

'Your heart speaks?'

Another pause.

'Yes,' said Sween. 'Yes. It does.' And although this was not a lie, he flushed.

'These are personal questions, Tiler,' said the grey-haired boy.

'We need to know,' said Tiler. 'Unless we are going to go hungry for another night.'

The other boy shrugged. 'Well, perhaps you would like to meet the chess champion. She's just finishing another game, I think.'

'The trees have offered us shelter,' said Tiler. 'Follow us, Sween the Tuneful.'

The dammerung walked fast, even in their human form, and Sween followed them. At last he saw the Karmidee Tower, except it wasn't *the* Tower, it was the third one, just like the others. They were near the Southern end of the Boulevard. He recognized the Park. He was used to the grand buildings continuing, dividing themselves among other streets where the Boulevard ended in a grand square with a fountain in the middle.

However, now, beyond the familiar faces of the apartments overlooking the Park Gates, he saw that there

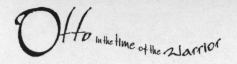

was rubble, and tents and campfires, and the City dwindled into scrubland. The rest, it seemed, had not yet been built.

The unexpected Karmidee Tower stood where the fountain should be. A narrow crack ran along the ground underneath it and continued some way along the Boulevard before it closed again.

There was a small crowd at the base of the Tower. Not underneath, outside in the sun. Citizens. Glinting and glittering with their gold.

Tiler turned and beckoned to him to come closer.

Tiler's Otter

Sween edged in among the Citizens. No one looked at him, of course, but some shuffled very slightly to one side, as if to make sure that he didn't touch them.

A man was sitting on a cushion at the edge of the space under the Tower. There was a chess board in front of him, and on the other side of the chess board, sitting on a small carpet, there was a girl wearing a broad-brimmed hat and ragged clothes.

She moved a piece and the man on the cushion shook his head and clicked his tongue. He wore big jewelled rings and a gold and silver chain mail coat.

Sween suspected that the game was nearly over. He looked through the crowd and saw Tiler and his friend,

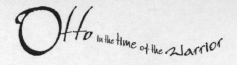

both with their mysterious eyes fixed on the board.

The man moved a piece.

There was mutter from the onlookers.

The girl moved again.

'Checkmate,' she said, in a rather clear, precise voice. She pushed the hat back on her head, revealing her grimy face.

'Norah?' whispered Sween, unheard in the chatter of activity around him.

People were pushing forward to try and see the board. Pieces of gold were exchanging hands. The man who had lost flicked a lump of gold in among his defeated pieces and the girl picked it up and inclined her head.

They stood up.

Sween recognized Otto's carpet. She had been sitting on Otto's carpet all the time. As the crowd turned away, still talking and exclaiming, he pushed forwards. The girl was collecting the chess pieces. It was a travelling chess board, of course, ideal for its purpose.

Was this why she had been so desperate to travel back in time? To find more people to defeat at chess?

'Norah,' he exclaimed, as soon as he could get near her. 'Are you all right? Where's Otto?'

He stopped short. She looked so different. Her sallow skin was tanned, her hair was extremely short, she had a moonstone stud in her nose. Years of meeting his father's rich and famous friends had equipped Sween with spectacular good manners for use in unexpected situations. He used them now. Instead of yelling in amazement he just raised his eyebrows.

'I'm sure I have no idea where your friend is,' said Norah, as if Otto was a parcel, carelessly mislaid. 'He didn't do up his safety harness properly. He fell off the bench. Then the weight distribution was unbalanced, I presume your harness snapped where you had tied all those bags to it. You fell off too, as you no doubt realize. I can only assume you both travelled some distance in space as well as in the other, er,' she lowered her voice to a whisper, 'as in *time*. I *had* done my harness up properly, and I *hadn't* hooked heavy bags on to it. Without you two the bench was too light. It went further back in time than it was supposed to do . . .' She looked past Sween, who turned and saw that the crowd had disbanded, leaving Tiler and his friend, who were watching from a distance. Not a very great distance. Two cats had joined them. One had jumped on to Tiler's shoulder.

'I've been here three months,' whispered Norah. 'And the machine leaves tomorrow night.'

'What! I've only been here since last night! You can't have been here three months . . . it's not, well, it's not—'

'Possible?'

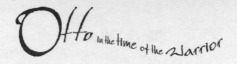

He stared at her. It was certainly hard to see how she could have changed so much in less than a day.

'But what about Otto? We've got to find him.'

The chess board folded to make a box. She snapped it shut. 'He has landed somewhere and at some time no doubt quite soon after you did. I imagine he'll go back to the Amaze. I'm afraid I've got other things to worry about. There's almost no time left and I need to get into—'

'Honourable greetings, honourable greetings,' said Tiler, arriving silently beside Sween. 'Do please introduce us to your friend. Now that we've been so kind as to find her for you.'

Sween frowned at Norah. He didn't know if she was using her real name.

'Norah,' she said. 'Norah the Champion.'

'This is Tiler of the Rooftops,' said Sween.

Tiler swept off his hat and bowed.

'May the trees guide you,' said Norah. She certainly seemed to know what to say. Twenty-four hours ago, as far as Sween was concerned, she had barely even spoken to a Karmidee. Now she had turned into one.

'We have a business proposition for you both,' said Tiler.

Sween tried to pull a warning face at her. Something touched his leg and he glanced down and saw a cat, and then another and another, gliding towards him.

'I am not interested in propositions, brother,' said Norah.
'I have been asked many times if I want a partner to handle
my affairs, or a body guard. With respect, I do not.'

Sween stared at her, marvelling.

She removed her hat and wiped her forehead with
her palm. She wore a silver bracelet and several rings
like Mab's.

'Those are not my suggestions,' said Tiler. 'I have a
friend who greatly enjoys the game of chess. I am sure he
would like to play against you.' He nodded towards Sween.
'He is also a lover of music. He is a man with great
responsibilities who craves entertainment.' He paused. 'A
very powerful, wealthy man. You would benefit from
meeting him. In many ways.'

'Anyone may come and challenge me to play chess in the
street,' said Norah. 'Your friend is welcome to do the same.'

'We're really not interested, thank you,' said Sween.
'And we must search for our lost friend.' Although he
suspected that Norah would not be interested in this
proposition either.

'I cannot help you,' continued Norah, as if Sween hadn't
spoken. 'I have something important to do for my family.'

'You would not have been so pleasantly reunited with this
friend without our help,' said Tiler, his voice even and
smooth. 'We have spent some hours looking for you. My

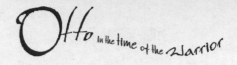

brothers and sisters are hungry. All Karmidee are one family, are we not?'

There were more cats now, plenty more. In the shadows.

Sween looked sideways at Norah, trying to catch her eye. She was staring straight ahead. Otto's carpet and her chess board under her arm. Her bag seemed to have gone and her coat bulged as if something was hidden inside it. He guessed that after three months spent winning at chess she must be a walking treasure chest of gold pieces.

Thank goodness, more than somewhat, that she wasn't being taken in by Tiler's invitations.

'My friend is Jack Sargasso,' said Tiler. 'He is living in the castle in the Forest of the Blue Cat. People call him the Rook.'

'I'll do it,' said Norah.

'What?' exclaimed Sween

'I'll do it,' repeated Norah. 'Take me to the castle. Now.'

Even Tiler seemed disconcerted. He turned to the girl with the striped freckles and muttered something in a low voice. Sween grabbed Norah's arm and pulled her further under the Tower.

'Are you crazy?' he hissed. 'These people are dangerous, they could rob you of all the gold you've been winning and leave you in a gutter—'

'Don't come then,' she said. Sharp as teeth.

'I'm not, I'm not.' He still had hold of her arm. 'I'm not going and neither are you.'

'Let go of me, Sween, and keep out of this. I've got to go. It's very, very important.'

'Yes, brother, let go of the lady,' said Tiler. Walking towards them.

He gestured to the cats. 'The musician wishes to leave. Let him do so.'

The cats looked away. Some sat down. Some wandered, apparently aimless, into the sunshine.

Sween stood where he was. 'Don't go with them, Norah,' he said, not bothering to even lower his voice. 'There is such a man, a Citizen chief, a warlord, he is not—'

'Just go,' said Norah. 'I know what I'm doing.'

'No you don't. No, you don't. I can't believe—'

'She has made up her mind,' said Tiler.

Sween looked quickly around him. As he thought, the cats had not gone very far. Now in the darkest corners under the Tower some of them had already turned into children.

'*Don't go with them,*' he said, clenching his fists, trying to keep himself from shouting at the top of his voice.

'All you have to do is go on your way, brother,' said Tiler.

Sween thought of the Karmidee who had been dragged out of his house by the men in chain mail. The Rook's men. He thought of the castle, remote in its forest. He thought of

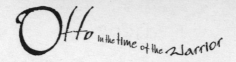

the Foundling Wagon and the faces of the children staring out through the bars. There was no one to tell. No one to go to for help.

He went cold with the realization of what he had to do.

'I'll come with her,' he said. 'To entertain your friend.'

'You don't need to come with me,' said Norah harshly. 'I am the chess player, you are an afterthought. I don't expect there's a shortage of musicians.'

'I need to come with you,' he whispered. 'Because although you're so clever it is now completely obvious that you are also an idiot.'

She didn't reply.

He couldn't remember ever having felt so angry with anyone in his life.

Discovery
In The Forest

Blue needed him. The last message had been from the castle. He would go there now and find some way inside.

Otto had barely slept. He was stiff and sore. He had washed his face in the river. The dawn had reached into the forest with cold fingers of light and it didn't care about anything or anyone.

He started to walk, calling Herzull's name as he went, climbing and sliding, as the path followed the curve of the river. He grew warmer as the day grew warmer.

And then he stopped absolutely still.

The light was brighter here. He put up his hand to shield his eyes and saw that trees around him had shed all their leaves. They were bone-bare, stricken. Green summer

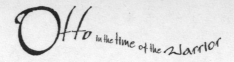

leaves lay everywhere on the path and on the ground.

Many things were strewn about, half hidden by this sudden shroud of green. A leather shoe. A broken axe handle. There was the remains of a camp fire, half-burnt sticks, blackened stones.

And something else.

The pallet of rushes which the hunters had been dragging along behind them. And the body of the caver tied on to it with chains.

Otto still couldn't move.

Then, his heart thundering in his ears, he crept towards the body. He had only seen adult cavers before. They lived safe in their warm caves in the mountains. His father's friend, Megrafrix, was half as tall again as a tall man and many, many times stronger. A great, scaled lizard who walked like a man. Proud, dignified. A keeper of ancient customs.

But this was a child.

His eyes were closed and his mouth was slightly open. Otto could see the tips of his forked purple tongue between his lips. His hands and feet were bound and his scales were caked with dried blood. He wore a studded waistcoat, just as cavers did in Otto's time. Only most of these moonstones had been torn off.

Otto shuddered. He couldn't look. He couldn't look

away. He knew that cavers hate the cold. He took off his coat and laid it very carefully over the caver's body.

Then he saw something more, out of the corner of his eye, black among the bracken and he turned, sick with fright.

One of the hunters lay there.

It must be one of the hunters.

Face down. His helmet gone.

His armoured clothes, his splayed, clawing hands. All covered in dew.

A bolt from a crossbow in the back of his neck.

Otto screamed.

He set off to run. His legs were giving way. He looked back at the caver.

Stopped.

Almost screamed again.

The caver child's emerald-green eyes were opening. A third eyelid, like a film of cloud, slid across the surface and was gone.

There was a terrible stillness in this place, where there had been violence that could never be healed.

But the caver child was alive, and Otto, trembling, made his way back to him, with the dead man, inescapable, at the edge of his vision.

The caver's lips moved. He was trying to speak.

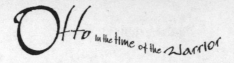

Otto began to do things. He cupped his hands full of river water and the caver drank a little and spat out some foamy blood and then drank some more. Otto broke the chain that bound him to the pallet by hitting it over and over again between two rocks. He found a knife in the pocket of the caver's waistcoat and cut through the bonds around his wrists and ankles.

The caver, very slowly, sat, very painfully, stood up.

Otto's coat did not reach around his massive shoulders, it draped over his neck like a scarf.

Cavers do not have as many facial expressions as people. The Karmidee call them the ancestors; they were in the mountains long before the City was built. They live to great ages.

Now this ancestor looked down at Otto with his large, slanting eyes.

'They would never have caught me,' he said, his voice cracked and dry, speaking with effort. 'I was weak. I slept through the winter. I came out to look for a certain . . . plant.' He gestured towards the forest with a clawed hand. 'I lay down to rest. I was sleeping. They had nets . . .'

Otto nodded. He understood that for a caver to be overpowered by humans was a terrible humiliation. Even if that caver happened to be a child.

'They would have killed me later,' the caver continued.

'For my skin. But they like it to be fresh. My skin is worth a great deal of their gold . . .'

As long as Otto kept his back to the hunter lying in the forest he could hold his thoughts steady.

'Are you hurt?' he asked.

The caver shook his head.

Otto looked down at the ground and the scattered remains of the fire.

'What happened here?'

'They are celebrating. They did not think they would ever succeed in catching one of us. I am the first. What they are going to do with all the gold? Enough to buy everything they ever want. They do not need to work for their boss any more. They have a flask of their stinking bloodberry juice.

'But I am listening. I begin to understand. Only one is drinking and drinking. The other is clever. He pretends to drink. He laughs and sings but he pours his drink away. On to the ground. Near my face. I see him pour it.

'In the end one is very dazed out on the juice. He goes into the trees for . . . to relieve himself. But he has only just stood up and turned his back and started walking and the other, quick as that,' the caver snapped his scaled fingers, 'he jumps for his bow and his death arrows. Sshtum! One shot. Then he makes sure that I am tightly bound. Then he hurries away.'

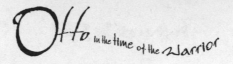

He fell silent.

'He's coming back to get you,' said Otto. 'He's gone to get someone to help him.'

'Yes,' said the caver. 'And then he will have all the gold for himself.'

Although he was, of course, much bigger than Otto, he seemed very young. His skin, where it was not coated with dirt, was sleek and supple, fading from gold and green on his back to a pale orange on his throat and chest. Megrafrix, as Otto remembered him, was covered in scales that looked like slices of stone.

'I think we should get out of here,' said Otto. 'Now.'

'I know,' said the caver. Not moving. Sounding younger than ever.

'Let's get off the path,' said Otto, quickly. 'Let's just get right away from here. Where is your home? Is there an entrance? A cave or something?'

'Yes,' said the caver, almost whispering.

'Is it far?'

'I don't think so.'

'Well what about your family, will they be looking for you?'

'I don't think so.'

Otto could hardly keep still. Now he thought he heard voices further up the path. Now he realized that it was a crowd of birds, cawing and plunging above the trees.

'My name is Turnix,' said the caver, bowing.

'Otto,' said Otto. 'Otto the Stranger.'

'I have nothing to give you for saving my life, Otto the Stranger.'

'*It really doesn't matter*,' said Otto, through clenched teeth. 'Please, please, can we *move*.'

He grabbed Turnix's arm and tugged without effect, like someone tugging at a statue.

'It is a matter of honour,' said Turnix.

'COME ON,' yelled Otto.

Turnix did move then. He seemed suddenly to have an idea. He shook Otto's hand away and set off past him on his big clawed feet and almost knocked him over with his tail.

Otto spun round.

Oh no. Oh no, no, no.

Turnix was bending over the body of the hunter, dragging on some sort of gold necklace around the hunter's neck. He fumbled in the tattered remains of his waistcoat, pulled out his knife, there was a glint of metal and he cut the necklace free. He came back with it dangling from his hand.

Otto groaned in horror.

'Do you know what this is?' asked Turnix, with a triumphant lift of his chin.

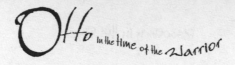

'I have no idea,' said Otto. 'And I really, really don't—'

'You are some sort of traveller? You are walking towards the City?'

'Well, yes, yes I am, but—'

'The Citizens all wear these. All of them. The Karmidee don't. It is like a badge, do you understand? Are you a Karmidee?'

'Yes,' exclaimed Otto. 'Now, let's—'

'I thought so. All the Citizens wear gold. Gold is their love and their breath and their heartbeat. You may need to pretend to be one of them. You cannot do it without this around your neck.' He grinned, undoubtedly he was feeling better. 'Look at their pathetic metal clothes. They don't dare to come into the forest without them.' He gestured towards the hunter. 'And almost always they travel in the two or the three or the four—'

'Let's just *get off the path* and then we can talk and things.'

'There is science in it,' continued Turnix. 'We don't know yet, but the Karmidee cannot wear these things for long. They look like lumps of gold, don't they, but they are not, they are some sort of stones, gilded to look like gold. It is very important, you cannot wear it very long.'

He forced the dreadful gift into Otto's hands and picked up a jewelled knife that had been dropped by the fire. Then, at last, he allowed Otto to steer him back between the trees and set off with purpose, splintering a number of lower branches as he pushed his way ahead.

'Come with me,' he called over his shoulder. 'The one who shot the metal arrow will have gone to get some friend. He will come back. Even a young ancestor is of much value and I am not so small. We must not be on the path.'

Otto, struggling behind him, managed, despite everything, to roll his eyes like Mab.

A few minutes later, after climbing steeply, Turnix stopped beside a rock about the size of Albert and Dolores's wardrobe back at 15 Herschell Buildings. He pushed it to one side, revealing a tunnel sloping into the ground.

'You must come too,' he said. 'This passage takes us to the edge of the City close by the castle, in the Forest of the Blue Hare.'

'That's where I need to go,' said Otto, breathlessly. Lowering himself inside.

'The passage is much quicker,' added Turnix. 'The path by the river is not so straight.'

He lifted the rock back into place over their heads, sealing the tunnel like a lid. The air was warm and welcoming and full of dull, red light.

No comfort to Otto, thinking of Herzull, outside in the forest maybe. Alone. Unable to hide. And he saw her in his mind, curled among dead leaves, her fur the colour of the

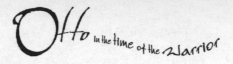

Hush family fridge, dotted with alphabet letters because she was hungry.

'I've lost my friend who's a bear,' he said. 'She might be in the forest like me, or she might be in the City at a place called the Amaze. But I have been searching and calling for her. Please help her if you see her. Perhaps someone could even take her to the Amaze, if it is still there, that would be best, because when I have completed what I have to do I will be going there. She's a chameleon bear but she never turns the right colour. She's only a baby.'

'I will tell everyone I know,' said Turnix. 'I know many, many ancestors.'

'And a boy with a pale bony face and two long black plaits and smart clothes and a guitar case, and a girl.'

'I will tell everyone,' repeated Turnix.

They walked on.

'If you wish to enter the castle,' said Turnix, after a while, 'maybe I can help you with a plan.'

THE *Castle*

Otto remembered at the last moment to knot the string of golden stones around his neck. They were heavy and cold against his skin, clearly visible above the collar of his pyjama shirt. As clearly visible, in fact, as they had been around the throat of the hunter to whom they had so recently belonged. He shuddered. He most certainly did not want to wear them at all but Turnix had insisted that no Citizen was ever seen without them and that only Citizens could safely enter the castle. 'Karmidee might go in that gate,' he had said. 'But only as prisoners.'

Turnix had also warned him that he should only wear them for a short time. However, Otto had forgotten to ask him how long a short time was and what would

301

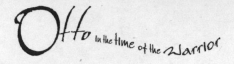

happen if he didn't take them off soon enough.

They had said a formal goodbye in a small cave, one of many ways in and out of the tunnel, which continued on deeper into the mountain.

Now Otto stood alone, blinking in the sunlight. He could see the rockface and the castle wall towering up through the trees. He scrambled, clinging to roots and low branches, until, at last, he came to the carved steps and the steep path that led down towards the streets and squares of BlueCat Wood.

Except the streets and squares were not there. The wood was a forest, stretching away and down and he could see the river glimmering beyond it, winding across a green plain.

He started up the steps. Out of the corner of his eye he thought he saw the hunter lying in his bed of bracken. He kept going, climbing faster, as if he could leave the picture behind, as if it had not scorched his mind like fire.

Missing everybody, tired, hungry and scared, he tried to rehearse what he was going to say to the sentry at the castle gate.

The plan had seemed good enough when he and Turnix had devised it in the warmth and safety of the mountain. Here, on the outside, he was considerably less certain.

Playing Chess

'A chess player,' said the man at the window. 'Excellent. The company of idiots like you, Clumber, is sapping my brain of its wit.' He turned to face into the room, blocking light. The guard, Clumber, went to stand by the door.

Jack Sargasso, known as the Rook, was short and heavily built. Yellow-haired and monstrously decked in gold. The gold stones around his neck.

'A Karmidee who plays the game of skill and cunning?' he said, approaching Sween, his eyes not unlike the eyes of the boar at the jeweller's shop.

'That's the musician,' said Tiler, very smooth. 'He is the accompaniment. The girl is the chess player. She has been

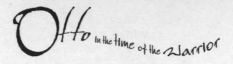

playing in the streets every day for weeks and no one has ever defeated her.'

'Two Karmidee,' said the Rook. 'I usually only entertain visitors of your kind in the dungeon.' He paused and Clumber laughed.

'Take a seat, musical magico,' he continued. 'It is my experience that some of your people are excellent musicians, despite your inferiority. I own a number of exquisite musical instruments. Later, perhaps, you can try your skill on a clavichord or a lute. I am a collector of valuable and beautiful things . . . however they are obtained.'

Clumber laughed again.

'And you,' the Rook gestured to Norah, 'come and see my chess board. I have only recently had it made. You will be my first opponent.'

He undid a purse on his belt and counted out a number of gold pieces. These were for Tiler. Clumber opened the door and Tiler went out, looking only straight ahead, the money in his hand.

'Well, start your music,' said the Rook. 'It will soothe your friend's nerves while I defeat her.'

Sween sat down on an embroidered cushion. In three hundred years' time this would be the living room of his home. The wooden door, with the small carved animals along the top, was familiar. In his own time the bear in the middle was split almost in two. Today, eerily, it was whole. All around him the floor was covered in overlapping carpets and rugs in reds and blues and, of course, gold. The walls were hung with charts and tapestries and helmets and weapons. A chandelier hung from the centre of the ceiling like a huge, threatening insect.

He undid the leather straps of his guitar case. It had occurred to him that the Rook might be puzzled by the guitar, an instrument not yet properly invented, and might ask questions that would be difficult to answer.

However the Rook was setting out gold and rose quartz chess pieces on a board made of some shiny stone.

'Play on, magico,' he said, without looking up.

Sween gritted his teeth.

Rosie climbed out of his pocket and up on to his shoulder. He hissed at her, as quietly and fiercely as he could, and put her back again. Then, ignoring her squirms of rage, he cradled the guitar for a moment, taking a bit of strength. He picked out a few notes. Then he stopped.

'This is for Otto, wherever he is,' he whispered.

And he began to play, very quietly, a wild, private tune, raw and hurting and fierce, that he had invented in his head while they were all walking to the castle.

Norah took her place on a low stool. The Rook had

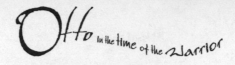

chosen the gold pieces for himself. The rose quartz pieces gleamed invitingly. They were full of soft misty light. The Rook held the gold queen between his finger and thumb. Turning it. It was inlaid with tiny emeralds and rubies.

'Magnificient, is it not?' he said, smiling his robber's smile. 'Made to order. Unique.'

'Very beautiful,' said Norah. She had seen it before, of course. It was the same set that she and her father played with at home. Inherited by Sargassos down three hundred years.

The golden tablecloth, studded with tiny nuggets which resembled those worn by the Citizens on their necklaces, was also familiar to her. Her father used it as a blanket. He wrapped himself in it as he sat every day beside the kitchen stove.

She looked around the room. The stained glass windows gleamed fresh and bright. Everywhere there were jewels and ornaments and everything seemed to be made of gold or silver or wood inlaid with stones.

But Norah had treasure of her own. Nearly a hundred gold pieces that she had won at chess, sewn into her coat. Too heavy to take home on the time machine. All she had to do now was find the place where she was going to hide it.

'Your move, sweetheart,' said the Rook, cheery and cold.

She gazed at the sparkling pieces and they played out their possibilities.

'Do you know why they call me the Rook?'

'No,' she said, moving a pawn, sliding it on the polished stone.

'Not curious? You seem very calm for a child of your species in the presence of the most powerful man in the City.'

'I am thinking about the game,' said Norah, who was thinking about treasure.

'After all the Rook is another name for the castle, is it not?'

She nodded without looking up.

'Perhaps you think they call me the Rook because I live in a castle. That would be a reason but it is not the real one. I called myself the Rook long before I lived in a castle, long before I even saw your strange and beautiful City. I chose my name as a little private joke with myself. The Rook on the chess board is a fighter, is he not? He is more powerful than the Knight and the Bishop and the sorry little pawns. The Rook can be very powerful indeed.'

Norah understood what he was saying. She narrowed her eyes at the chess board. She believed that any piece, even a pawn, could be powerful in skilled hands.

'In chess. And in life,' continued the Rook, 'your people

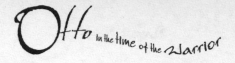
always have someone they call a King. Some kind of leader, a philosopher, an advisor. You will know that they have a new one, we have heard that his name is the Warrior. I will finish him. I have an excellent plan.' He moved a golden piece, stroking it with his finger as he put it down.

There was a knock on the door.

'Enter,' shouted the Rook.

The guard, Clumber, strode in, accompanied by another guard and a boy.

Sween stopped playing his guitar. He almost dropped it. He cracked his biggest grin. He coughed and went red.

Norah looked round, barely able to see because of the moves and counter moves which were bouncing like ballroom dancers in her imagination. Even she looked shocked. For a moment she almost lost her concentration.

'This boy was hunting for rabbits and found something which he wishes to show you,' said Clumber. 'Step forward, boy.'

Otto looked from Sween to Norah and back again. He nearly lost his balance. His mouth fell open, his eyes went round.

'Sween!' he exclaimed. 'Where the skink—'

'You know this magico?' snapped the Rook.

Sween stopped smiling. With his eyes fixed on Otto's he shook his head from side to side by the tiniest amount.

'No,' said Otto.

'You just addressed him by name, did you not? What is your name, magico?'

'Herzull the Crumb,' said Sween.

Otto made a spluttering noise.

'I used to work in a bakery,' said Sween.

The Rook frowned. 'I had the impression that you just called this magico, Sween, Citizen.'

Otto was cold with fright. He guessed that he had put them all in danger. He ran his fingers under the stones around his neck.

'I called him Swine, Mr Sargasso,' he said, slowly. 'And I called him Swine because I thought he was someone else. Someone I don't like. Someone I got into a fight with recently. But he isn't. His hair is the same. But now I look,' he breathed in, almost dizzy, 'it is not the same magico at all.'

'He's brought you a knife that was dropped on the path,' said Clumber. 'He thought it might belong to someone from the castle. He seems an honest young—'

'Thank you, Clumber,' said the Rook. 'You go. And you, boy, sit down. We are playing chess but it will not take long. After I have won you can show me this knife. It interests me.'

Otto walked across the soft carpets. The relief, the wonderful relief of seeing Sween was flooding through him like heat from a fire. It wasn't easy to understand how or

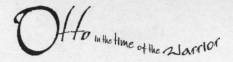

why Sween was here, of course, but surely, somehow, everything would be all right now. They would rescue Blue together. They would find Herzull and get home.

Sween began to play a moody tune from the mud towns.

'As I was saying,' said the Rook. 'The Karmidee have a new King and I intend to ambush him, secretly, just myself and a couple of trusted men. Your people are only a problem if they gather together. They will not gather so successfully if they do not have a leader.'

The game was progressing, move followed move.

'I like chess because it is like life,' said the Rook. 'The winner traps the King of the enemy. Then the winner possesses the whole board. No room for any one else. Just like here, when I trap the King of the magicos.'

Otto, on his cushion on the floor, had become very alert.

'Where I come from, we know how these matters are conducted. New people arrive. Stronger. More numerous. Ruthless and hungry. Old people sign treaties. Sign more treaties. Keep trying to make peace. New people don't want peace. They want everything.'

Norah took one of the Rook's pieces off the board. She had taken several already.

'Ah,' he added, 'you are better than I expected.'

For some reason Otto's skin had started to burn and ache all over. His head hurt, his palms were sweating. He struggled to keep still. He forced himself not to try and catch Sween's eye. And he listened to the plan to trap the person the Rook thought was called the Warrior.

It was to be that very night. The night before the Red Moon. The Rook had heard that the Warrior was alone, somewhere along the river. His spies had not actually seen him. Here the Rook took one of Norah's knights with a chuckle of triumph. The rumour, it seemed, was that there was someone of importance to the magicos down there, by themselves, and it was hardly likely to be anyone else, was it?

Otto thought of Delilah and her dog and their little tent. He imagined this square-faced man creeping down through the trees.

'It's the King you need. Just like chess,' said the Rook, taking another of the rose quartz pieces. 'You kill him and everybody else goes home.' He grinned at his own wit. 'Or, in this case, *leaves* home.'

Looking down at his hand, turning it over. Otto found a strange rash flowering on his palm.

'Checkmate,' said Norah.

Sween stopped playing his guitar.

The Rook glared at the board.

For the first time since Otto had come he saw that Norah was wearing a nose stud. She removed her hat and wiped her forehead and he saw her shorn hair.

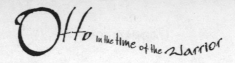

'I concede,' grunted the Rook. 'We'll play again after I've eaten.'

'We have to go now,' said Sween. 'We are expected home.'

The Rook stood up and stretched and laughed. The gold gleamed on his hands and wrists and clothes.

'You'll stay here tonight, until I've dealt with your friend by the river.' And he drew his finger across his throat. 'I think it is not impossible that you are spies.'

He turned to Otto. 'Show me the knife, boy, and make it a good story. I've just lost a chess game to an ugly-faced magico kid and I don't lose to anyone. You'll have to take my mind off it.'

Otto, desperate in several horrible desperate ways, pulled a short knife with a jewelled handle out of his coat. It was the one Turnix had found on the ground beside the hunters' camp fire.

'Your clothes are mighty unusual, Citizen,' said the Rook, taking the knife. 'What part of the City do you come from?'

This had been rehearsed with Turnix. Otto's mouth was dry.

'Near the Bridge of the Black Dog,' he said. 'I found the knife on the path. When I was hunting rabbits. It's . . .' His skin was screaming. He was starting to see strange black lines curling and uncurling wherever he looked.

'It's richly decorated. I thought it might be yours, or someone who—'

'I recognize this,' said the Rook. 'This belongs to one of my men, I was admiring these rubies and pearls not so long ago, and hoping he might give it to me out of respect and loyalty . . . or fear,' he smiled. 'You've brought it to the right place, do you seek a reward?'

Otto and Turnix hadn't planned much further than this. The idea had been to get into the castle.

'No, thank you,' he said, rubbing his palms against the sleeves of his coat.

'No thank you!' laughed the Rook. 'Everybody wants something, Citizen—'

The door burst open and Clumber thudded, breathless, into the room.

'Marco is murdered, Captain!'

'Murdered?' snarled the Rook.

'Yes. He was out hunting last night, in the great forest, him and his brother, looking for a lizard—'

'Greedy stupid fools! Be patient and I'll make all your fortunes! No one has caught a lizard in that forest for a twelvemonth but plenty have died trying! Do you think I have men to spare?'

'No-oo, Captain,' stammered Clumber.

'Haven't I ordered every single man in my pay not to go

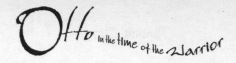

into these forests at night? We do not yet understand all the dangers we face—'

'They caught one, Captain.'

'A lizard? They actually caught a lizard?'

'His brother says it's a fine one – young, still alive, skin as sweet as silk and as strong as steel, he says.'

The Rook was silent for a moment. 'You amaze me. I would not have thought them capable of such a feat.'

'Marco was on watch while his brother slept. Someone, the assassin, has crept up and shot Marco in the back.'

The Rook laughed. 'And stolen the lizard, no doubt, so all is wasted.'

Clumber swallowed noisily. 'Marco's brother wants someone to go back with him. When he woke up, and found Marco dead, the lizard was still there. He thinks the attacker tried to drag it away, but it must have been too heavy. He thinks it may still be there now. He will give ten gold pieces to the man who will dare go back with him. He's coming now, Captain.'

'Ten gold pieces?' said the Rook, softly. 'For a skin that will be worth at least a thousand? I will have to keep a watch on Marco's brother, perhaps he is not such a fool as I thought.'

A second man stepped through the doorway. He stood there in his simple, horrible ordinariness. This, then, was the man who had hunted Turnix down. The man who had killed his own brother with a crossbow bolt in the back of the neck. He worked for the Rook and this castle was his home.

Otto felt as if the floor was melting under him. In the tunnel, with Turnix, this possibility hadn't entered his head.

The Rook stared at Clumber and the hunter. He seemed to be thinking fiercely. Then he spoke fast.

'Has anyone caught that wretched hare yet. Clumber? The one wandering around this castle as it pleases? Or am I surrounded by imbeciles?'

'Not yet, Captain,' said Clumber, backing towards the door.

'Well catch it. I saw it again in the courtyard this morning. I'll warrant it's a shape-shifter, a magico spy. The devil knows how it's done. Very likely this business with Marco and this spy and these children with their music and their chess are all connected and are part of some plan to stop us dealing with the Warrior. When you catch the hare, wring its neck—'

'No!' cried Otto, before he could stop himself.

But something else was happening. The Rook had fallen silent and was staring at him. Otto felt, among other things, as if his bones were restless in his flesh. As if his own burning, throbbing skin was starting to creep and crawl all over him.

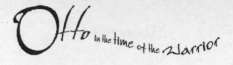

The murderer stared too. So did Sween, his face filled with horror.

But no one stared more than Norah. She stood up slowly, her hands over her mouth.

She began walking, a step, another step, across the sumptuous carpets.

'STAND STILL, MAGICO!' shouted the Rook.

She stood still, eyes wild and questioning, hands still held to her face. The Rook leapt forward and seized the string of golden stones around Otto's neck. He sliced the strip of leather with the jewelled knife.

In an instant Sween had flung down the guitar and jumped forwards. The guard, Clumber, caught him and twisted his arms behind his back. The Rook had Otto by the hair. Norah, in the midst, still stood transfixed.

'A skinking magico all along,' snarled the Rook. 'Thought he could trick us. Whose stones are these, little freak? Let's look, shall we?' He was holding the stones up close to his face, narrowing his sand-coloured eyes.

The murderer, slender, oval-faced, quiet on the edge of the drama, suddenly struck like a snake.

'Those are my brother's stones, I recognize the clasp, there, look, his initials.'

Otto was down on one knee, his neck pulled sideways, the Rook's hand still savagely wound and clenched into his hair.

The murderer's eyes gleamed. 'Here's your bowman,' he said. 'Shot my brother right in the back, left him lying like a dog . . .'

'Don't you know what we do to magicos who dare to wear the stones, little freak?' whispered the Rook. 'We sew stones into their clothes. Real stones, big stones. And we throw them into the deep river, where the water sucks out their eyes and grinds their skulls into sand.'

Otto couldn't speak.

'You must have wanted to get into my castle very much,' continued the Rook. 'You have killed a man. You have risked your life . . .' He hauled Otto to his feet. 'I don't think you would do all that just to get a reward for this trinket.' Otto saw the gleam of rubies and pearls, too close. He felt the blade pressed flat and cold against his cheek. 'I choose the little dancing bear,' whispered the Rook. And he suddenly threw the knife, very fast, the whole length of the room, and it cut the air and embedded exactly in the tiny carved bear at the top of the door, trembling. 'We are too quick and too ruthless for you and all your sorry people. We are the future. You are the dead, lost past—'

'Leave him alone!' screamed Sween, white-faced and writhing in Clumber's grip. 'Let him go!'

Norah, in the same instant, jumped back to the chess set, grabbed one of the pieces and threw it. It hit the Rook on the

temple and he yelled, almost let go of Otto . . . another chess man, a gold one, hit Clumber on the ear as he tried to duck behind Sween.

Sween broke free. Otto, contorted, through eyes blurred with pain, saw him snatch up his beloved guitar and turn to face Clumber, now lunging at him, fist raised.

Sween swung his guitar like an axe.

'Stop them, you idiots,' snarled the Rook, kicking a stool out of his way, using Otto as a shield as the chess men flew at him like shots from a sling.

The hunter, dodging and jumping, reached the table with the chess board. He snatched up the gold cloth that covered it, sending everything crashing to the floor. He held the cloth up, took a step towards Norah . . .

But before anything else could happen the door flew open and two, three, more men rushed in . . . and very quickly all the children were held prisoner.

'This one will go to the dungeon. Take the other two to the storeroom upstairs,' ordered the Rook. 'We'll talk to them in the morning.'

Clumber was still sitting on the floor among the shattered remains of Sween's guitar. He rose unsteadily and helped push and pull Sween and Norah out of the room. Sween looked back at Otto and they managed to see each other clearly for a moment.

Then the door closed, leaving Otto alone with the Rook and the quiet-eyed murderer.

The Rook let go of Otto abruptly and Otto toppled sideways on to the carpet. He struggled to his feet. There was a gilt framed mirror propped up against the wall and he saw himself there. He gasped. Astonished. He saw his own face, some blood drying under his nose, his white locks, matted and tangled, and his skin, light brown, and on his skin . . . no, *under* his skin, twisting, crawling, glowing . . .'

He screamed and clawed, he tried to wipe them away, but they were still there, he couldn't touch them, *little writhing worms* . . .

The two men laughed.

'Anyone would think he had never seen them before,' said the Rook. 'A magico trying to wear the lodestones. Entertaining. That is all your sorry magical energy, Ignoramus, that is why your people cannot wear the lodestones. They are iron ore, magnetic power, they draw your energy out. Put it on the surface for everyone to see.' He gestured towards the gold cloth on the table. 'It would be very interesting if we wrapped you in that. It has lodestones sewn all over it. Lethal.'

'I haven't killed anybody,' shouted Otto. 'I found the knife by the camp fire . . .' He was trying so hard to think, to make his innocence clear, to make the Rook believe him. 'I

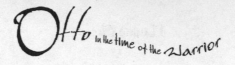

saw a dead man in the bracken. There was a caver—'

'No doubt you did,' said the Rook, laughing. 'No doubt there was.'

'*He did it*,' said Otto, pointing at the hunter. 'The caver saw it all. The caver told me. He let his brother get dazed out on bloodberry juice. He shot him when his back was turned—'

'Let me kill him now, Captain,' hissed the hunter, his voice truly terrible in its softness. 'He slanders my name.'

'All in good time,' said the Rook smoothly. 'If it was all as you say, magico, I do not think you would come here pretending to be one of your betters, talking about a lost knife, failing to tell me the most important part of the story.'

He smiled. 'No, you are a spy and you have killed a man just to get this knife, or some other object, that you could use to cheat your way into my castle. It is good that you were so foolhardy. The stones gave you away, my friend, just as they are supposed to do. Why are you so concerned about that wretched hare that has been seen here? Because, like you, that hare is working for the Warrior, trying to obtain news of my plans and designs.'

Otto stared at him. The room was filled with dusk and shadows. The Rook and the murderer loomed, their faces indistinct.

'We will be leaving soon to deal with your so-called

King,' said the Rook. 'The one who sent you on this escapade. You will have some useful things to tell us tomorrow. We will swaddle you in the lodestone blanket and cradle you. And you will scream like a baby.'

Clumber came back into the room. This room where one day Max Softly would entertain his elegant, brainless guests.

'Take him down to the dungeon,' said the Rook, turning away.

Rosie

Sween didn't recognize anything. He was shoved and cursed through one door and then another. Up a staircase, through another door. He was bent forward, he saw the paved floor, the stone stairs, his own bare, dirty, bleeding feet. Then, abruptly he was alone with Norah and a door was being eloquently bolted behind them.

'It's your music room,' whispered Norah.

He looked around in the dim light and recognized the shape of the windows on to the parapet. All locked and barred.

'Look at all these *things*,' continued Norah. Her voice sounded strange, as if she was going to laugh.

Sween sat down on a pile of carpets. His eyes were

getting used to the light. There were chests and wooden boxes, carved figures, a harp . . .

'There's no way out of here,' he said.

'I know. Did you see Otto's skin? All those little worms?'

'Yes, thanks.'

'Have you ever seen anything like that before?'

'No.'

'What I mean is, have you ever seen anyone with those things on their skin at home?'

'No.' How could she ask these things now?

'But you've got friends who are Karmidee haven't you? Otto is a Karmidee. I mean, he *is*, isn't he?'

Sween stood up. He had just realized that it wasn't a pile of carpets that he was sitting on. Whatever they were felt like snake skin, but they were much too big. And the wrong shape.

'Did you see that man with the gold cloth? He was going to trap me inside it. It had little stones on it. Did you see that? Those were lodestones. Like the necklaces. He thought I'd get those evil worms all over me because he thought I am a Karmidee. Do you think they're going to kill Otto?'

Sween didn't reply.

Rosie, confined far too long, had suddenly started to bite through his coat, something she had never done before. She didn't eat fabric. He could hear tiny coughing sounds as she

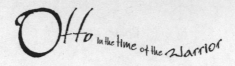

spat out each mouthful. He unbuttoned the pocket and she scrambled into view with threads of lining trailing from her jaws.

'She's hungry,' he said. Mechanically. As if there was a point in saying anything at all.

Then suddenly the shadows began to shrink back. Norah was revealed, her face like a carving. She had found a worm torch.

'Do you think they're going to kill him?' she repeated. 'Why did he want to travel on the time machine anyway?'

'To save someone's life,' said Sween, staring at Rosie, who was sniffing at a statue, which was lying on its side. He thought perhaps he was crying. His face felt wet. Never mind.

'And you?'

He couldn't see her very well any more. She was bending down looking at something. Her nose stud gleamed very faintly.

'I came along to help him,' he said. 'And I didn't like watching my father getting so fascinated with your mother. And I also thought maybe I could buy a lute from Domenico Nocte, the greatest lute maker who ever lived.' Nothing had ever sounded so ridiculous.

'I came here to save someone's life too,' said Norah. 'There's a skeleton here, it's got gold teeth.'

She didn't sound as if she was going to laugh. Perhaps, after all, she had been starting to cry.

Rosie seemed to have rejected the statue. No doubt it was made of wood. Unlike the walls of the music room which Sween happened to know were at least half a metre of solid stone.

Solid stone.

'I've got an idea,' said Sween suddenly. 'Maybe Rosie could eat through the wall.'

'Eat through the wall! But it's rock—'

'That's what she eats. She's a rock-nibbler. That's how she got all the rubies in her shell.'

He had picked Rosie up. He stumbled over something finding his way back to the door. There were crates and piles of parchment.

'All she has to do is eat around the lock.'

'But where will we go then? We'll just be in the passageway outside.'

'Well, anything's better than sitting here waiting for—'

'I know!' Norah waved the torch beam away from him and it danced across the walls to the row of windows. 'She can eat round the bars on the windows. We'll go out on to the flat bit outside.'

'And?'

'I've got that carpet.'

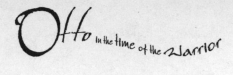

'What?'

'I hid it in my coat when I sat down to play that idiot at chess. We can fly down. We can look in windows. Maybe we can see Otto.'

'It's better than that,' said Sween. 'There's a passageway to the cellars under the forest. At least there is in our time. We can try and get him out.'

'If he's still there,' said Norah, softly.

She unfolded her coat. Otto's mat, with its pattern of butterflies, slipped out on to the floor.

In The unqeon

Otto was hurried down the stone staircase to the cellars. The guard, Clumber, was close behind him, cursing. The ceilings were low, Clumber couldn't stand straight. The passageways were full of gold. Gold paintings on the curved, scooped out walls and alcoves and gold piled up, lumps of it, on the floor.

Otto stumbled into bolts of fabric. He tripped over heaps of chain, piles of canvas. He saw a wooden wheel as wide as he was tall. A ship's wheel.

'Slow down there, Clumber!' shouted someone behind them. 'I've got the rabbit.'

Otto's heart lurched. Surely not a rabbit. Surely this was Blue. She had been here. She had scratched the

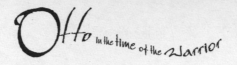

message on the piece of red glass.

Sween tell Otto please get me . . . She had hidden the message in a box here in the castle.

'I thought we were under orders to wring its neck,' shouted Clumber, slowing down only slightly, keen no doubt to stand up straight again.

'Captain's changed his mind,' the voice grew nearer now. Otto could hear something else, the muffled squeals of an animal in pain. 'Wants us to keep it until morning, thinks he might be able to make it talk.'

Clumber snorted. 'I can't abide these half and half creatures,' he said, quickening his pace again. 'Neither one thing or the other. Against nature. Has it ever crossed your mind that it might be catching? I heard there's a woman given birth to a giant frog up in HighNoon.'

More squeals from the hare. Right behind them.

'Well it's free and easy up there,' said the other guard, who was holding Blue by her ears. 'My sister's had two kids with a magico. Not that I shout about it . . .'

They had reached an iron gate.

'They're not frogs, at least, I don't think . . .'

Clumber opened the gate with much rattling and kicking.

'The only thing about them is that the big one tends to float about—'

'Don't talk about it too much,' said Clumber. 'Captain might think you're a spy too.'

The rattling and kicking was repeated. This time Otto and the hare were on the other side of the gate. Clumber lit a candle and put it on the floor of the passageway and shadow bars were flung across the stone floor, black and magnified.

'Don't touch the wine, magico,' said Clumber. 'And don't touch that table. That's something special the Rook's saving for his wedding. He's going to marry a Karmidee wench. Thinks he can make her into a Citizen.' And they both grinned horribly at Otto and stamped off, starting some other conversation, their voices and footsteps dwindling, until it became very quiet in the cellar.

This room, which was really a cave, should have had Max and Sween's billiard table standing in the middle. A wooden door on the far side should have filled the entrance to another tunnel, the one that led out into BlueCat Wood. The table, of course, wasn't there. Instead, there was another one, with carved legs, and feet like the great clawed feet of a lion. The wooden door was missing too. The far wall of the cave was smooth, ancient and untouched. Crates of wine bottles were stacked on the floor.

'Blue, it's me, Otto Hush,' said Otto rapidly. 'Don't be afraid. I'm here. I've came to help you. I got your messages. I travelled in time. I'll protect you.'

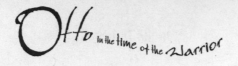

The hare sat in the candlelight, staring at him. Its fur was golden brown. It blinked slowly. Eyes beautiful and mysterious.

'Please don't be scared,' continued Otto. 'I'm so glad I've found you. I'll get us out of here.'

The hare dropped on to all four feet. Otto saw its shadow spring up across the wall as it came towards him. At the last moment, just as he was about to reach out, he drew back, without knowing why.

Now it blurred. It was lost in tiny fragments of colour. Otto had seen dammerung change before. He stood his ground. He was about to see Blue again.

A moment later he jumped back in horror.

It was not Blue.

It was TumbleMan.

TumbleMan grinned, electric with energy.

Otto stepped backwards into the iron gate. His mind wiped clean with shock.

'Honourable greetings, you are not a hare. You say you travel in time. How do you do it?'

'Bicycle,' said Otto. Numb.

'Well, whatever that may mean, your adventure is over,' said TumbleMan. 'Give me the KeepSafe and I will let you go.'

'The what?'

'I give you credit for your bravery. You are stronger than you look. But what happened outside my caravan is over now.' He brought his face close. Tall over Otto.

'I don't know what you're talking about,' said Otto. 'I've never seen your caravan. Where is Blue? Have you hurt her?'

TumbleMan put his head on one side.

'Stop acting,' he said. 'You really are a little nobody, time bicycle or not, and you know nothing. Perhaps you think you are important because you stole the KeepSafe. But I have caught you now. And you will give it back to me.'

He was not holding Otto. He wasn't touching him at all. But Otto felt as locked and powerless as if he were chained to the floor.

'I don't know what any of this is about,' he whispered at last. And he spoke the oath of the mountain. Too sacred to write down.

TumbleMan stared at him for a moment and then, suddenly, seized him by the shoulder and searched the pockets of his coat. Only a little handful of rings and a chip of blue stone. He snarled and pushed Otto away.

'Then why are you here? Why did you come to this castle? Why are you looking for her?' He mimicked Otto's voice. 'Don't be afraid. I'm here. I came to help you. I got your messages . . .' He smiled. 'You came here because you thought she might be here. This castle was ours once, in the

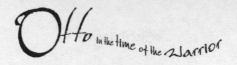

long ago. Often it is empty. A good place for a rest when you are hurtling about in time. Some idiot is living here at present it seems. But that will be undone.'

'How?' demanded Otto. 'How will it be undone? What is a KeepSafe? What are you going to do with it?'

'My Circus is here on the mountain at this moment,' said TumbleMan. 'But when I have the KeepSafe I will take them to a safe time, an early time, before the Outsiders came. Then I will take the KeepSafe to the night before the earthquake and spin the City and the mountains into it and keep it in my pocket until the earthquake is over. Then I will spin everything out again. There will be no crack in the mountain. No Citizens will come. Our City will be safe.'

Otto's imagination stretched and shuddered.

'You use the KeepSafe to travel in time with your Circus.'

TumbleMan nodded. 'We made it. Me, Blue, Rainmaker, all the first children. When we came here and planned the City in the beginning. The cavers helped us, they gave us the blackglass. We built the Towers to warn us in case the earth should ever begin to shake.

'But when the earthquake came and they gave their warning the KeepSafe was far away. I had stolen it to travel with my Circus and it was with me, far away in time, and there was no way to protect the City when the earthquake came.

'I've been travelling with my Circus for a long time now. Too long. But when I get the KeepSafe back now I am going to make everything right. She's trying to stop me. Ever since I said that was what I was going to do, she's been trying to find me. Chasing me.'

'I don't have it,' said Otto, managing to match TumbleMan's steady voice with a calm he didn't feel. 'I don't have it. I don't know where it is. I've only met Blue once and she didn't give me anything.'

He didn't add that he had seen the sphere. That TumbleMan himself had already almost spun him into it and taken him away with his Circus, on a visit to three hundred years in the future, when Otto's face had been painted to look like a lion.

He didn't say that TumbleMan had stolen Mab. If the Circus was on the Mountain now, was she there too? Mab. Who didn't want to come home.

And now there was a faint sound of footsteps and voices.

TumbleMan seized his arm. He pulled Otto into the familiar fresh, cool air that surrounded him. He stared down into his face, just as he had done when he had balanced the sphere on the tip of his finger and the caravans and the tent had swerved and blurred around them.

'Time travel can be complicated, little nobody,' he said. 'Maybe you are telling your own truth. I have been coming

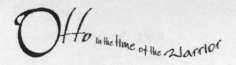

and going. My past could be your future. I think the moment when you have the KeepSafe is yet to come. But you are not a real time traveller. I have many, many friends. This bicycle device of yours will not be hard to find. I will destroy it. And you will stay here in the Year of the Red Moon, in the Time of the Warrior. And then I will get the KeepSafe from you because I know everything about this City and there will be nowhere for you to hide. And when I have taken it back to the night of the earthquake, and saved our City from the Outsiders, everything will be rewritten. There will be a wonderful clean, new page. Everyone you know, little nobody. Everyone you love. Gone. You will never have existed.'

Voices. Definitely. Growing louder.

TumbleMan, however, lowered his voice to a whisper. 'I think I will set you free to complete your destiny.'

He grinned and stamped his foot. The iron gate rattled in its hinges. The floor shook. The crates of bottles leapt and shattered, gushing wine. The far wall of the cellar cracked with a crash that threw Otto on to the floor, his hands over his ears. A fissure opened in the rock. Meanwhile TumbleMan sprang upwards and disappeared into nothing, sending a great wave of dazzling blue light.

The voices had grown louder still. Perhaps someone had come to check on the prisoners. But a grown man couldn't follow Otto. He struggled and squeezed into the slice of space. TumbleMan had splintered a way through the side of the mountain. An eye of moonlight winked at Otto somewhere ahead. Soon he was able to walk easily. The sweet clear smell of the forest was the breath of life itself.

Return to The River

Otto stood still among the trees. He breathed in lungfuls of warm, night air. The valley below, usually chaotic with lights, lay in velvet darkness. Further to the North, towards BrokenHeart, he could see the shape of the City in this Year of the Red Moon. The Boulevard, the Old Town, HighNoon, SteepSide silver and grey and black in the moonlight.

He leant against the nearest tree trunk, dragging his thoughts together. Delilah the Worrier was about to be ambushed down there by the river. Later tonight. Soon. Very soon. He must warn her. But how?

The path would not be safe. The Rook and his men would go that way.

'Otto?'

Otto became as still as a stoat. His heart thudded. His eyes grew huge.

'Otto, is that you?'

'Turnix?'

'Otto?'

'Turnix!' He was so relieved he was fighting not to cry. 'Turnix, whatever—'

'I have been waiting to see you come out of the castle with your friend. The one you went to rescue. But you didn't come out. And now you have come out of a hole in the mountain. But your friend hasn't come out—'

'She wasn't there, she wasn't there,' said Otto hurriedly. 'And these two other friends, the ones I was looking for, the ones I told you about, the ones I travelled with, are still in there. It's really complicated. But the first thing I have to do is go immediately at once to the river. Further down from where I met you. There is someone there I have to warn.'

Turnix was sitting on a fallen tree, his face like metal in the moonlight. He put his head on one side, spoke slowly and carefully. 'You have not found the first friend. You are leaving two friends trapped in the castle. You want to go into the forest again, all the way back, and more, to help another friend—'

'Yes, yes,' cried Otto. 'All the way back. Can we go in

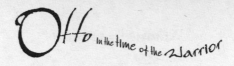

your tunnel? It's much quicker. That way we can get there before them.'

'Before the friend?'

'The Citizens. The ones from the castle. They're going, they're going to, hurt her, they think she is a Warrior. A Karmidee King. And even when they find out that she isn't a warrior I'm sure they'll still want to stop her. To get rid of her—'

'You mean kill her?'

'Yes. Please, Turnix, it's very important.'

'I will help, of course, because you saved my life,' said Turnix. 'And because you seem to be a good human type deeply wading in confusion.'

Turnix led the way, he seemed to see very well in the dark, and Otto crashed and scrambled behind him. He would never have found the entrance to the tunnel on his own. Nor would he have been able to lift the stone that concealed it. However, now it was only a few minutes before he was following Turnix through the dim reddish light with the entrance safely closed again behind them.

'I was going to come after you anyway,' said Turnix, over his shoulder. 'I also have news for you. I have heard that there is a stranger bear in the forest. A small chameleon bear with difficulty in colours—'

'Herzull! Where?'

'It seems this bear friend of yours arrived unexpectedly in the forest last night and is being cared for by chameleon bears like himself. Except they change at the right time.'

'Herself, herself—'

'My plan was to try and meet you when you came out of the castle with your friend you went to rescue but didn't, and take you to meet these bears. It is all arranged to meet them.'

'Why didn't you say?' gasped Otto, now having to jog briskly to keep up. He tripped over a tree root and fell heavily.

'I *have* said,' said Turnix. 'I am saying now.'

'What are you doing?' yelled Otto.

'I am picking you up. It is easy for me to carry a small human type. If you are to continue trying to rescue everybody you must not be late.'

And so they sped down the long passageway in the mountain. Otto hunched over on Turnix's back, his arms around the caver's scaled and sinewed neck, bouncing and lurching.

Turnix was right, of course. They travelled much more quickly this way. They passed the entrance where they had come into the tunnel that morning. Turnix had explained that there was another way out, further South again, which would be much nearer to the place by the river where

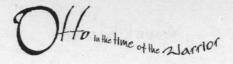

Delilah had made her camp. Turnix knew the place, he had seen the girl and the crooked tent. For someone who was supposed to live inside the mountain he seemed to have been spending a lot of time out of doors.

'The hunters came from the castle, they work for the Rook, the other one came back while I was there, they thought I had stolen the knife,' said Otto. 'It was terrible. I was accused of, you know, of . . .'

He trailed off. Dreadful pictures were pounding through his head. The dead hunter's hands, grey and wet in the bracken. Sween's face as he was bundled out of the door . . .

When Turnix spoke his voice was calm and quiet and frightening. 'If I see that hunter again,' he said, 'it will be terrible for *him*.'

Over two hours had passed since they set out. Turnix slowed and halted, his breath rasping. Otto, speechless with relief, slid from his back and stood shakily on the floor. A short length of tunnel led off directly to the right and ended in a wall of stone. They had reached the place where they were to go outside into the forest.

'Thank you,' began Otto. 'I wish you safe travelling, may the trees—'

'I am coming with you,' interrupted Turnix, pushing his shoulder against the stone.

'No. You don't need to, really,' Otto floundered for the

right sort of words. 'You have repaid your debt already.'

The stone shifted. Pale light and cool air flooded the tunnel. Turnix put his finger to his lips. He crept outside and Otto followed.

THE Hares ON THE Wall

Meanwhile Rosie the pink-footed, rock-nibbling armadillo, was growing weary of nibbling rock. No doubt she was much less hungry than she had been at the beginning. She had eaten round one end of the bar across the bottom of the northernmost window and now she was curled up in the space she had made in the stone around the other end. The bar was loose. There was not much more to do. However, for the moment she was resting. Her velvety rose-coloured stomach was as round as an orange and her paws were crossed daintily upon it.

Sween Softly was asleep on the floor at the foot of the wall immediately below her. Only Norah was awake. Very much so. She had been climbing about amongst the great hoard of treasure, picking things up, looking in chests and boxes and sacks. She had found something which interested her greatly. It was in a wooden crate.

Now she began to search the walls themselves. She started by the door and felt her way from stone to stone.

She found a carving of three hares on the wall opposite the windows, running in their circle inside the moon. Norah had seen this before, of course, when she had visited the castle with her mother. It was the only part of the carving which had survived into her own time. Now there were nine other carved blocks in this wall, dotted here and there around the hares, some close by, some far away. They were immediately recognizable as the distinctive shapes of the mountains which ring the City.

Norah began to press the mountain blocks one by one, starting with BrokenHeart, the mountain of the North, then BlueRemembered, almost at the ceiling, then SmokeStack, then Midsummer Night . . . as if she were reading their names from a map and going clockwise around the City. She stopped when she had pressed them all once. That was the end of the advice she had left for herself in the back of the guide book, after that her handwriting had been washed away.

She was not disconcerted. She worked for a long time, systematically experimenting with combinations and possibilities.

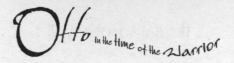

Then, suddenly, there was a dull sound of stone grating on stone, a creaking, and a small door swung open, a stone door that until that moment had been impossible to see.

Norah gave a squeak of excitement that would have shocked her fans. She made her way back to the crate. Perhaps it contained glass or china: certainly she pushed it very, very carefully. Then, when it was safely inside the door, she closed the secret cupboard again, muttering to herself as she pressed the stones. She took all the hidden gold out of her coat and piled it where the crate had stood.

'I have taken something from your stolen hoard, Jack Sargasso,' she whispered. 'And this gold is recompense. But you have given me something else which is beyond price. Information.'

She closed the secret cupboard again, muttering to herself as she pressed the stones.

She had already found a pile of parchment sheets, like newspapers, but more crudely printed and without pictures. She shuffled through them in the light of the worm torch, biting her lip, listening to Sween's breathing, and the sound of tiny, muffled snoring from the hole beside the window.

There it was, *BlueCat Wood, Essential Information for the Inexperienced Adventurer*. The familiar pages were new and fresh and sewn together with waxed thread. She took her pen out of her pocket and wrote herself a message in her own personal code.

First of all she identified the position of each of the nine carved mountain blocks. BlueRemembered, for example, was three blocks above the hares and two to the right.

Then she recorded the sequence of blocks which were required to be pressed to open the cupboard. Some of her message would be washed away, but she knew now that enough would be left for her to open it.

'That's it,' she whispered. 'I've just done what I needed to do to be able to do what I've just done.' And despite the fact that they were all still in mortal danger, she managed a smile.

Then she rolled up her sleeve and drew a diagram on her arm. It showed the exact positions of all the carved blocks on the wall, so that she could open the cupboard in a time when all but the running hares in the moon had disappeared.

Sween stirred and then suddenly opened his eyes wide. He was not safely in his bed in his tower. He scrabbled to his feet.

'I think we'd better wake your armadillo up now,' whispered Norah. 'She only has a bit more to do. Then we must get out of the window and go and rescue Otto.'

At The  Campsite

Otto and Turnix pushed their way through damp bracken as tall as a man. Turnix could see over it. Otto only knew that the ground sloped steeply downwards and they were getting closer to the river.

The forest was full of birdsong. The bracken came to an end and they emerged on moss among massive, ancient trees. Then, suddenly, they were beside the river, lazy and pale and gold in the dawn.

Turnix stopped and pointed, and there was the shingle beach and the tent and the washing line, and Delilah and her dog sitting by the camp fire.

She was worrying already. Otto could see a grey fish swimming round in the air over her head. She swatted at it half-heartedly as they walked towards her. Then, seeing them, she stood up.

'Otto the Strangest,' she said, swatting at another, larger fish. 'What brings you back here. And who is your friend?'

Her dog, on seeing Turnix, had made himself flat on the pebbles.

Turnix bowed.

'Delilah the Warrior, I mean Worrier,' gabbled Otto, 'you are in danger.' He stopped, took a breath. Started again, more slowly. 'We have come to warn you that the Rook is on his way here now. He has maybe two trusted men with him. He plans to kill you.'

'Is this the one?' asked Turnix.

Otto and Delilah looked up the slope towards the edge of the watching trees.

There was the Rook, a purple scarf tied around his head, climbing down towards them. A sword in his hand like a slice of light. And, as he had told Norah so sweetly across the chess board, he had brought only two men with him. One of them was Clumber, slipping on the wet grass, coming from up river. The other was the hunter, who stood some way off, down river, with a crossbow in his hands. They had surrounded Delilah the way wolves surround their prey before they strike.

The Rook held up his hand and the archer became very

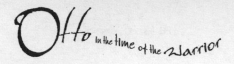

still. The forest, and the river and the sky seemed to hold their breath.

'What is our plan?' hissed Turnix.

Otto couldn't speak.

The Rook was staring straight at him.

'It is our friend from last night,' he said. 'Now, I would really like to learn from him how he comes to be here so quickly, after his magical and demonish escape from the hold.'

'Sorcery, Captain, and no mistaking it,' said Clumber.

'That is the same hunter. He has his arrow pointing personally at you,' whispered Turnix.

This fact had not escaped Otto's notice.

'Don't move, magico,' called the Rook to Otto. 'He has only to loose his crossbow and you will be dead before you hit the ground.'

The bowman, of course, was accustomed to murder. He shifted very slightly where he stood, smiling.

The Rook stepped up to Delilah. 'You, girl, where is the Warrior? Is he your father? Where is he?'

'Do we *have* a plan?' whispered Turnix.

'What do you want with the Warrior?' asked Delilah, very proud.

Clumber laughed.

'I'd just like a little talk with him,' said the Rook.

'A confidential talk, man to man, King to King, as you might say . . .' his bantering voice trailed off. He still held his sword, the deadly point close to Delilah's thin face, but he was looking at the ground. There were shadows and shapes flickering on the shingle around her feet. They looked a little like rats.

'Just magico trickery,' said Clumber.

'I know that,' said the Rook. 'It puts me in mind of a plague of jellyfish.'

The shapes swarmed and spread. Then rose and began to fade.

Turnix, perhaps not surprised at the absence of a plan, had crept sideways and picked up a sizeable rock.

'Everybody keep still!' commanded the Rook, roused from some private memory.

But something in among the trees did not keep still.

There was a rustling, a pounding of excited paws and a very small bear hurtled across the shingle, scattering stones, and threw itself at Otto's legs.

This bear then changed colour from a bright orange, possibly inspired by the dawn, to the russet-red of Hepzibah and Zeborah's hair.

Otto reached down without bending and touched the top of her head.

'Tell us where we can find the Warrior,' said the Rook.

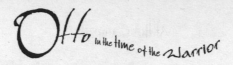

'The one held so dear by the Karmidee. Their *advisor*.'

Clumber and the hunter sniggered.

'I am the Queen of the Karmidee,' said Delilah. 'If you wish to speak, speak to me.' And she stood there, unarmed, ill-fed, ragged. As proud and brave as any warrior there has ever been.

'She is a she-wolf,' whispered Turnix.

Otto saw the triumph flicker across the Rook's face as he glanced at the hunter and at Clumber. All of them were grinning greedily now.

At that moment Herzull, cowering at Otto's feet, gave a tiny, clear cry. And cried again. As if she was calling for help.

'*You* are the Warrior?' said the Rook. Savouring the moment.

Delilah stared up at him. Then she answered him very clearly. 'Yes,' said Delilah. 'I am the Warrior.'

The sunlight reached his sword. It lit like a flame.

'We'll charge,' whispered Otto desperately. 'Yes? We'll try to get her to the tunnel, yes?'

Turnix didn't look at him. He spoke, barely moving his lips. 'Agreed. We may give her time to escape. We die with honour.'

Otto didn't allow himself any more thoughts.

He seized a rock from the shingle and ran forwards with a yell, his coat flying open, his pyjama legs flapping against his ankles. He held the rock with both hands as high as he could, which wasn't as high as he wanted.

He didn't expect to have time to throw it.

Then suddenly he realized that he couldn't see the hunter or Clumber. The Rook and Delilah were still there.

Then they weren't.

There was a lot of shouting. There was a strange uneven, moving wall of forest and shingle around him. He stumbled forward and collided with this wall. It was warm and hard.

Extraordinary, inexplicable sounds mingled with shouts from the Rook and his men. Herzull started yelping. Turnix, somewhere, threw his rock with a mighty war cry. It sailed over the turmoil, crashed into the ground next to the Rook, who leapt to one side with a scream.

The air rippled. Everything was changing.

Huge, towering bears revealed themselves everywhere. They had paws that could knock a man to the ground. Jaws that could snatch off his head. No longer covered with the illusions that would hide them, they were brown, black, dark boiling red.

They crowded across the shingle, too many to count. Some nuzzled Herzull. One licked her face. The others advanced on the Rook and the hunter and the grovelling Clumber, already fallen and struggling on the ground.

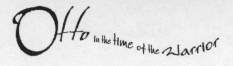

'Demons!' shouted the hunter. 'Apparitions, Captain! Ghosts!'

No doubt he had much to fear from ghosts. He threw down his crossbow and ran for the trees and Clumber stumbled after him.

The Rook was left, transfixed. Wild-eyed.

Otto pushed his way forwards, the bears flickering in and out of sight all around him. They smelt like deepest unknown forest. Their breath was hot. A false step and one might crush him by mistake. He heard Delilah scream, very near and then, suddenly, he saw her.

The Rook had grabbed her in the chaos. His sword was across her throat. He held her in front of him.

Trees, half-formed, swayed all around them. A great smitten, rotting stump, looming next to Otto, shimmered and became a bear, fur the colour of coal, standing on its hind legs.

'Put down the Queen of the Karmidee,' shouted Otto.

'I have sailed the great seething, breathing world,' gasped the Rook. 'No demons will frighten me!'

The coal-coloured bear gave a snarl of rage. Its gleaming fur began to change. Not the trees this time, or the shingle, or the grass. The bear became the colour of the river. The exact colour of the river behind him. At once, everywhere, the other bears did the same.

At the Campsite

Turnix, armed with a glowing branch from Delilah's fire, arrived at Otto's side as if striding between waves.

The Rook bared his teeth. He staggered like a man on the deck of a heaving ship.

'Let go of her!' yelled Otto. 'We are more powerful than you know! Leave us! We will build our own sanctuary! Here! Don't set foot in it! Keep your men away! Never come back!'

The Rook was trembling. His eyes darted. Walls of water shimmered around him.

Turnix raised the burning branch. Took a terrible step forward.

'Release the human!' he yelled.

But the Rook seemed to have forgotten where he was. He began to gasp for air as if he were drowning. He dropped the sword. He pushed Delilah away from him.

'No!' he screamed, clawing at the waves. 'It can't be!'

Delilah raised her hands and the air around her began to take shape. Great rope-like tentacles flexed and groped and seized the air. A creature with flapping gills, rolling eyes, teeth like spears, crawling and reaching, reaching for the Rook.

He made some sign of protection, of warding away evil, and crashed into the trees. Otto saw a dark shape beyond him. The hunter was up there. Turnix leapt forward and the bears let him through.

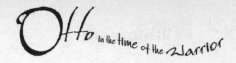

Otto started running, Herzull lurching and bounding beside him.

'Turnix!' he shouted. 'Turnix!'

He rushed on, scrambling over tree trunks and rocks that the caver had taken in a leap. He plunged and staggered and struggled, sinking into soaking, glittering moss and clouds of flies.

He thought he heard a distant, choking scream.

Herzull rolled into a gulley. He hauled her out, gasping for breath, climbed up between shadows on to roots and higher ground.

The forest was silent. Every leaf seemed to be watching him. He snatched up something dropped on the moss. It was a piece of purple material. The Rook's headscarf. Herzull jumped into his arms and he turned round in terror and she screamed.

But it was only Turnix, marching towards them.

'Turnix!' yelped Otto. One of Herzull's paws was over his eye.

'I greet you, brother,' said Turnix. He seemed to be wiping his hands on his waistcoat. 'Do you wish me to remove that bear?'

'No, no! This is the friend I was telling you about.' Otto sat down.

'This is no time for seating and contemplation,' said

Turnix. 'You have other friends for us to rescue. Back at the castle.'

'Oh. Yes,' said Otto, weakly. 'Turnix, what happened to the Rook and the hunter and—'

'Gone,' said Turnix. 'No danger any more.'

'Did you see them?'

Turnix glanced at the purple scarf, hanging from Otto's pocket.

'The Citizen with the sword and his friend ran away. First one. Then the other, shouting about evil spirits.'

'And the hunter?' persisted Otto, feeling cold. 'The one with the crossbow. The one who—'

'The one who jumped on me with nets and chains the night before last and killed his brother and planned to kill me is also no danger,' said Turnix.

'He ran away too?'

But Turnix did not reply. He only narrowed his jewel eyes and looked down at Otto as if from very far away.

On The Shingle

'We can't stay,' explained Turnix, although Otto had sat down, was almost lying down, next to the embers and the ring of stones.

'So that's the bear you were looking for,' said Delilah.

Otto nodded.

'And those others?'

'Not my bears.'

'No. Well, they seem a bit big.'

'Yes.'

Even talking was tiring.

The other bears, magnificent and moody, were reclining in the sunshine. Most were pale blue now, with traces of cloud.

'Would you like some strips of dried fish to take with you?'

'Thank you,' said Otto.

Turnix sat down too and Herzull climbed on to his shoulder.

Delilah's dog sat in front of the little tent, chewing a piece of driftwood.

Delilah picked up a pebble from the shingle, one that was small and oval and and extremely smooth. Then she scratched a letter D on it with the point of her fish hook. Then, next to the D, she scratched an O.

'You take that, Otto the Strange, and remember me one day, in your home, when you are three hundred years away.'

Otto gave her the fragment of lapis lazuli from his pocket. The blue stone that was Rosie's favourite.

They rested a little longer.

'I won't forget you,' said Delilah, when only goodbye was left.

Back Down Through The Tunnel

The walk back through the tunnel was very different from the journey during the night and the more recent and rapid one before dawn. Much to Otto's relief Turnix did not insist on carrying him. They walked rather than ran. And Herzull, who had turned green and gold and glimmering in honour of Turnix, trotted beside them.

This time, however, they did not have the tunnel to themselves. Karmidee were coming towards them, going to Delilah's meeting place, ready for the night of the Red Moon. They carried baskets and bundles and babies. The tunnel was repeatedly flooded with light and colour and dissolving images like the ones Delilah so frequently had around her. Otto guessed that these Karmidee, his ancestors, had more powerful energy than the Karmidee in his own time, or perhaps they were not so skilled in the art of concealing it.

There were unicorns walking down the tunnel, some had blunted horns, as if they had tried to rub them away against rocks or trees.

They tried to eat the strips of dried fish. It made them very thirsty. Fortunately there was a spring in the tunnel, in a cavern to one side. Here they washed their faces and drank.

Now that Delilah was safe, Otto's mind was starting to scream with ideas about what might be going to happen to Sween and Norah, still prisoners in the castle.

And there were other, deeper and even greater terrors. He understood now what Blue had thought he would have in his care, that night on the roof. He understood the purpose of the KeepSafe. He understood that TumbleMan intended to use it to undo the history of the City. To wipe out, in one single moment, millions and millions of lives.

Including his own life.

And the lives of everyone he knew and loved.

The tunnel grew steep again. Turnix, who clearly never admitted to hunger, tiredness or fear, slowed only slightly. Otto felt as if he were going to collapse. Then they were at the entrance, the one in the Forest of the Blue Hare, later to be called BlueCat Wood. They stepped out into sunlight.

'So?' whispered Turnix. 'What is our plan?'

THE Teapot

'What is our plan?'

Otto winced. He had, of course, no plan whatsoever. The gate was out of the question. The way he had escaped would only lead back into the cellars. He craned his neck and peered up at the parapet. If only he had his mat he could fly up there. Maybe land. Look in a window.

'You have a plan?' enquired Turnix. 'You would like me to crack a hole in the wall with my fist?'

'No. No. NO, thanks.'

'I think the Rook is not yet back from our meeting in the forest,' persisted Turnix. 'It is a hole in their armour. Now is the time to strike.' He clenched one substantial scaled hand and smacked it solidly into the palm of the other.

'What's that?' exclaimed Otto. 'Look!'

There was something on the edge of the parapet. Two things. Heads? Yes. One of them had plaits.

They disappeared again.

'I think it's them. I think I saw them . . . up there . . .'

Turnix squared his shoulders, staring upwards. 'The Citizen scum are going to throw them to be smashed on the mountain. But we will catch them.'

Otto, his eyes fixed on the parapet, started to croak some sort of question and at that moment the heads reappeared, Herzull, at his feet, gave a squeal of fright and excitement and Sween and Norah, hunched and strangely bundled, plunged forwards into the air. Otto screamed. Turnix stepped back and held out his arms. Sween and Norah hovered and then started to jiggle about up there as if in time to music.

'They're on a carpet,' cried Otto. 'Look! Norah's at the front. Oh, sweet shade—'

The carpet bucked like an angry horse. It dropped height, rose, rocked sideways, bounced up and down.

'Sween!' yelled Otto. 'Get it down!'

He saw Sween look over the edge of the mat. Then Norah looked too. And then he realized that they had seen him because the mat immediately soared upwards, surely the opposite direction from the one Norah intended, higher

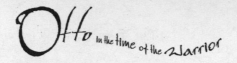

even than the top of the tower. Up and up until it was very small.

Otto gripped Turnix by a massive arm. 'She's a Citizen. She doesn't even *like* the Karmidee. She'll never be able to fly that thing. Flying is Impossible. She's about as Impossible as a teapot.'

'Teapot,' breathed Turnix, gazing up in admiration. 'Your friend flies like a teapot.'

The distant carpet was now jolting and jittering away from them. Sween yelled something that sounded like 'Otto!' and pointed to the South West. The carpet spun round and was rapidly lost from view in the other direction.

'Sween!' screamed Otto, pointlessly. 'Come back! You've got to help me!'

'So,' said Turnix, after a moment. 'Is there anyone else to rescue?'

But Otto wasn't listening. 'How the skink are they going to land?' he whispered.

It took him a moment to realize that Turnix had become very silent beside him. It was not just that he wasn't speaking. His silence had become something cold and frightening.

'It is lucky for you that you saved my life,' said Turnix, his voice adult and slow.

'Why? What's the matter?'

'By using that word you insult me, my family and every caver. You know that?'

'No. No. I don't. I'm sorry. What word?' For a wild moment Otto thought that perhaps it was teapot.

'Don't you know what skink means?' Turnix managed to make the word sound like spitting.

'Well, yes, I mean it's a way of cursing, really, but I didn't mean to—'

'You know that the Citizens make things out of skin. Out of the skin of cavers. Cavers like me, my father and my mother?'

'Well. I, yes, I did see something in the castle. And you told me about it—'

Turnix's eyes had narrowed. 'That word you just used, it means caver. It is the Citizen word for caver.'

They were both hidden from the castle on the steep slope among the trees. Otto was holding on to a tree trunk. He dislodged a stone somehow with his foot and it rolled away, striking off rocks and roots, down and down, lost . . . he suddenly felt as if he were falling too. Then another forest surrounded him. It was night. He heard shouting. There were the lights of torches carried in the air.

Branches snapping.

He was entering a heartsight, his own Karmidee ability, to see into another person's mind and memories,

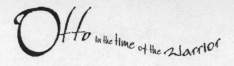

often those scenes they had stored most deeply away.

He heard a cry. The cry of a terrified child. The smoke made him cough, he held up his arm to shield his eyes from the glare of the torches.

But this time was different. As soon as the scene around him had appeared, alive with cries and fear and bitter smoke, as soon as this had formed it began to waver and fade. He blinked. Saw Turnix, staring at him. The other forest and the darkness surged back. Then, finally, it was gone.

'You are ill?' said Turnix, coldly.

'No,' said Otto. He steadied himself against the tree beside him. He had just witnessed something in Turnix's life, he was sure of it. Something terrible. He had experienced very few heartsights, and like this one they had almost all come to him unbidden. However this was the first that had finished almost as soon as it had begun. It was as if the caver's mind had slammed shut.

'I'm sorry I said that word,' he added. 'It's just that in my time it definitely doesn't mean caver. It is a Karmidee way of cursing. Skink means money to us, in our time. Money. You know how the Karmidee despise money. I expect the meaning has changed with time, you know, that could happen, if the Citizens, well, if they make, well, purses out of, er, it—'

'In your *time*,' said Turnix, slowly.

'Yes.' In his nervousness Otto had dislodged another

stone. A rust-coloured deer suddenly sprang out of the shadows and was gone, followed by a smaller, dappled fawn. 'I have travelled in time. I used a time machine. A bicycle. It's in the Amaze. We came three hundred years, from the future. I really am sorry about saying that word, I just didn't know—'

'Tell me,' said Turnix, looking him very definitely in the eye. 'How is it for the cavers in your time? Do they still hunt us with nets and arrows?'

'No,' said Otto. 'I have never heard of anything like that. The cavers live in the mountains, in their tunnels and caverns. Nobody hunts them. Most Citizens don't even know they are there. And the Karmidee respect them and go to them for minerals and medicines and things. We call them ancestors, because they, you, were here first.'

Turnix gave a deep sigh. 'And how long do you plan to be here rescuing?'

'Three days, no, two now, I have to be back at the machine at midnight on the night of the Red Moon.'

'Then you do not have two days. You have to go back tonight.'

'What?'

'It is easy to lose count of the time if you are very much by yourself,' said Turnix. 'This is something I know about very well.'

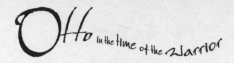

'That must be why my friend was pointing, on the carpet. He must have been telling me to hurry back to the Amaze! But there's somewhere else I have to go first.'

Otto jumped from foot to foot with panic. He looked around for Herzull. She was the colour of Dolores's dressing gown.

'I dare not accompany you through the City in daylight,' said Turnix. 'I would be no use to you. I would be captured. It would need about thirty of them. And not all of them would live. But it would be done.'

He put his hand in the pocket of his waistcoat and pulled out some fragments of gold. 'You may need these, going among the Citizens.'

'But, what about—'

'I have no interest,' said Turnix. 'Ancestors do not use money.'

Otto held them in his palm, where the worms which had tortured him were fading like an old scar. He thought of Turnix when he had first found him and the dread scene by the hunter's camp fire . . . He remembered the hunter who came back with his crossbow when they were trying to save Delilah. He cleared his throat. 'Turnix, where did you get—'

'May the forest shield you, Otto Hush,' said Turnix. 'I bid you solemn good wishes from the heart.'

They both stared at the ground.

Then Otto bowed. He picked up Herzull, nodded, bowed again, stumbled and set off towards where the path should have led down to the houses which were not yet there.

He looked back and saw that Turnix had not moved, although his green and gold scales, and his stillness, made him very hard to see.

THE Apple Seller

Otto Hush, I hope you'll see this.
Come and help me to get out. I'll be in the dome

Blue had not been in the castle. But she might still be in the Town Hall. Under the dome of the Banqueting Hall. Not a window this time. Real. He must find her. There would be some sort of danger. He would save her from something. Then she must give him the KeepSafe. Then, somehow, he must escape with it. Before TumbleMan found and destroyed the time machine.

He crossed scrubland and deserted Karmidee campsites and entered the edge of the City unnoticed. He looked like yet another ragged Karmidee boy.

However, there was one obvious difference, apart from the fact that he was wearing pyjamas under his coat. He was the only Karmidee walking in that direction. All the others were going out of the City, down towards the river path and the forest. Often, as they passed, someone would advise him to join them. The Queen had summoned them, they said. Didn't he know? To a great meeting far down the river, tonight, the night of the Red Moon.

He stopped on the strange, windblown Boulevard, looking for something familiar. He pulled the knotted string with its small cluster of rings out of his pocket and held them in his hand.

'Lost someone have you, dear?' said a voice close by. A Karmidee woman, heading in the other direction, of course, pushing a barrow full of large red apples. Herzull began cooing and chuntering beside him.

'Always sad to see empty rings,' the woman said. 'Dead is she?'

'No!' exclaimed Otto. 'No. At least,' he hesitated with the horror of the thought, 'at least, I don't think so.'

'Didn't expect to see you again, I reckon,' added the woman. 'Terrible sad it is to part from those we love. Sister, was she, dear? Does your bear want to pay for that apple?'

Herzull had elected to help herself. She held a very large, very round apple neatly between her front paws.

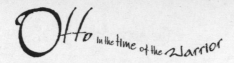

Otto in the time of the Warrior

Otto handed the woman one of the gold fragments given him by Turnix and she bit it and put it in her pocket. Hungry-faced.

'I'm looking for a big building,' he said. 'With big doors and all sorts of things on the roof. And stained glass windows . . .' This wasn't much help. There was stained glass, and mosaics and wall paintings wherever he looked.

'You mean the Artists' Guild,' said the woman.

'I do?'

'That's got all manner of magical devices and such on the roof, not that *they* know or care. The Rook's making it into something called a Town Hall. He's going to be a Chief or King or something, some word I hadn't heard and had no wish to learn—'

'Mayor?' asked Otto.

'That's it. The place is crawling with Normos now. You know what they're like about our pictures and things. Covered a lot of it up. Although they do say that the Rook has a fondness for windows. What are you going there for? You know the Queen has called us all to the river. Some say we're going to give up on the City. Try to build ourselves a new town all our own down there.'

'There's someone in the Town Hall I need to see, I think,' said Otto. 'I think she's in trouble.'

The woman's face snatched itself into a frown. She looked

up and down the Boulevard, pulled the canvas over the top of the apple barrow and made ready to move.

'I'd stay away from there if I were you, brother,' she said quietly. 'We don't know who she is but we know that girl is a prisoner because the Rook intends to marry her when she's old enough. Cared for, but trapped. And it would take more than you to get her out. Even if you've the blood of heroes in your veins. Guarded night and day, so they say.'

He stood speechless. He had found Blue at last.

'Is that little bear teething? Only I don't appreciate her chewing the wheel of my cart.'

'I'm sorry,' said Otto. He picked up Herzull and she yawned obligingly. A ferocious new tooth twinkled briefly among the innocent cub-sized ones.

'Don't you worry about your friend in the Artists' Guild,' said the woman, still whispering. 'Don't worry about any of it. TumbleMan's been here. He says all the Normos are going to disappear. The mountain's going to close again. TumbleMan's going to make everything right.'

Otto managed to speak. 'Using the KeepSafe.'

'Oh, I don't know how he's going to do it,' said the woman. 'I don't go into things deeply. I leave that to clever people like TumbleMan. The Blue Hare was hopping around, a while back. Trying to find him, spreading lies. But TumbleMan spoke to me himself. Have you ever met him?

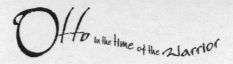

He's got energy round him like a tornado. A real traveller, if you know what I mean. I asked him what would happen to my baby. Her dad's a Normo. Met him up in HighNoon. Gone prospecting up on CrabFace. Coming back for us when he's rich. Anyway, do you know what TumbleMan said? He said it specially to me. He said. No harm will come to your man or your baby, my darling, he said. No harm at all.'

She looked at Otto, triumphant, smiling, waiting, it seemed, for a reply.

'I think your man will disappear, and your baby will disappear. You will be back as if the earthquake had never happened and you won't even remember any of this,' he said. Shocked by his own words.

Her eyes widened. The warmth drained from her face. Then, suddenly, she was all hate.

'TumbleMan cares about us! He'll do what's right for us!'

'I don't know what *is* right,' Otto discovered that he was yelling back at her. 'I only know that TumbleMan cares about nobody but himself.'

THE  Artists' Guild

The Artists' Guild, soon to become the Town Hall, was massive and formidable and familiar. The great wooden doors were standing open and workmen and women came in and out with wheelbarrows of rubble and bricks. Otto walked in, the front of his coat bulging with bear. The floor of the foyer was extraordinary. It seemed to be absolutely transparent, as if he was standing on the cleanest, clearest glass imaginable. Under his feet he saw the shapes of drifting clouds. He was walking on the sky.

Carvings on the walls shifted and changed. Washes of colour poured off the walls and seemed to swirl around his feet as if he were wading in the river. He kept walking, staring straight ahead, and, as he came along the side of

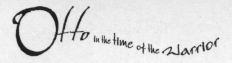

the cloisters where he and Sween would one day follow the fast moving porter, he was engulfed with the smell of lavender. The walled garden was planted full of it. A carpet of flowers.

He reached the door to the lift. The Karmidee had invented such a thing, then. And there was a guard, wearing the uniform of the Rook's men, sitting on a stool with a half eaten tray of food on the floor beside him.

'I've brought a gift from the Rook, for his bride to be,' said Otto Hush. This was it then.

He opened his coat and put Herzull carefully on the floor. She was still the colour of the red apple which she had so recently enjoyed. She might easily be taken for some sort of ordinary, though rather red, bear. Otto held his breath. His heart was beating so loudly that he wondered if the guard could hear it.

Then, wondrously and beautifully, Herzull noticed the ceiling. She became a deep blue, spangled with gilded stars.

The guard's mouth dropped open.

'Do you think she'll like it?' enquired Otto, pleasantly.

'Maybe,' said the guard. 'But I wouldn't count on it. She certainly didn't like her dinner, but that's nothing new.' He gazed some more at Herzull, who gazed back at him and began to assemble white eyebrows and a white handlebar moustache.

'You take her up, if you would be so kind. Only that demon box makes me powerful sick.'

'Of course,' said Otto, scooping Herzull up. Pushing buttons. Trees bless the Karmidee for inventing a lift, or something like a lift, so long ago.

'She's not to come down,' added the guard. 'Seems cruel to me, she's only a kid. But she's safe up there, he says. You know what he's like when he wants something.'

'I do,' said Otto, closing the door of the demon box behind him.

ON THE Gallery

The lift was not called the demon box for nothing. Otto and Herzull huddled on the floor in the corner. It went even faster than it had done last time he rode in it, when he and Sween had seen Blue's window. The single blow on her face. She had looked so beautiful, so real. As if she could step right out of the glass.

And now he was going to see her. And she would be real at last. As real and powerful and magical as she had been on the roof of his own Herschell Buildings.

The demon box thundered to a halt. He stood up and opened the door and stepped on to the narrow gallery into light and space. Herzull leant against his ankle.

The gallery curved away from them, decorated with the

colours of the stained glass windows. They were clean and bright. There was the Rainmaker, and the Ice King and Midsummer. Already Otto could see someone, a girl, surely, wearing a long dress, crouching in front of the window where Blue stood, undamaged, glittering with jet and obsidian.

He kept walking, his footsteps creaking softly. Beyond the gilded handrail the great cavern of the Banqueting Hall echoed with the rumble and clatter of barrows and workers below.

What must it be like for her to be a prisoner up here? Alone, and yet not alone. Out of reach. And why, since she could travel through time, did she just not leap away from this moment and leave her captor wondering where she could have gone?

Never mind that now, though. This must be the place. TumbleMan might appear at any moment. He couldn't see the danger, but he must be walking towards it.

The girl stood up slowly. She had been chipping at a block of jet with a chisel. There were jars on the boards around her feet. A brush dipped in silver.

The image of Blue towered behind her.

But she was not Blue.

'Otto!'

Otto couldn't move. He couldn't speak.

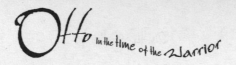

She ran to him. She flung her arms around his neck. 'Otto, I knew you'd come! Thank you! Thank you! Thank you!'

It was Mab. Taller, even thinner than he remembered. Decked out in gold jewellery, at her wrists, her throat. On her fingers.

'You got my messages,' she said, letting go of him. Tears in her eyes. Smiling.

After another long moment he found some words. '*Your* messages?'

'Yes. One in that place in the wall in the Library. In the back of that book. I was working at the Library, restoring windows. That's what I do. They were mending the wall. But I knew it would break open again because you told me it would, when the Library was struck by lightning. They'd said I was going to be sent here next. One of the builders was coming. I couldn't finish it properly.

'But that wasn't the first message. The first one was when I was working at the Rook's castle. I found that box among all his stolen stuff. I hid a message in it and buried it. I didn't dare sign it, Otto. Just in case. But I knew Sween would find the box. I just hoped he was going to get it open. How is Sween? How is everyone?' She was still smiling. He didn't remember her ever smiling so much.

'You were at the castle?'

'Yes. I went there to make a window. I was in something called a Foundling Shop, Otto, terrible. Then the Rook came in, looking for servants, you know, and he asked if anyone could draw or paint so I said yes and I ended up at the castle. But it's even worse than that because he wants to marry me, Otto, when I'm old enough. He's keeping me prisoner. I'm guarded wherever I go.' She looked around her. Then back at him. 'But now you've come, it'll be all right. I know it will.'

Otto spoke again. He chose his words most unwisely. He said, 'So where's Blue?'

Mab's smile faltered. 'What do you mean?'

'I thought she was here,' he mumbled.

'You mean the girl you met on the roof?'

He looked dumbly at the window and at Blue's serene, purposeful face. 'I met her on the roof and she said that I was going to save her life,' he said. 'Then I started getting messages.'

'But they were from me,' said Mab, her smile gone, very far away. 'The Circus travels in time. Did you know that? When we got here, last winter, TumbleMan had told us that we would never go back to that time again. I mean our time. He's never taking the Circus there again. I wanted to get back home. I think he *let* me run away. He only let me *join* to hurt Genevieve. He hated her for wanting to leave . . .' she stopped. Now she was looking scared. 'I want to go home,

379

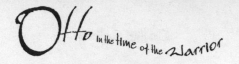

Otto In the time of the Warrior

Otto. It turns out Genevieve had adopted these other two children. They're still there, with the Circus. I told them you would come and we would go back for them, and somehow we'd all go home together.'

'You mean Morwenna and Cal?'

'Yes, yes. How did you know their names? Did Genevieve tell you about them?'

He shook his head.

'This is what happened. Genevieve was a really successful artist in the Time Before the Gates. Thet's not long ago. She was actually Head of the Artists' Guild, Otto. Her name is on the wall downstairs. Then, not long after everything happened and the Citizens came, she rescued Morwenna and Cal from a horrific Citizen family. You can't even say they were servants. They were slaves. The Citizen family were very powerful and they were looking for her, and the children, everywhere.

'The Circus was visiting. Somehow TumbleMan heard about her and invited her to join them because she can make things fly. It was her only way of escaping and saving Morwenna and Cal. So she joined.

'Then, after a lot of travelling the Circus came to our time. They call it the Time of Albert the Quiet. The Circus came to our time and she found *me*. I was a little baby. I'd been *left*. She found me under a tree somewhere near

TigerHouse. Anyway TumbleMan let her look after me for twelve years. Then he came back for her.'

'But what about Morwenna and Cal? Who looked after them while she was looking after you?'

He waited for her to roll her eyes. She didn't.

'Don't you see? TumbleMan brought the Circus back to a day twelve years later. But he's a hare. He can jump from one time to another with the Circus in the KeepSafe. As far as he was concerned, he came back for Genevieve the next day. Don't you remember, when we saw them talking in the tent and he was being so terrible to her? Saying how old she looked? He's just a boy himself, he comes from the very beginning of the City. The Circus is like a toy for him.'

Otto stared into the hollows and shadows of her face. This was almost too difficult. But perhaps he was cleverer than he thought. 'If Genevieve found you in our time, I mean the time when we were little, why didn't she just take you back with her to the Circus and look after all three of you together. And keep travelling?'

'She wouldn't tell me. She just kept saying I must stay in my own time and there was a reason. I had to grow up there. And be there. Maybe she was going to tell me, but I didn't really give her a chance.'

'I thought you were Blue,' said Otto. 'She and TumbleMan are fighting over something. Something to do with the City

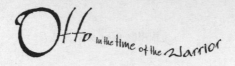

and the earthquake. I was supposed to help her. I thought you were her.'

'Well, I'm not,' said Mab. And, suddenly and dangerously, her expression changed. 'I'm just Mab and I've been missing you, and everybody else, from the moment I left.'

'But that window is just like her,' said Otto. 'How did you know what she looks like?'

'I didn't make these stupid windows,' said Mab, almost shouting. 'They're really, really old. I'm just repairing them. I don't know what your stupid friend looks like. I've never seen her.'

'She's not stupid,' yelled Otto. 'TumbleMan wants to take the KeepSafe back in time. He wants to put it back where he stole it from so that when the earthquake comes they can spin the City and the mountains and everything into it until the earthquake is over. And then BrokenHeart won't get broken. And the Normals won't come. Which might sound good, *except that everything will be different and nobody that you want to go home to, will be there.*'

Mab said nothing. He thought perhaps she understood. He continued more calmly.

'I'm going to save her life. She's going to give me the KeepSafe. I've got to take it with me. But now there's hardly any time. I thought she was here. The time machine goes back tonight. And now I've no idea where she is.'

He stopped because Mab was walking back to the window, the one with the portrait of Blue. She picked up the chisel she had been using to chip away the shards of jet.

They stared at each other for an electric moment. He was suddenly terrified.

'I've been waiting, and hoping, and waiting,' said Mab, finally, almost slowly, 'for almost a whole year. And now you've come. And it's not me you've come for.'

She swung the chisel, it was only quite small, she swung it with her arm straight, and as she did so she jumped high and she smashed the tip of it into Blue's forehead and the sound was like ice breaking.

'NO!' screamed Otto. 'YOU RAN AWAY!'

Mab let the chisel drop. It skidded a little way across the polished boards.

There was a silence. Then the sound of Herzull's paws as she ran back towards the lift, and the same sound, echoing back, tiny, almost lost.

'I didn't want to run away,' said Mab. 'I just couldn't stay.'

Otto stood like stone. He stared at Blue's shattered face. Tears of exhaustion and loneliness and fear welled up in his eyes.

'GO!' screamed Mab. 'GET OUT!'

He stepped backwards. Almost slipped.

'Go on! Go home! Now! I hate you!'

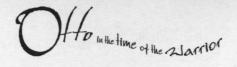

She started throwing things at him. Fragments of obsidian and jet, hard, sharp, spinning up and chipping the glass of the Rainmaker's cloak, splinters showering the floor.

'Go home to your family and your friends with your cuddly little bear! And take your stupid stories with you!'

He stayed where he was. Held his hands in front of him.

'Mab, please, Mab . . . It's all of us. Everything. We're all in danger. Don't you see . . .'

'I hate you!' she screamed.

There was a thud behind him. He half turned, ducking his head as she threw something else, and saw the door of the demon box standing open and the guard peering queasily along the gallery.

'Go and find her,' hissed Mab.

'What's going on here?' asked the guard, managing to walk, taller than Otto had expected now that he was standing and carrying a long staff with the carved shape of a rook on the top.

'Don't you like the gift, my dear?' he called to Mab.

She said nothing. Tears were pouring down her face.

'Better be on your way, young man,' said the guard. 'Not everybody likes bears.'

'But—'

'The Rook doesn't like her upset.'

He took hold of Otto by the elbow and steered him mightily back to the lift.

Otto twisted his head round for a last look and saw Mab watching him, her face white and set, her eyes like caves.

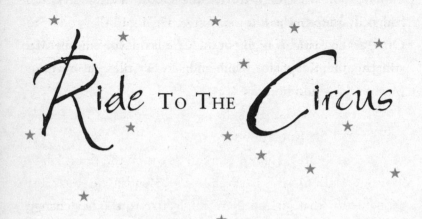

Ride to the Circus

'Don't blame yourself,' said the guard unexpectedly, sitting down with a thud in his chair. 'She's often crying. Poor kid.'

Otto couldn't speak. He held on to Herzull tightly. He pushed his face into her fur.

'I'm off in a minute anyway,' added the guard. 'Second watch takes over in five minutes. I'm off to the Circus with my grandchildren. It won't be here long, so they say.'

'The Circus?' said Otto, muffled.

'Up on TumbleMan Mountain. I don't know if they let magicos in though, if that's what you're wondering.'

It was not what Otto was wondering. A simple idea had come to him. Simple and beautiful. TumbleMan would have to be at his Circus for the performance tonight. And

TumbleMan, who jumped backwards and forwards in time, had said, *Maybe my past is your future.* He'd said that today, to Otto, at the castle. Tonight, at the Circus, maybe TumbleMan still had the KeepSafe. Maybe Blue was still chasing him. Maybe she would be there . . .

'That's a pretty amazing bear,' said the guard. 'You taking her back to the Rook now, are you?'

'No,' said Otto. He put Herzull down on the floor. 'She's mine, actually. Or at least, well, we're friends. The Rook just thought that that girl up there might like to see her change colour. To cheer her up.'

Another guard was coming down the passageway towards them. The building was quiet now. His feet echoed on the mosaic.

'Here's my replacement,' said the guard, standing up, stretching.

Herzull, no doubt still very shaken by the events on the gallery, had adopted her most personal and comforting colours on their way down in the demon box. These were the stripes on the towel Dolores wore around her head after she had washed her hair. Otto saw them and felt reckless with misery.

'Perhaps your grandchildren would like to see my bear,' he said.

'I was just thinking that myself,' said the guard.

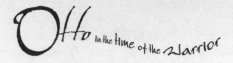

'I've got a friend who might be working at the Circus,' added Otto, quickly, before the new man was upon them. 'If you could see your way to giving me a lift there, maybe they'd have a chance to see her before the show.'

'I'll meet you outside,' said the guard, suddenly whispering and looking away as he spoke. 'Good evening, Citizen,' he added, at normal volume, to the man who was taking over, now unpacking a bundle of bread and sausage.

It took a moment for Otto to realize that the guard didn't want to be seen speaking to him. He picked Herzull up again, just in time to save the sausages, and set off back the way he had come along the passageway to the entrance hall.

Outside the light had softened. He could see BrokenHeart, far and blue in the summer evening haze. 'The colour of time,' he said. Out loud. He was holding Mab's rings . . . So tightly, he might break his own fingers.

The guard appeared out of another, lesser door, and waved and Otto set off towards him, past raw tree stumps and piles of branches. The guard hurried ahead around the side of the building. By the time Otto caught up with him he was already busy with the harness of a piebald pony, hitched to a small open cart.

Despite everything, Otto managed to be mindful of possible dangers. He concluded that, if necessary, he could jump off the cart, even if it was moving. This was small comfort.

'I'm meeting the kiddies at the third Tower,' said the guard, climbing up and taking the reins. Otto climbed in behind him. He couldn't let go of Mab's rings. He had to haul himself up with one hand.

'I'll tell them you work for the Rook,' added the guard. 'They're very well brought up, they don't normally meet magico kids. You let them see your bear.'

The pony began to trot surprisingly fast. The cart jiggled and rocked.

'When we get there, well, just before we get there, you hop off and we'll say no more about it. You haven't got any diseases have you? Their mother is always worrying about them catching things from people like you.'

'I'm fine,' said Otto, his face burning.

Herzull settled on his knee, once more wearing the white eyebrows and moustache elsewhere garlanded with pictures of sausages. She began to gnaw very quietly on the side of the cart.

THE *Red* AND *Yellow* *Caravan*

The tent shimmered on the side of the mountain, gorgeous and mysterious. The sun was setting, already there were lights glowing at many of the caravan windows. Smoke drifted from their chimneys. As he climbed nearer Otto heard music and voices.

He was already higher than the path, now busy with people crowding and queuing and having their faces painted. Below them, in another meadow, he could see carts and carriages and horses tethered. The guard and his three grandchildren would be there by now. The guard satisfied that no one had seen him giving a lift to a magico. The children still disappointed that Otto wouldn't sell his bear.

Herzull scrambled ahead. Perhaps she could smell food.

They had crept through the rocks and the flowers, round the sweep of caravans, so that now they were as far from the entrance as possible.

Otto had no mat, no magical devices. No friend, except a small, teething bear. He had, Turnix would not have been surprised to know, no plan. He had very little time.

And he was walking right into TumbleMan's heart.

He reached the first caravans and crept between them. He had forgotten how tall they were, some three storeys high. Pitched roofs. Chimneys at wild angles. Porches. Bits added on.

And there was TumbleMan. The first person he saw. Walking slowly, spinning the gold club on his fingertip.

For a moment Otto couldn't move or think. TumbleMan saw him. He smiled.

Honourable greetings, brother, the queue is that way.' He pointed with his free hand. The club still spinning.

A thought sparked in Otto's terrified brain. TumbleMan hadn't seen him before. At least he had, but Otto's face had been expertly and magically painted to look like a lion at the time. TumbleMan might have noticed Herzull but Otto was prepared to gamble that he hadn't. The encounter in the castle cellar, from TumbleMan's point of view, was yet to come.

'Honourable greetings, I'm interested in joining the Circus,' he said.

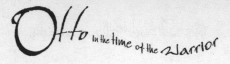

TumblcMan laughed.

'I'm a three sixty,' continued Otto. 'But my ability is heartsight. I don't know if you can really use that in a Circus.'

'Heartsight?'

'Yes.'

'That's an unusual one. We might be able to use you. You could pick someone from the audience. Tell everyone their deepest secrets and make them cry. People love that, as long as it's someone else.'

Otto nodded.

'Think you could do that?'

He nodded again.

'Any family?'

'No, not really.'

'Only this is a travelling Circus.'

'Yes.'

'And we're not coming back here.'

'I know,' said Otto. 'Some in the City, among the Karmidee, I mean, say that you are going to get rid of all the Citizens for us and close the mountain one day. And then this time now will be wiped away.'

TumbleMan flicked the club into the air and caught it on a different fingertip. He began to spin it the other way. 'Not everyone is grateful,' he said softly. 'The Blue Hare has managed to deceive a few with her talk of life and death and futures already blossomed into fruit. There are those with the mark of the Blue Hare drawn on their skin, to show their loyalty to her as she chases me and torments me.' He turned his quick eyes on Otto. 'Do you have that mark, brother? The mark of the running hares?'

'I have no tattoos,' said Otto. His heart jumped in fright.

'Once you join my Circus, you cannot leave,' said TumbleMan. 'The Circus is my family. Too many secrets. Too much confusion. Travelling in time is a delicate matter. Follow me, heartsight. We'll go to my caravan.'

Otto followed. Herzull, purple with alarm, followed Otto.

TumbleMan's caravan was close to the tent, painted in his colours of red and yellow. He opened the door and it was immediately brightly lit inside. Neat shelves, pictures like windows on to different times and seasons. The real windows were shuttered.

He clicked his fingers at the kettle and it began to boil. Fire lizards the size of baby mice dozed in the embers in the grate.

'Show me that you can perform a heartsight,' said TumbleMan.

'What?'

'Look into my heart. We can't allow you to join us unless you are speaking the truth. Someone tried to fool me not

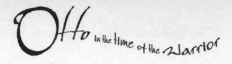

long ago by claiming that he could fly. Not a pretty sight.'

Otto, beginning to sweat, nodded. He hadn't foreseen this. He never foresaw anything.

The energy of the Circus, so strong and alive, was even more powerful here in this caravan. Ancient power. The power of the first children. In comparison his own abilities were frail indeed.

'I'm waiting,' said TumbleMan. 'It shouldn't be difficult. I have many memories. I'm layered like the mountains. I'm a thousand years old.'

'You are angry,' began Otto. This wasn't a heartsight. That wouldn't happen just because someone was demanding it. He closed his eyes. Sat down. Should have done that first. 'Yes, you are angry. You are trying to right a wrong that you believe you have done. Someone is chasing you. They want to stop you. They won't let you rest. They are trying to take something away from you. A sphere. It's made of blackglass . . .'

He paused. The little room had suddenly grown cold.

'That's not a heartsight,' said TumbleMan. And his voice was as soft and cold as snow. 'You are not who you pretend to be, are you . . . brother? . . . And you know things you should not know . . .'

There was a flash of blue light and the sound of screams from outside.

'Don't move,' snarled TumbleMan. He flung the door open.

Blue was standing there.

TumbleMan gave a howl of rage.

'Give me the KeepSafe, TumbleMan,' she said, 'I have hunted you through the centuries. I have crossed canyons and deserts of time. At last I have found you. Give me what you stole.'

He stared at her. Then he nodded, slowly. When he spoke it was almost a whisper. 'I have warned you not to chase me, sister. I have warned you and I have run from you and I will not do either of those things again. Let us settle the matter. For ever.'

He stamped his foot and the steps where Blue was standing split down the middle. She fell, he jumped after her and in the instant of their falling they were lost in a great gust of colour and shadows and turned into two hares.

Herzull dropped whatever she was chewing, gave a huge jump and scrabbled into the caravan.

The hares circled each other.

The Circus people were running from all sides, in their wild and gaudy costumes, shouting and screaming.

Otto stood completely still for a moment and then he began pulling out drawers, emptying jars and boxes and sacks. He ran to the tiny staircase, which hooked round like

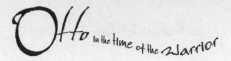

the staircase on a tram. Up here there were books from his own time, from other unknown times, maps and charts and musical instruments. Several costumes hung on the wall. He tore at the bedding, threw pillows and cushions, scattered a jar of glass marbles. They rushed backwards and forwards across the floor, skidding in front of him, bouncing around his feet. Almost tripping him at every step. They were looking for him. He was sure of it.

He stepped backwards and fell over Herzull, who had come upstairs, chewing a wooden doll. There was a terrible quiet outside. He pulled the doll out of her mouth and pushed open the slats on the window.

The two hares were on a circle of grass, surrounded by the crowd. They were still and silent. Staring. Unblinking.

He struggled across the room towards the second staircase, Herzull in his arms, the marbles, faster and faster, circling and darting around him. Then up the narrow stairs, pushing Herzull in front of him, into a tiny room which sat on top of the caravan like a hat.

This room was full of toys. Toys, surely, from every time TumbleMan had ever visited. Toys that moved, that flew, that sang. A puppet theatre. A row of puppets hanging, strings unknotted, costumes fresh, ready to perform.

The marbles had not followed them up the stairs. Otto stopped his frantic search for a moment. Could not help stopping. As the silence outside deepened like a well he looked at these puppets with their delicate hands and their beautiful bright clothes.

Then he noticed a glass dome. The kind that is picked up and shaken and fills with snow. There was TumbleMan himself, his small wooden face lit by a smile. The single gold juggling club balanced on his finger. Next to him was a white wolf. His fur like frost.

Without thinking, or meaning to do so, Otto picked up the dome and turned it upside down. A blizzard swirled inside the glass. For a moment it seemed to him that the white wolf moved its head.

Herzull snuffled around the floor. She picked up a wooden tram and began to chew it. He grabbed it out of her mouth with a curse and scoured the cluttered room. It was full of toys and sadness. But no KeepSafe.

He stood there a moment longer and felt everything begin to stir. Heard the creak of wooden wheels on the carpet. A drum began to play a slow rhythm. A ball rolled towards them.

There was a scream outside. A scream of many people at once.

Otto pounded down the stairs, and the next stairs, Herzull following, crashing into his legs. They ran to the doorway.

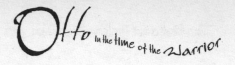

The crowd of Circus people had backed as if from a fire. In the centre TumbleMan had become a boy again. He had his back to Otto and the caravan. He stood tall, his hat gone, his hair and cloak crackling, and a wolf was on the ground in front of him. A white wolf, huge, made of light and ice and sparks and a dust of glittering rock.

The wolf held the Blue Hare under one massive paw. Blue had not changed back into the girl Otto had come so far and so dangerously to save. She was still a hare, struggling, gasping for breath.

In a moment, he was sure, some sign, some command, would bring the wolf's jaws down on her throat. This was a trial of strength. Perhaps it was already over. TumbleMan could split the ground, he could break open the walls of caves. As Otto stared, locked and terrified, Blue twisted her head and looked straight back at him. He heard her voice as if she was calling right into his mind, as if she was screaming, 'HELP ME . . . HELP ME . . .'

Herzull dropped something with a thud on to the wooden floor.

Otto, in anguish, half crying, about to throw himself at the soulless, deadly wolf, looked down and saw TumbleMan's golden juggling club. The one he so loved to spin on his finger. Herzull had fractured the side. Teeth marks gone deep.

'Give up your quest, Blue Hare,' shouted TumbleMan. 'You will never find the KeepSafe. Leave me to do what is right.'

Blue didn't move. She lay on her side. Her eyes burned.

Everything, everybody was waiting for her.

Only Otto moved.

Very slowly.

Going from standing to stooping to crouching, he reached for the golden club, the split ran down the slender neck, half way along the body, like a thick black line drawn on the side of a bottle.

Something gleamed.

Something inside the club.

He closed the fingers of his right hand around the neck. His left hand was the stronger, but throughout everything he had not properly let go of Mab's rings.

Slowly, slowly he stood up again.

Voices were jangling up from the crowd. 'Finish it, TumbleMan!' and, much outnumbered, 'Let her go!' Now the crowd was writhing and boiling like an angry sea, fighting itself.

Otto tightened his grip on the golden club. Behind him he heard a crash as a jar of nails hit the caravan wall. He looked over his shoulder and saw shadows in the curve of the stairs. Unknown, unknowable energy taking form and flesh,

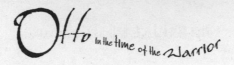

creaking towards him. In front of him the white wolf breathed closer to Blue's neck.

'TumbleMan!' shouted Otto. 'Look at this!'

He smashed the club as hard as he could against the doorframe of the caravan. It broke open and the KeepSafe fell out, full of its own dark, swirling colours.

TumbleMan spun around as the wood splintered. He saw the KeepSafe, spinning by itself next to Otto's foot, leapt at it with a cry. But Otto, nearer and forewarned, was quicker. He snatched it up, jammed it into his pocket and TumbleMan was upon him like a storm.

As Otto fell he saw the white wolf dissolve and explode into particles of light. Blue shimmered and was gone. Then his shoulders hit the floor. TumbleMan's hands closed around his neck. Everything began to pound and blur.

Suddenly TumbleMan gave a savage, angry scream. His strong fingers loosened their grip. Herzull had jumped on to his back. She had sunk her teeth into his shoulder, through his cloak and his costume. He cursed, half turned, fighting to throw her off and Otto glimpsed her small face, her eyes screwed shut with effort, blood on her black nose, clinging on, rigid . . . TumbleMan swung round, she was almost crushed against the wall of the caravan, he swung again, snarling, and Otto rolled free, staggered to the doorway and made a desperate lunge to seize Herzull, had his hands, for a moment, around her, although this way TumbleMan would have him for sure, and was then suddenly yanked into the air by one arm and dangling in merciless space over the crowd.

The whirring wheels of the wicker chair blasted his ears. Cal's grip on his arm was like iron. He felt as if his shoulder was going to rip apart.

'Get in!' yelled Cal.

'No!' he yelled. 'My bear!'

TumbleMan staggered out on to the broken steps. Herzull was still clinging to his back. He raised his hand. A burning rock seared through the air past Otto.

People were screaming and climbing over one another to get away. Cal steered the chair upwards with one hand.

Otto could see Herzull. Small and far below. She was green and gold now, like the fearless Turnix. Her teeth were still sunk into TumbleMan's shoulder. Surely she was doomed.

'Put me back down!' Otto cried. 'I've got to get the bear!'

Cal held the chair still for a moment. Despite all, he was calm. With a great gasp of effort he dragged Otto up and inside. The chair swerved through the air and climbed higher. Morwenna, crammed beside her brother, locked her small arms around Otto's chest.

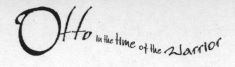
'NO!' cried Otto, in anguish.

'Yes,' shouted Cal. 'Call to your bear. Tell her to let go. Tell her to get on the roof. It's the only chance.'

Another bolt of lightning. The whole mountain seemed to shake. TumbleMan, cursing and staggering.

'Herzull!' shouted Otto. 'Jump! Jump on to the roof!'

They lurched sideways. He shouted into Cal's ear. 'She can't understand!'

'She's heard you!' cried Morwenna. 'Call her again!'

The chair shuddered. A fireball shot past. The air smelt of smoke.

Otto leant forward, almost fell, Morwenna's small hands wrenching at his shirt. He fixed his eyes on Herzull. She had saved his life.

There was a flash of light and Blue was on the roof of the caravan. Not as a hare. As a girl. She reached both her arms into the air. Stood still as stone.

'Herzull!' screamed Otto. 'Let go of him! Jump on to the roof!'

Light began to flare and stream from Blue's hands.

THE Colour OF Time

It was like a mist. It muffled every sound. More than a mist. It was the blue of mountains far away. The blue of the distance, of that which has passed and that which is yet to be.

And they were in the centre of it, and everything else had disappeared.

'She's holding a moment of time for us,' said Cal, somewhere.

The chair dropped.

The roof of TumbleMan's caravan loomed up towards them.

Blue was standing there, with Herzull in her arms.

The chair landed and Otto, stumbling, climbed out.

They were alone.

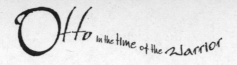

'I've got the KeepSafe,' he said immediately, holding it up. 'I know what it's for. I can take it away from here. To my own time. Three hundred years from now.'

'What is your name?' said Blue softly, because he was a stranger to her.

'Otto. Otto Hush, son of Albert the Quiet. And this is my bear, Herzull. It was supposed to be Herschell.' He couldn't stop speaking. He wanted to stand there with her for as long as he could, wrapped in light. 'My mum thought of it, but my sisters, the twins . . . they couldn't pronounce it, you see.'

She smiled. It was like the beautiful night smiling down at him from the sky. 'I called for help and you saved me. You are a hero, Otto Hush.'

The words like a blessing.

'You have some way to travel back to your time?'

'Yes. I hope so, yes.'

'You have injured your hand, I think.'

He looked down in surprise at his clenched fist. She closed her own hands over his.

Nothing else existed.

'My friend Mab,' he said. 'She's trapped in the Town Hall. It all went wrong . . . I don't think she'll ever come home . . .'

Blue uncurled his fingers, one by one.

There were the rings and the string and the deep marks on his palm where they had cut into him as he clutched them so tightly.

'I see,' said Blue.

The light was changing. The colour was deepening around them.

She swayed a little, as if someone had pushed her.

'Go,' she said, quietly. Intense. 'Go now. Give the KeepSafe to the King. I will try to find you.'

Was she falling? He reached to catch her.

But Cal had the chair hovering right behind him. He put his hand on Otto's shoulder and tipped him backwards into it with Herzull yelping on his chest.

The chair soared upwards. The mantle of blue light was gone. They circled long enough to see TumbleMan below, screaming curses at them.

'Where's Blue? gasped Otto, leaning forward, almost falling out. 'Where's she gone?'

'She's probably managed to leap into another time,' said Cal. Tilting the chair back. Climbing higher. Everything accelerating. 'Let's hope so.'

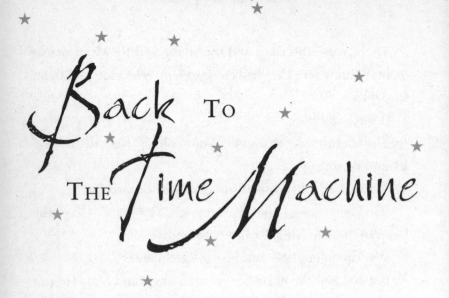

Back To The Time Machine

The wicker chair hung motionless above the vast and shadowed Amaze.

There was a warm wind blowing in Otto's face as he looked down. He saw the roof of the shed, the bench . . .

'They're there,' he whispered.

Cal and Morwenna had spoken on the journey. Asking questions. Asking about Mab. Telling Otto things. Now they became very quiet. Morwenna was holding Otto's arm. Her grip tightened. The chair dropped gently through the air, creaking as it landed in the long grass.

Otto jumped out.

'Ah, Hush,' said Sween Softly, stepping out of the shadow beside the shed. 'You're here. I am more than somewhat pleased to see you. We haven't been here very long ourselves because there were problems flying the mat. Also Norah had to take a little book to the Library. I've no idea why.' His voice shook very slightly. His teeth flashed a huge, unsteady smile. 'And you've got a visitor.' Otto looked round in terror.

But it was not TumbleMan. Not yet.

It was Turnix. Washed clean and gleaming as a water snake. Wearing a different, undamaged waistcoat.

'Honourable greetings, Otto,' he began, starting his bow, his voice grave. 'May your—'

'I'm sorry but he can't come with us,' interrupted Norah. She was already sitting on the bench. 'It can only take three. That's what went wrong when we came here. The bags were extra. It was too heavy. Harnesses broke. You and Sween and your dogbear fell off. It leaves in five minutes.'

Otto didn't even need to look round at the wicker chair. He could feel Cal and Morwenna's eyes on his back.

'There must be a way,' he said. 'These are Genevieve's children, Cal and Morwenna. They've got to come too.'

'Mab?' asked Sween.

Otto shook his head. 'Someone's after me,' he whispered. 'We are all in danger.'

Morwenna, meanwhile, jumped down from the wicker chair. 'Are we going to see Jenny now?'

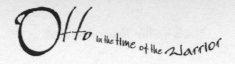

'Is it TumbleMan?' whispered Sween.

'Yes.'

'And did you save—'

'Yes. Yes, and I've got the KeepSafe here, the thing he was spinning on his finger that time at the Circus when he wanted me to join, that's what it's all been about. And he could appear any moment now. He's going to use it to wipe everything out, Sween. He's going to go back in time. Then, when the earthquake comes, he'll spin the whole City and the mountains and everything, into the KeepSafe. That's what it was made for. Then, afterwards, he'll just spin everything out again. BrokenHeart won't have cracked open. The Citizens won't have come . . .'

He paused. His mouth was dry. What was it Blue had said on the roof the first time he had seen her? *There's a battle for time. For the future and the present and the past.*

'I know,' said Sween. 'He's famous.'

Sween, Norah, Turnix, Cal and Morwenna. They were all looking at him.

'Maybe TumbleMan's right,' said Sween, very quietly. 'The Karmidee would have been better off if the Outsiders had never come. If none of it had happened.'

There was a silence.

'But it did happen,' said Otto. 'And now we must all live together, or die.'

The wind rustled through the Amaze. The hedges shuddered.

'I am amazed that you have chosen the powerful traveller as your enemy, Otto,' said Turnix. 'But I will stand by you and help you.'

Otto nodded. Even Turnix, huge and fearless and true, would not be able to protect him from TumbleMan.

'Can't we all just climb on the bench together?' said Sween.

'I've already told you,' snapped Norah. 'It won't travel far enough if it's too heavy. And anything over three is too heavy. And we now have four minutes. And then it goes back whether we are on it or not.'

'I will forgo my place,' said Turnix. 'Maybe then the children from the Circus can travel safely with you. I will return to my family.'

But Otto had guessed that Turnix had been living alone in the forest and the tunnels. He had no family. 'There must be a way,' he began—

But he was interrupted.

'Can I assist?' asked someone.

A boy in a woollen hat had come out of one of the many passages between the hedges. He stepped forward, looking at Norah, but it seemed that he was eager to assist everyone in sight.

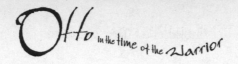

Turnix also stepped forward. He had been holding a small sack. He put it down.

'You are not TumbleMan,' he said to the boy. 'You are not TumbleMan in another form—'

'No. NO!' exclaimed Otto. 'He's NOT—'

'I know him,' said Norah. 'I've met him before. He built the machine. He knows how we got here.'

'My name is Ignatius,' said the boy, beaming at everyone.

Then she and Sween both began to speak to Ignatius very rapidly at the same time, trying to explain.

Otto could feel the weight of the KeepSafe in his pocket. He looked across at the bench. 'Please,' he said softly, to no one, 'please, we must go somehow.'

Ignatius, whoever he was, seemed to have seized on the problem with glee. He rushed into the shed, and out again, and in again. The moonlight changed. It became sombre, the colour of rust. Everything became harder to see.

'There's the eclipse,' he exclaimed. 'Immensely interesting.'

'Red Moon,' thought Otto. 'In the Time of the Warrior.'

He was exhausted beyond endurance. He felt as if he had run for days and was in sight of safety and home. And couldn't run any more. Or walk. Or even think properly. And everyone seemed to be hurrying backwards and forwards. Now Turnix was carrying Cal from the wicker chair to the bench. Morwenna was to sit on Cal's knees. Ignatius had mended the harnesses since they arrived. They'd been broken apparently. Otto sat on the damp grass. The strange dim light enveloped him.

'If I adjust this dial here,' called Ignatius from the shed, 'this is called the chronometric adjuster. It is for emergencies. I can adjust it so that the bicycle goes *further*, it's a sort of additional tightening mechanism, and then we put more *weight* on, which there will be, three extra people, and then you should still arrive back at the time you left. It is just a question of estimating the nature of the *weight increase* we expect to be carrying and how much further I need to, er, *set* the chronometric adjuster . . . and whether the bicycle will break in *half* under the *strain* created by the additional *tightening* . . .'

Norah was already strapped into the middle seat. Turnix was to go at one end with Herzull held to his chest under one powerful arm.

'Get up,' said Sween, in Otto's ear.

'I'm not sure I can.'

Sween tried to pull him up. Otto stayed on the ground.

'That's the best I can do,' shouted Ignatius, pounding across from the shed, dragging a length of rope. 'I've locked the door now. I'm going to tie you two on with this. More towards that end, to balance, the, er, caver gentleman . . .'

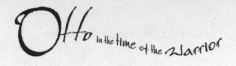

'Get up,' hissed Sween.

'Where's your guitar?' asked Otto. Stupidly. He knew where it was. He'd just never seen Sween without it before.

The light from the bicycle was growing brighter and brighter. It became a faint eerie purple under the red moon.

'Two minutes to go,' called Ignatius.

Then blue light blasted the scene like lightning and suddenly Otto managed to stand. He felt a surge of strength. The sort that comes from terror. He felt the ground very solid under his feet. This light was nothing to do with the bicycle. This was TumbleMan.

TumbleMan, smiling, with a cat on his shoulder. He stood lightly balanced, as he always did, untroubled by the pull and turn of the earth. He was not enraged as he had been when Otto had escaped him in the sky above his Circus. He had instead an air of confident menace, layer upon layer of danger and pride and lonely hunger, one thousand years old.

The great wave of light drew back and the cat jumped down and turned into a boy.

'Well, honourable greetings,' whispered Sween, and Otto had never heard such contempt in his voice before. 'Tiler who works for everyone. You sold us to the Rook and now you're selling us to TumbleMan.'

Tiler's face was locked shut. Maybe he was going to reply. TumbleMan spoke first.

'Honourable greetings, Nobody,' he said. 'What a happy chance. We came to destroy your pathetic machine and we've found you as well.' He surveyed them all. No one moved.

'Ah, I recognize the Whisperer's waifs. The ones who helped you steal the KeepSafe. Do you think they're planning some little journey, Tiler? On their so-called time machine?'

Tiler nodded. Shifting his eyes away from Sween's relentless stare.

'Give me the KeepSafe. Nobody, and I will let you all go.'

About two minutes left now.

'If I give you the KeepSafe, TumbleMan,' said Otto, 'it will not matter where we go in place or time. We will be unwritten. Wiped out. As you well know.'

'Come back with me to my Circus,' said TumbleMan. 'We are going to be perfectly safe. Back at the beginning. No Citizens though.' He looked at Sween. 'At least three of your little band are Citizens. I suspect, from the energy, or should I say, lack of energy, which I detect. The caver can come with us, of course.'

'Never,' said Turnix.

Tiler was creeping away from them. Towards the shed and the time machine.

'In fact I detect that you yourself may have Citizen blood, little nobody,' added TumbleMan. 'How humorous, not only

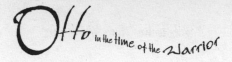

is Blue trying to betray her people, she has someone such as *you* to help her.'

He tilted his head, as if he were listening to something. Then he pointed at Norah, back on the bench, holding Herzull.

'And here we have a Citizen, with a trace of Karmidee running through her family tree. A thread of gold. An ancestor somewhere in her past. Such a muddle and all my fault. But I am going to put it right.'

The light in the shed was growing brighter. It could be clearly seen through every crack and joint in the wood. Inside, the bicycle was alive with energy. The illogical and Impossible energy which had propelled it here and which, like a spring, was about to fling it back, with or without passengers.

Tiler was almost at the door.

One kick could be enough, lock or no lock. And then the bicycle, after all, was made out of glass.

'Everybody get on the bench!' yelled Otto.

Turnix swung his fist at TumbleMan like a blacksmith swinging a hammer. TumbleMan disappeared, laughing.

Reappeared instantly right next to Otto.

'What's the hurry, Nobody?' he whispered. 'Is it going to go without you?' He disappeared again, sending sparks like crystals of turquoise burning through the air.

Now he too was outside the door of the shed.

He stamped his foot, almost lazily, and a great crack opened in the ground. He was on one side with Tiler and the shed. Everyone else was on the other with the bench. Otto looked down and saw a fine band of reflected light running deep across the chasm, from one side to the other. Something that had been buried in the ground. The gold connection between the bicycle and the bench. Unbroken.

'You go,' whispered Turnix. He dropped his shoulders. His power seemed to concentrate. 'I will jump over there,' he whispered. 'I will jump—'

'No! NO. Get on the bench!' cried Otto. At the same moment Ignatius was from nowhere, beside him, shoving rope into his hands, flinging a loop to Turnix, who snatched it out of the air. There was a splintering crash. Tiler had kicked down the door of the shed.

Otto saw TumbleMan clap his hands, raise his arm, expecting burning rocks . . . expecting everything to be over, everything and everything . . . lost and over and gone.

He was blasted with the blue light, screwed his eyes shut. Hung on to the rope.

Professor Flowers

Otto still didn't open his eyes. There was somewhere out there. He could hear and smell it. But he didn't want to know, straight away, exactly where and when that somewhere might be.

'Hush?'

That sounded like Sween.

'Is that you, Sween?'

'Open your eyes. We've travelled. TumbleMan's not here.'

Otto opened his eyes. He was sitting on the grass. The short, dry, parched grass in the secret centre of the Amaze. A rope was around his chest. It had been wound round him twice.

Sween was sitting nearby with Rosie on his shoulder.

Norah, Herzull, Cal and Morwenna were all on the bench. The rope was tied to one of the legs, then to Sween, then to him. Turnix lay a little further away. The rope ended with him.

'What happened to Ignatius?' said Otto.

Someone sobbed. A deep, choking sob. Quickly mufffled by a large, scaled hand.

'Turnix, what's the matter?' whispered Otto. 'Where's Ignatius?'

'He gave me the rope,' said Turnix. 'He wanted to come too. I held him. By the hand. It was all so fast. I held him but he slipped.' He wiped tears away from his eyes. 'I let him go.'

'Oh, sweet trees,' said Otto.

Norah stood up and walked quietly over to the shed. She went inside. Herzull crept over to Otto. It was hard to tell what colour she was in the dark, despite the lamps. He suspected stripes but could not be sure.

'We're back,' said Norah, emerging from the shed. 'We've done it. This is the night we left. The bicycle is smashed.'

'Oh, sweet trees,' said Otto again.

'He could be anywhere,' said Sween. 'Perhaps he fell back to where we left. To TumbleMan and Tiler.'

'Or somewhere else, where he knew nobody and had to find out how people live and how to fit in and not be

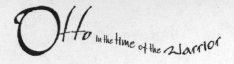

noticed,' said Norah. 'That's hard. I should know.'

'Perhaps he died,' said Turnix.

'No,' said a voice. Not Ignatius, surely. A grown man. And yet . . .' 'And you must not blame yourself, Turnix. Without you and your exceptional strength I would not have escaped at all. As it was I just landed thirty years ago. In a pond, but it wasn't deep.'

And Professor Flowers came from between the hedges. 'And I am so very, very pleased to find that you are all safely here,' he added. 'I have waited thirty years, you see, to know that all went well.'

He wiped his eyes.

They all gazed at him.

'You're Ignatius,' said Otto, trying to keep a grip on the puzzle.

'Don't you see?' said Norah.

'Well, yes, sort of . . .'

'Me and Otto came to ask you all about the time machine,' exclaimed Sween. 'Didn't you realize who we were? Didn't you recognize us?'

'Thirty years is a long time,' said the Professor, gravely. 'You must remember that we only met in the dark, for a few desperate minutes, on the night of the Red Moon.'

They all stared at him. Even in the lamplight the exhaustion in his face was clear.

'Did you recognize me?' whispered Otto.

'It is true, Otto, that I have met you several times. I did begin to wonder . . . And I told your parents after you came to see the machine, just a few days ago. And I believe they told Sween's father, Mr Softly.'

'WHAT!'

'We discussed it for many hours. Myself, Mr Softly, your parents, Otto. We consulted Megrafrix—'

'But my dad never said anything to me,' whispered Sween.

'Nor did mine,' said Otto.

'We realized that you must already be a part of the history of the City. Your visit to the past had already happened. It was beyond anyone's intelligence to know what to do for the best. We had only a very few pieces of a very large and dangerous puzzle. It was decided that they would speak to you about it if *you* raised the matter. But neither of you did.'

'Perhaps you did not wish to suddenly fly forward in time, perhaps you left family behind. You only fled because of TumbleMan,' said Turnix abruptly.

'Not at all,' said the Professor. His face lit by a smile. 'I built the glass bicycle to try and escape. Then I realized that I had made the whole mechanism the wrong way round. It only went backwards and I wanted to go forwards. I couldn't work out how to make it go into the future, unless it was

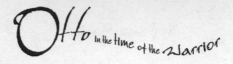

returning there. If it had not been for you coming backwards from the future, I might never have travelled at all.' He sighed. 'Time travel is full of loops and confusions. Not unlike the Amaze. I myself have never seen it from the air but I am fairly certain that it is actually in the shape of running hares. The symbol of the Blue Hare herself.'

'Yes,' said Otto. 'It is.'

'Well it is a very unusual maze. I managed to buy the whole place when I had grown up and been here for a few years. I'd made some money from the flower shop, and a number of my more successful inventions. It had not been looked after very well and I was able to restore it. I discovered that it had many loops but no dead ends. Every single path leads somewhere. It is all joined together. I believe it dates from the beginning of the City and it represents the, er *possibilities* of journeying through time.'

Otto's mind was electric with the memory of Albert and Miss Fringe showing him the message that day at the Library. The one that started with his name, *Otto Hush*. Albert's knuckles had bleached white as he clutched the scrap of parchment . . . and Miss Fringe, covered in paper clips. And then Dolores, after they had been to see the time machine, frantically practising magic on tea towels . . .

'I need to go home,' said Norah. 'I need to see my father. There's something I need to tell him.'

'Your father?' said Sween. 'Bibi's married?' He looked almost too tired to care. But not quite.

Norah nodded and frowned. 'Thanks for coming with me into the castle,' she said abruptly. 'I'd like to come over tomorrow, or the day after. I hid something there for you. To make up for what happened to your guitar.'

'You hid something? What do you mean, you hid something?'

'Treasure,' she said quietly. And she smiled, just for a moment.

Otto stood up.

'Are we going to see Jenny soon?' asked Morwenna.

'Very soon,' whispered Cal, hugging her tightly. 'Everything will be all right now.'

'We must take Cal and Morwenna to Genevieve,' said Otto. 'And you must come home with me, Turnix. I've got to go home now. Before they wake up and think I've run away.'

THE Party AT 15 Herschell Buildings

The kitchen was full of steam and the clatter of dishes in the sink. Herzull was sitting on top of the fridge, chewing a shoe. Turnix, wearing a specially enlarged apron, was washing up. A pool of soapy water was forming around his feet on the tiled floor.

Hepzie hovered over the draining board. 'Ottie threw a cup once,' she informed Turnix. 'Very large crash.'

She was wearing a fantastically beaded dress, all black. It was a fairy costume. Confusingly, it had pretend wings sewn on the back.

The Hush family was having a party.

'You should be joining with everyone in the other room. Otto,' said Turnix.

'So should you,' said Otto. He was on the floor in the corner.

'I am unused to these events,' said Turnix. 'And I like the hot water and bubbles.'

He blew a bubble off the back of his hand and Hepzie drifted after it, waving a wooden spoon.

'Put that down,' said Otto.

'No. Is wand.'

He glared at her.

She waved it.

'There's no such thing as fairies,' he said.

She hit him on the head with the spoon.

He lunged at her, snatching at the air as she bobbed daintily out of reach and out of the door.

Otto was about to say a short sentence with the word skinking in it. He managed to stop himself.

'Sween is playing his lute, Cal is playing his musical pipe. We are honoured by the presence of Mayor Crumb. Professor Flowers and his esteemed wife, Madame Doriel have brought delicious grapes. It is pleasant and soothing in the living room,' said Turnix.

'You're not in there,' Otto pointed out. 'You go and get soothed and I'll finish the washing up.'

No reply.

Otto looked at Turnix's massive back. The hunched set of

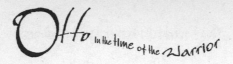

his shoulders. He forgot his own misery for a moment. 'It's because of Megrafrix, isn't it?'

Still no reply. Megrafrix had made a rare journey out of the mountains. He would be discussing with Albert where best to hide the KeepSafe. However, he had also come to meet Turnix, who had been staying with the Hush family for the last month. It was possible that Turnix might go and live with Megrafrix and his children and grandchildren. Nothing had been decided.

The music sang sweetly from the living room. Morwenna was playing a little drum, very softly. Sween's lute had been made by Domenico Nocte. Otto knew now that Norah had hidden it in the castle when they were back in the Time of the Warrior.

There was a lot more about Norah. Her mother had suddenly stopped being so interested in Max Softly. It was all to do with the reason why Norah had wanted to go back in time in the first place, which was somehow connected with a golden blanket and the lodestones that Citizens used to wear around their necks. Sween had been very willing to explain it all. It was just that Otto wasn't interesting in listening.

'Yes,' said Turnix.

Otto looked up to find his friend staring at him. Yet more soapy water dripping from his hands on to the floor. 'You are right. If he doesn't like me perhaps they will send me back on the time machine.'

'Of course they won't,' exclaimed Otto. 'And anyway, he *will* like you.'

'Because I have no one, Otto,' added Turnix. 'My parents died when I was very small.'

Otto had guessed as much already.

'Citizens?' he said, leaning his head back against the wall, ready for the wave of sadness and shame.

'Before that,' said Turnix. 'Caver wars.'

'Caver wars?'

'Turnix, I was just looking for you.' It was Dolores at the kitchen door. Dark red dress. A single amber earring like a drop of honey, against the darker honey of her skin.

'Mr Megrafrix is very much hoping to meet you, you know. He asked me to tell you that he has gone to the roof garden. He wanted to be able to stand up straight for a little while.'

Turnix nodded. He dried his hands on a tea towel.

'I'm sure it will be all right,' said Dolores. 'And if you like, you know, you can always have a home with us.'

There was a yell. Zebbie's voice raised in rage over the murmur of the music. 'Fairies need more cake! Vittingmins and minerbals for the glowing child!'

'Excuse me,' whispered Dolores.

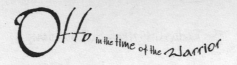

Turnix banged his head on the ceiling lamp. This was not unusual. The shade was bent in several places.

'Your mother is very kind,' he said. 'And she is considered beautiful, for a human type?'

'Yes,' said Otto.

'I thought so.' Turnix stroked Herzull's head. She was black and beaded. 'You know your parents and Mr Max Softly were already trying to find a hare, a traveller, in the mud towns. In case you did not come back and the time machine was damaged. Which it was.' He removed the apron.

'Really?'

'Your mother told me she would have found a hare if it is taking her the rest of her life.'

Otto coughed. 'Go on, go and see Megrafrix.'

'You come too.'

'Good plan,' said Otto.

It was past midsummer. The crate eggs had hatched and the babies, as big as turkeys, had taken to wandering about on the roof garden, knocking things over. There were banana skins everywhere.

Megrafrix and Turnix were sitting on a bench beyond the massive, tilting nest.

Otto, after the initial greetings, had needed to provide

only distant, back-up support. He was doing this now, sitting near the door to the stairs, under the huge sky and the stars. Cal's new wicker chair was parked nearby. Herzull was chewing a log.

It was not an easy place to sit.

It was here on the roof that he had first seen TumbleMan.

Otto knew that TumbleMan had no way of knowing where in time to search for him, and for the KeepSafe.

Furthermore, Cal and Genevieve had assured him that TumbleMan would never leave his Circus for long, and, without the KeepSafe, he could not take the Circus with him.

Nevertheless, several times a day, Otto would think he saw TumbleMan out of the corner of his eye.

He leant his head back against the wall. He hoped no one would come up from the party to look for him. There was only one person he wanted to see, and she was three hundred years away.

'Otto?' A whisper. Almost shy.

It was Genevieve. Fidgeting her big hands.

'Otto, can I ask you a favour?'

Megrafrix and Turnix were sharing a joke. Sounds of caver laughter. All well there, then.

'Of course,' said Otto.

'I want you to take me up on to BlueRemembered. On your carpet.'

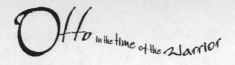

'Of course,' said Otto. 'Why?'

'There's a place I need to visit. A private place.'

'When would you like to go?'

'Now,' she said simply. 'We will be there at dawn.'

'Now?'

'Yes, please.'

Otto went back down to the flat to get his mat. Professor Flowers was in the kitchen making a drink. Green and purple vapour was drifting out along the corridor, towards the singing, talking and music in the living room.

'Can you keep an eye on Herzull?' said Otto. 'She's chewing things on the roof. I'm taking someone for a ride up to BlueRemembered.'

The Professor nodded. Moist with steam.

On *Blue Remembered*

Genevieve said almost nothing as they flew over the City. The sun was just rising, lighting the far Western mountains with turquoise and gold. In the City the street lamps were still on. They climbed over the rooftops of SteepSide and HighNoon, higher and higher, until everything was washed in grey, up over the forests where the wolves ran like ghosts between the trees and further, beyond the crags and the barren rock.

'Almost there,' whispered Genevieve.

Otto looked down and saw dim-lit fields of grass and flowers. Ancient trees with gaunt, uneven branches.

'There are trees here,' he whispered back. Because they were much too high up the mountain for trees to grow. And these trees were like no trees he had ever seen.

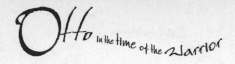

'There are always trees,' said Genevieve. 'This is the place.'

They spiralled down.

It was very, very quiet. Otto stood up slowly. Rock and plunging slopes hid the City below, no doubt full of light by now, while here everything was still in shadow.

'Where are we, Genevieve?'

'Do you know why I stayed here to bring her up? Why I parted myself from my other children for twelve years, just to keep her here, in *this* time?'

'No.'

'Can you imagine how I longed to see Cal and Morwenna in those twelve years even though I knew, for them, it would only be a day?'

'Yes.' There were now many things that Otto could imagine.

'I stayed here because she belonged here. Where she was born. The day was sure to come, not yet, not for a long time I hope, but it would come, when she would be needed.'

She looked at him as if she were asking a question.

'What is it, Genevieve? What do you mean?'

'This is an ancient place, Otto. Nowadays the Karmidee have forgotten it. It is a burial ground. The burial ground for those born with the mark. The Kings and Queens of the Karmidee.'

He looked around. There were low, crooked stones around them, almost hidden by the long grass.

'Mab had the mark, Otto. On her head. Hidden by her hair.'

'WHAT?'

'I found her. Someone had put her in a basket and left her on the edge of the forest path. They knew someone would find her, Otto. Maybe they were taking her to the Tree Scholars themselves and then they were too afraid. They left her and I found her and I took her back to my caravan at the Circus. She had the mark. I saw it then, very faint. Perhaps her mother was ill. Perhaps the mark frightened her with all it might mean.'

'You are saying that Mab had the butterfly? She was the next Karmidee Queen?'

'Yes, Otto.'

'Did she know?'

'No, I planned to tell her when she was older. Sometimes the mark fades. There can be more than one born, you know.'

Otto was so shocked that he felt scared.

'It's on the back of her head, under her hair,' said Genevieve, her voice faltering.

'And did it fade?'

'No.' She stared around her. Lost. 'Your father has been

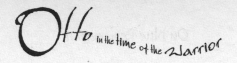

trying to find someone who would go back to fetch her home, Otto. But we do not think there have been any hares for many, many years. And she chose to go. And then she chose not to come back with you. She was so terribly angry with me, Otto, so very, very angry . . .'

Neither of them spoke for a moment.

Then Otto walked to the nearest stone. It was covered in carving. There were some letters, but they were too worn to read.

Silence.

'Have we come here to try and find Mab's grave?' asked Otto at last.

Genevieve nodded.

'She might have become a Karmidee Queen,' she said softly. 'When she grew up. There are no clear records. The Warrior may have died young. Mab may have been asked to take her place. They would have found the mark, you know . . . A friend . . . someone dressing her hair one day . . .'

'The Warrior? You mean Delilah? She might have died young?'

'It could have happened, Otto. You know yourself, they were terrible times.'

Otto began to run from stone to stone. His heart beating fast. His thoughts rushing ahead. Looking for names he didn't want to find.

Genevieve slower, stooping slightly, running her fingers over ancient words. Picking at moss.

There was a place where the stones looked cleaner. Newer. Here Otto stopped. He could read these letters.

Almost immediately, shouting for Genevieve, he found a name.

DELILAH THE WORRIER
QUEEN OF THE KARMIDEE DIED AGED 9
BRAVE AND WISE

'Genevieve!' screamed Otto. 'Come here!'

She came towards him. Her face like a skull.

'It's Delilah, Genevieve. She was only nine! Only nine! Maybe the Rook went back for her. Maybe he went back that same day!'

There was another stone nearby. They both looked towards it.

'Wait,' said Genevieve. 'You are the traveller who came out of the forest. Turnix is the giant. The chameleon bears are the forest spirits. We know you saved her. It is part of our history.'

She drew the comb out of her hair and began to scrape at the stone. Cleaning it. Bringing away lichen.

Gradually more letters became visible.

Otto, next to her, clenched his hand around the string of

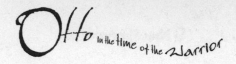

rings in his pocket. He couldn't bear to step across to read the next stone.

'Ninety-eight!' cried Genevieve.

He looked back at the writing, scratched and scraped into sight.

DELILAH THE WORRIER later called WARRIOR QUEEN OF THE KARMIDEE DIED AGED 98 YEARS BRAVE AND WISE FOUNDER OF THE MUD TOWNS MUCH LOVED

'Perhaps Mab is not here,' said Genevieve.

'Ninety-eight years,' whispered Otto. He half laughed. Wiped his eyes.

Then they gazed around the quiet meadow of stones. A bird flew from one tree to another.

There was a flash of light. A surging wave of blue that hit Otto, hit Genevieve, flooded the grass. Two figures were standing near the carpet, among the first most worn and ancient stones. Two figures holding hands.

One was dressed in tattered trousers and a loose embroidered shirt. A single diamond burned like ice against her lovely skin.

The other was a girl in a long dress. Her pale hair fell to her waist and she seemed weighed down with gold. She raised her hand to shield her eyes.

The Blue Hare walked towards Otto and Genevieve, as light on her feet as her careless, lonesome brother.

'Otto Hush,' she said, 'I have brought your friend. She is longing to be home. We went first to your roof garden. They told us you would be on the mountain. Do you have the KeepSafe, Otto Hush? Is it well guarded?'

But Otto did not reply at once.

He was watching Mab as she came slowly towards them. As she walked she unclasped first one, then another heavy necklace and let them fall through her fingers like water. Bracelets, rings, a chain from her ankle. Last of all the gleaming circlet from her hair.

And so it was that when she finally reached them a trail of gold lay behind her in the grass, gleaming and bright and already forgotten, as the sun lit the meadow, and the new day began.

A Note from Miss Fringe of the Central Library, City of Trees

I understand that hares exist on the Outside too. If you would like to know more about them and how to protect them you might find the following sources of information to be of value:

British Brown Hare Preservation Society
www.brown-hare-preservation.co.uk

North Wales Wildlife Trust
www.wildlifetrust.org.uk/northwales

Partnership for Action Against Wildlife Crime
www.snh.org.uk/wildlifecrimeschools/

Gentle reader, I extend honourable greetings to you. May you always be in the right place at the right time. And may those who have had to travel to find safety, find kindness and hope and a home.

Edna Fringe